IDIOT'S GUIDES®
AS EASY AS IT GETS!

RV Vacations

by Jeremy Puglisi and Stephanie Puglisi

ALPHA

A member of Penguin Random House LLC

Publisher: Mike Sanders
Associate Publisher: Billy Fields
Managing Editor: Lori Cates Hand
Cover and Book Designer: Becky Batchelor
Cover Photographer: Monica Bennett (MonicaBennett.com)
Prepress Technician: Brian Massey
Proofreader: Amy Borrelli
Indexer: Celia McCoy

First American Edition, 2016
Published in the United States by DK Publishing
6081 E. 82nd Street, Indianapolis, Indiana 46250

ISBN:9781615648924

Library of Congress Catalog Card Number: 20155951805

Printed and bound in China

idiotsguides.com

Contents

WEST

Introduction

We went on our first road trip together when we were teenagers, driving a small Pontiac hatchback through the night toward New Orleans, where we stayed at the YMCA in the French Quarter for $60. Countless road trips followed, and we slowly upgraded to hotel rooms, bed and breakfasts, and lodges. We both had done our share of international travel, but we loved exploring the American landscape, from the mountains to the sea.

When our children arrived, we were determined to keep traveling. However, it only took a couple horrible hotel experiences for us to start seeking another option. We determined that a pop-up camper would be the ideal solution, even though we had limited experience with camping and no experience whatsoever with RVs. Happily, we were right. RV travel was perfect for us and our kids, and over the hundreds of nights we've spent at campgrounds, we've met so many other campers who feel the same way. The RV lifestyle allows young couples, families, and retirees to vacation in a comfortable, affordable, and adventurous way, with the potential to spontaneously extend a trip if you want to stay longer or to let inspiration guide you to your next stop.

We've also found that RVers are happy and social people, and our lives have been enriched by the many friendly folks we've met at campgrounds around the country. No matter where we go, we find people willing to help with a rig issue, recommend a great area attraction, dish about an all-time favorite destination, or just invite us to sit around their campfire. When you travel by RV, you're not only lucky enough to see the best places America has to offer—you also get to meet some of the best people.

In *Idiot's Guides: RV Vacations*, we share 40 great vacations, with recommendations for 120 great American campgrounds as diverse as our country's landscape and citizens. If you love to fall asleep to the sound of crashing waves, try a campground nestled along the Atlantic or Pacific oceans. If you prefer mountains and rivers, camp near a rushing stream in the Great Smoky Mountains. Do you enjoy shopping, nightlife, and culture? Try a campground with a view of the Manhattan skyline, or one just a few blocks away from the sounds of jazz in the French Quarter. Today's RV travelers can go anywhere and do anything in the comfort of their very own home on wheels.

Is the road calling your name? If it is, this book helps you map your adventures. There's never been a better time to see America in an RV—and the future only looks brighter.

Icon Legend

On each vacation's recommended campgrounds, restaurants, and attractions, you'll see several icons. Here's what they mean:

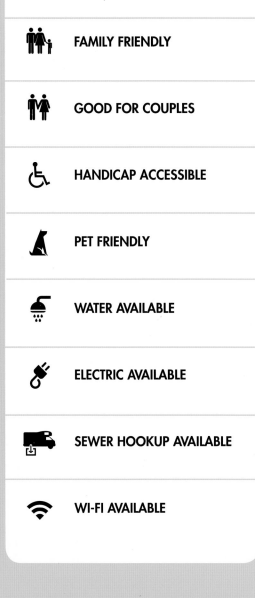

FAMILY FRIENDLY

GOOD FOR COUPLES

HANDICAP ACCESSIBLE

PET FRIENDLY

WATER AVAILABLE

ELECTRIC AVAILABLE

SEWER HOOKUP AVAILABLE

WI-FI AVAILABLE

Online Extras

As a bonus to this book, we've included helpful resources online. Point your browser to idiotsguides.com/rvvacations for more information.

Acknowledgments

This book is dedicated to Max, Theo, and Wes, our constant traveling companions who have turned every day of our lives into a great adventure. Without them, we might never have bought an RV. We'd like to thank Mike Ayars for offering encouragement and support before anyone else was looking. Thank you to Mary Puglisi for her endless help, love, and support. Thank you also to Jeremiah Drew, the king of Myrtle Beach, for giving us a campsite of our own. A huge thank you to all our industry partners who have welcomed the voice of a younger RV generation by publishing our writing and supporting our podcast. To Ashley Lehman, for publishing our first travel pieces in the RV industry. To Michele Wisher, for sending us on epic adventures—our boys are forever grateful. To Laurie Hallowell, for putting us onstage. To Anna Paige, for showing us the way. To Jessica Fix, for responding to every one of our emails, every time. To John Sullaway, for publishing us in digital and print. To Mike Gast and Polly Mulvaney, for understanding the value of a good utility piece. To Mark Nedved, for being a consummate fan and recognizing a well-crafted sentence. To Courtney Robey, for trying something new. To Lori Cates Hand, for somehow finding us and thinking we might be able to write a book. And a special thanks to Janine Pettit, our fairy godmother, and to all our podcast listeners who welcome us into their lives for an hour every week. RV travel has brought our family so much joy and adventure, and it's a blessing to be able to share that with others.

RVing
essentials

Entering the world of RV travel can be overwhelming at first, but you'll quickly get comfortable and confident in your rig. If you're just beginning your RV journey, be sure to read the safety and convenience tips in this section for an overview of important issues.

When you're ready to start planning your vacations, you have a range of camping options available, from rustic campgrounds in state or national parks to high-end resorts with pools, spas, fitness centers, on-site dining, and fun recreation schedules. If you're looking to camp off the grid, we give you some advice on boondocking, too.

safety and convenience

RV travel is an exciting and affordable way to see the country. With the proper precautions and advance planning, it also should be a safe way to travel. Purchasing or renting, using, and maintaining an RV can seem intimidating to novices, but it's not difficult. Follow these basic safety and convenience tips to ensure you spend your next trip relaxing at the campground—not stressing on the side of the road.

SAFETY TIPS

Mind these safety pointers for hassle-free travels:

Check your air pressure. The Recreation Vehicle Safety and Education Foundation (RVSEF) strongly advises that you check the tire pressure on your RV or on your tow vehicle and trailer every driving day. The most common cause of tire failure, by far, is driving with underinflated tires. You can avoid this easily by maintaining proper air pressure. Keep a portable air compressor in your rig at all times, and add air as needed.

Match your tow vehicle and RV. Don't try to pull a fifth wheel with a tiny car. Likewise, be sure your motor home is capable of towing your personal vehicle behind. *Do not* take the word of a salesman. Consult an expert resource such as the RVSEF at rvsafety.com, or see *The Complete Idiot's Guide to RVing, Third Edition,* by Brent Peterson and April Maher for more information.

Distribute weight evenly. The weight of your clothes, food, and other gear should be distributed evenly throughout your RV, and it should be properly secured so it doesn't shift and cause damage during travel. Remember, your RV's slide-outs might already be causing a weight imbalance. Store heavy items on the opposite side of your slide-outs to distribute the weight on the tires more evenly.

Drive by day. Driving your RV at night might be unavoidable, but consider driving only during daytime hours. Visibility is limited at night, and so is the availability of mechanics and parts distributors. Breaking down after dark might mean spending the night in an unfamiliar hotel room in an undesirable location.

Plan ahead for gas stops. Be thoughtful about selecting gas stations for refueling. Begin looking for an appropriate gas stop long before you hit empty, or map out your gas stops in advance using a reliable app or print resource. Look for gas stations at travel plazas that are visible from the highway and can clearly accommodate tractor-trailers. Avoid getting off on exits that send you into neighborhoods or urban areas where the gas stations are tight and highly trafficked. Never enter a gas station or parking lot if your exit strategy is not clear.

Test and maintain smoke and carbon monoxide detectors. Be sure your smoke detectors and carbon monoxide alarms are working properly. Consider adding a second carbon monoxide alarm as a backup. If these devices aren't hardwired into your rig, put in new batteries twice a year when you do the same in your house.

CONVENIENCE TIPS

Follow these hints to make your vacation more enjoyable:

Stop and cook. Sick of eating fast food and using yucky travel plaza restrooms? Take full advantage of your RV's kitchen and bathroom while on the road. Find a safe location to park, such as a state-maintained rest stop, and stop for a nice dinner. Never walk around and try to prep a meal while the RV is in motion.

Plan your route. Purchase an RV-specific GPS that knows which roads and routes are safest for RV travel. Or consult printed road atlases and set your course in advance. Using your smartphone's GPS might lead you into some tricky situations.

Keep an eye on your house. Purchase a home monitoring system that can be controlled wirelessly from your smartphone or tablet. These systems give you peace of mind about your sticks-and-bricks house while your enjoy your house on wheels. Or hire a house-sitter to watch over your home.

Pack efficiently. Download checklist apps for both packing and safety, and review them before departing for your trip.

Keep it legal. Be sure your license, registration, and car and RV insurance are up to date for the duration of your trip. If your RV insurance doesn't provide roadside assistance, purchase a separate plan. Your cell phone plan also might include roadside assistance.

campground **camping**

We've entered a new golden age for RV travel, partly because RV manufacturers are offering an astonishing variety of products at practically every price point. But this new golden age might owe even more to the increased quality and diversity of the American campground.

CHOOSING A CAMPGROUND

If you want to travel on a budget, with limited amenities, state parks offer beautiful options in prime locations. If you want a campground with full-hookup sites (water, electric, sewer), a pool, and a modern playground, however, state parks might not be for you. Instead, reserve a site at a well-reviewed private campground.

Some private campgrounds offer luxurious amenities, such as tasteful landscaping, high-quality grills, outdoor furniture, and stone fire pits. The campground industry's movement toward comfortable camping—or what some have called glamping—is more than just a trend.

In this book, we recommend a variety of campgrounds, but they lean slightly toward private campgrounds for one important reason: many of our state and federal campgrounds are outdated. Sadly, too many of these beautiful campgrounds, particularly the ones run by the National Park Service, cannot accommodate larger RVs. If your rig is shorter than 30 feet (9m) long, you might be able to find suitable sites in our national parks. But if your rig is longer than 30 feet, you're out of luck.

A variety of options are available at every great RV destination, and this book points you to the best of them.

MAKING RESERVATIONS

Experienced RVers often know how to navigate state parks' rather complicated reservation systems to book their favorite lakeside or oceanfront site. Novices might feel frustrated when trying to find a spot.

Call or book online at the minute they become available. These advance booking windows vary from park to park. Most state and federal parks use reserveamerica.com for

advanced reservations. Go directly to the campground's page within that site to find out how far ahead you can book.

Thankfully, reserving at private campgrounds is much easier. Most have online booking options, but we strongly recommend calling the campground directly to reserve the site that most suits your particular needs. Insiders know that a phone call likely gets you a better site than an online reservation. Most private campgrounds start reservations at least 1 year in advance.

Of course, it's always possible to book an amazing site at a popular destination with short notice. But you might have to call several times and check for cancellations.

MOVING IN

When you pull into the campground, look for a sign that directs you to temporary parking for the registration area, which is almost always in the camp store. After paying your bill, you'll either receive a map of the campground with directions to your site or, at many private campgrounds, a camp worker will take you there directly.

When you reach your site, locate and hook up to water, electric, and sewer, which are almost always clustered close together and easy to find, if the campground has them.

If you need additional help and you're staying at a private campground, ask. Camp staff are trained to help. If you're staying at a state or federal campground, which are often understaffed, you might need to ask for assistance from other campers. Many are friendly, handy people who are happy to help.

CAMPGROUND LIFE

Campgrounds provide safe places for children to play and spontaneous communities to form. They're also egalitarian places, where you might find a million-dollar motor home parked next to an old pop-up camper.

Show courtesy to your neighbors by obeying the campground's posted hours for quiet time. Generally speaking, quiet time is enforced more strictly at private campgrounds where the owners live on-site. Some state parks are notorious for attracting campers who want to stay up late and party. To avoid these campgrounds, use the recommendations in this book or check online reviews. For the most part, the rangers at federal campgrounds run a tight ship and don't tolerate noise after quiet time.

Most campers look at their campsite as their personal haven, so avoid using them as shortcuts, and if you're traveling with children, instruct them to do the same.

boondocking

Many American campers stay at public or private campgrounds, but some daring and resourceful campers choose to boondock.

Boondocking is completely self-contained, off-the-grid camping without the use of water, electric, and sewer hookups in a natural and undeveloped environment or in an environment such as a parking lot where the primary purpose is not to host RVs. Boondocking is often called *dispersed camping,* meaning camping outside the boundaries of a traditional campground.

The terms *boondocking* and *dry camping* are often used interchangeably, but boondocking purists would note a major distinction. Dry camping also refers to camping without hookups, but it implies doing so at an actual campground, such as one inside a national park. Those who dry camp in a campground might not have hookups for their RV, but they do have the use of running water, a dump station, and other limited amenities nearby.

WHY BOONDOCK?

For many RVers, escaping to a campground just isn't enough. They crave a closer connection to nature in a quieter environment. They crave solitude. They crave star-packed skies without light pollution. Other boondockers are frequent (if not full-time) travelers who budget to maximize their time on the road. But for most RV travelers, boondocking just means spending the occasional night in a big-box store or restaurant parking lot.

HOW TO BOONDOCK

When you boondock, you must rely entirely on your own batteries, propane, or generator for power, and you have to provide your own water. You also must store all your own black and gray wastewater in your RV's holding tanks. Some campers find this kind of self-reliance unappealing, while others wouldn't have it any other way.

The first two rules of boondocking are know thyself and know thy RV. Spend some time thinking about whether boondocking is right for you before you end up alone in the middle of the wilderness. Preparation is everything, and checklists are highly recommended.

If you find boondocking a good fit, consider adding solar panels to your RV's roof. They'll greatly extend your precious time off-grid.

WHERE TO BOONDOCK

Countless boondocking possibilities are available within the national forests and within lands governed by the Bureau of Land Management. Some of the state and national parks also offer boondocking opportunities.

The key to finding suitable and legal sites within these lands is to research their websites directly and acquire permits whenever necessary. A wealth of information about boondocking is available online, and several books and apps help provide an organized and systematic guide to a rather wild and decentralized world.

Boondocking Safety Tips

Keep these tips in mind when boondocking:

- Always keep a friend or family member informed of your travel plans.
- Consider caravanning with friends whenever possible.
- Don't announce your presence with loud music or bright lights.
- Be sure your batteries are fully charged and your fresh water and propane tanks are full.
- If you're camping in bear country, leave no trace of food or waste around your site.
- Lock your doors at night and whenever you leave your RV.
- Pay extra attention to engine maintenance and the running condition of your vehicle.
- Keep a well-stocked emergency medical kit in your RV.
- Keep a reliable emergency radio in your RV.
- Don't rely solely on GPS; carry print versions of relevant maps.

planning your trip

If you're like us, you spend weeks, if not months, looking forward to your next RV trip. Vacation time is precious, and you want everything to be perfect, so don't waste any time by picking the wrong campground or destination. Planning a fantastic trip requires research, self-knowledge, empathy for co-travelers, balanced expectations, and a little old-fashioned campground know-how.

Here are some tips for planning your perfect trip:

Pick a destination your whole family will love. For some families, that might mean theme parks for the kids and hiking, Civil War battlefields, or antiquing opportunities for Mom and Dad. Find a balance so everyone can have fun. Bored kids can ruin a trip, but so can bored adults.

Have realistic expectations when choosing a campground. Even the best campgrounds have limitations and imperfections. Do you want a campground with easy access to a city? Expect road noise nearby. Do you want a large, deeply wooded site next to a gurgling mountain stream? Don't expect a good Wi-Fi signal. Looking for campgrounds with friendly pricing? Don't expect an Olympic-size swimming pool and modern fitness room.

Reserve your perfect site. Do you want a site near the playground? Or a quiet spot tucked away from the sound of excited children? Experienced RV travelers know what kind of sites they like—and ask for them. If you have specific preferences, never book your site online and hope for the best. Instead, call and ask specific questions with a campground map open on your computer. Not getting the answers you want? Ask to speak to an owner or manager. Remember that even great campgrounds can have a few bad sites, so be sure it doesn't end up being yours.

Be selective with your wheels. When traveling by plane, many vacationers choose one destination and stick to it for the most part. When traveling by RV, it's tempting to

rush from one destination to another just because you have the wheels. But too much setting up and packing and unpacking eats away at precious vacation time. Great destinations, like the ones in this book, can reveal themselves slowly, and they often reward your patience in magnificent and unexpected ways. You rarely hear someone complain about spending too much time in Yellowstone, Glacier, or Acadia.

Balance exciting activities with campground relaxation. It's normal to try to pack too many exciting activities into your days, but that can quickly lead to burnout. Why not plan something exciting for the morning hours, find great local food for lunch, and head back to the campground for a relaxing afternoon? If the campground has a great pool, plan on swimming. If you're camping on a lake or river, drop your kayak and go for a paddle. Many RV travelers enjoy their time at the campground as much as any other part of a trip.

Overprepare rather than underprepare. Those who travel by plane have to deal with luggage size and weight restrictions. Most RV travelers have the luxury of ample storage space and can hit the road with all the comforts of home. Worried about sudden shifts of weather? Bring your rain gear and warm sweaters. Worried about getting sick on the road? Pack a pared-down version of your home medicine cabinet. Enjoy biking and kayaking? Skip overpriced rentals and bring all your favorite toys with you.

Leave room for spontaneous discoveries. Talk to locals and other campers to discover a swimming hole that wasn't in your guidebook, or a restaurant where only the locals eat. These conversations are a rewarding and enriching part of RV travel, and no amount of research can ever take their place.

the best rv
vacations

In this section, we share America's best RV vacations—40 in total, all across the United States, from top national parks, to iconic travel destinations, to thematic road trips. For each, we've listed the best campgrounds, top attractions, tastiest restaurants, and suggested itineraries. We selected campgrounds, both rustic and resort when possible, to provide a range of options for families as well as couples. Attractions were chosen for a variety of travelers, and restaurants were selected based on the regional specialties.

The recommendations are intentionally diverse so you can build your own personalized itinerary—because planning your trip is half the fun!

acadia
national park

Acadia National Park, one of America's top 10 most visited national parks, offers the grandeur of the mountains and the sea. The area around the park boasts excellent campgrounds with options at nearly every price point.

HIGHLIGHTS

★ Bundle up and bring your camera to watch the East Coast's earliest sunrise on top of **Cadillac Mountain.**

★ Feast on fresh lobster at one of Acadia's many famous **lobster pounds** with water views.

★ Enjoy a **romantic sunset kayak tour** around the rocky coast of Mount Desert Island.

BEST TIME TO GO

Summertime in Acadia is heavenly, but to avoid crowds, visit in the early fall. Skip the spring, when the black fly is abundant.

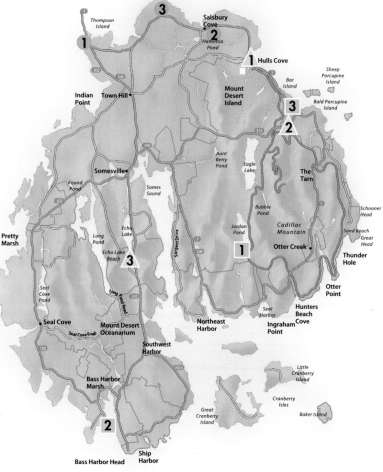

CAMPGROUNDS

1 BAR HARBOR/OCEANSIDE KOA

136 County Road, Bar Harbor, ME 04609. koa.com/campgrounds/bar-harbor-oceanside; barharbor@koa.net; 207-288-3520. 8 A.M. to 9 P.M. $50 to $110. Camp store, playground, kayak rentals, shuttle service, scheduled activities.

With more than 3,500 feet (1,067m) of shoreline, this campground is the perfect choice for RVers who love kayaking, fishing, tide pools, and spectacular sunsets. The playground, train rides, and crafts delights kids, while on-site lobster dinners and live music around the community campfire entertain couples.

Book early for the highly desirable waterfront sites, and keep your eyes peeled for seals. Although a bit on the pricey side, this KOA serves as the perfect base camp for your Acadian adventure.

2 BAR HARBOR CAMPGROUND

409 State Highway 3, Bar Harbor, ME 04609. thebarharborcampground.com; 207-288-5185. 8 A.M. to 9 P.M. $38 to $44. Camp store, playground, shuttle service, heated pool.

This affordable family favorite is the closest campground to Bar Harbor and Acadia National Park. It offers beautiful ocean views without direct water access. Many of the sites are large and wooded.

Be warned: bring cash because credit cards are not accepted. You also can't make advance reservations. Guests simply show up and pick an available campsite. (Checkout time is noon, so showing up before then would give you a good shot at claiming a spot as people leave.) Return campers insist you can always find a spot, with the exception of the busiest holiday weekends.

BASS HARBOR SHORELINE.

3 HADLEY'S POINT CAMPGROUND

33 Hadley Point Road, Bar Harbor, ME 04609. hadleyspoint.com; 207-288-4808. 8 A.M. to 8 P.M. $37 to $42. Camp store, playground, shuttle service, heated pool, shuffleboard, basketball courts.

Nestled in a quiet, wooded location, this campground is only 4 miles (6.5km) from the Acadia National Park visitor center. The same family has owned it since 1969.

Although it has no water views or direct water access, a 5-minute walk takes you to a pretty saltwater beach. The campground hosts a weekly Sunday church service with crafts and story time for young kids.

ATOP CADILLAC MOUNTAIN.

For much of the year, Cadillac Mountain is the first place in the United States to view the sunrise.

> The water temps at Sand Beach top out in the mid-50°Fs (10 to 12°C), even in the heat of summer!

RESTAURANTS

1 JORDAN POND HOUSE

Park Loop Road, Seal Harbor, ME 04675. acadiajordanpondhouse.com; 207-276-3316. Lunch 11 A.M. to 5 P.M.; dinner 5 P.M. to close. $11 to $32. American.

The Jordan Pond House is packed during the summer season, but the afternoon tea with popovers is definitely worth the wait. The traditional light and puffy muffins are served with local strawberry jam and butter. Years later, you'll crave these treats when remembering your trip to Acadia. The crab cakes and seafood chowder are also delicious, and a prix fixe menu is available if you're looking to keep costs down. Make a reservation ahead of time, and ask to sit outside so you can enjoy one of the most delightful views Acadia has to offer. After your meal, stretch your legs on the Jordan Pond Path.

Whether you visit for lunch, dinner, or high tea, eating at the Jordan Pond House is not just a meal. It's an event.

2 THURSTON'S LOBSTER POUND

9 Thurston Road, Bernard, ME 04612. thurstonslobster.com; 207-244-7600. 11 A.M. to 8 P.M. Market prices. Seafood.

No trip to Acadia is complete without a visit to a local lobster pound, and Thurston's is one of the best. The waterfront views of Mount Desert Island's busiest working harbor are picture-perfect. Add locally sourced lobster followed by homemade blueberry cake, and you have the quintessential lobster dinner.

To avoid the crowds, enjoy a late lunch after visiting the Bass Harbor Head Lighthouse. Order a lobster roll with a beer, and enjoy the local flavors while sitting on the screened-in dock.

3 LOMPOC CAFE

36 Roddick Street, Bar Harbor, ME 04609. lompoccafe.com; info@lompoccafe.com; 207-288-9392. 4:30 P.M. to 1 A.M. $8 to $14. New American.

When it comes to food, Bar Harbor is filled with tourist traps. But if you want to eat with the locals, head to the Lompoc Cafe, where you can enjoy music, drinks, and even bocce ball. Offering comfort foods like pulled pork and fresh salads full of local ingredients, the menu here is fun and affordable.

Eat outside on the covered patio, and enjoy a competitive game of bocce ball after dinner. Then indulge in another draft from the beer garden. You *are* on vacation, after all.

> John D. Rockefeller Jr. built more than 45 miles (72.5km) of carriage roads throughout Acadia.

ACADIA'S ONLY SAND BEACH.

ATTRACTIONS

1 PARK LOOP ROAD

👪 👫 ♿ ⚓

Acadia National Park Hulls Cove Visitor Center, Bar Harbor, ME. **nps.gov/acad**; 207-288-3338. April 15 to October 31. Entrance fees May to October: 7-day vehicle pass $25; 7-day individual pass $12

This 27-mile (43.5km) stretch of road seduces with the best views Acadia National Park has to offer. The drive takes you past Sand Beach, Thunder Hole, and Otter Cliff, where you can enjoy the view from your car or park and take a stroll to soak it all in. The Park Loop also gives you access to Jordan Pond and Cadillac Mountain.

The Park Loop Road is best experienced early in the morning before the crowds and shuttle buses arrive. The parking lot at Sand Beach is often packed by 10:30 A.M. If you start your drive by 9 A.M., you should have no problem parking and enjoying the views. Then you can finish your tour with lunch at Jordan Pond.

2 DOWNTOWN BAR HARBOR

👪 👫 ♿

Bar Harbor Chamber of Commerce, 2 Cottage Street, Bar Harbor, ME. **barharborinfo.com**; 800-345-4617. Metered parking.

If you want great shopping, the collection of stores in downtown Bar Harbor offering local art, beautiful pottery, handmade toys, and endless Acadian souvenirs is for you. The

downtown area offers so much more, too. You can rent bikes to tour the carriage roads, or you can take a guided kayak tour, whale-watching tour, or tall-ship cruise. During low tide, walk across the land bridge to hike on Bar Island. Just be sure you come back before the tide comes in!

Start off by visiting the Chamber of Commerce office in the heart of downtown on Cottage Street. The staff there can give you information on tour availability, times, and prices.

3 ECHO LAKE

👪 👫 ♿

Acadia National Park, ME 04660. **nps.gov/acad**; 207-288-3338. April 15 to October 31; lifeguard on duty Memorial Day to Labor Day. Park admission required.

This is one of the only two places to swim in Acadia; Sand Beach, where water is frigid year round, is the other. Freshwater Echo Lake isn't located on the Park Loop, so it tends to be less crowded. The beach is staffed by lifeguards during the summer, and the local Island Express Shuttle has a pickup and drop-off location in the parking lot.

If you're up for a challenge, take the Beech Mountain Trail from the parking lot to the summit of Beech Mountain for spectacular views of Echo Lake and the southwestern part of Mount Desert Island. Climb back down to enjoy a refreshing swim.

ITINERARIES

IF YOU HAVE 1 WEEK ...

Visit Hulls Cove Visitor Center, schedule a Ranger Program, and drive the Park Loop Road. Hike Gorham Mountain Trail and the Great Head Trail. Shop downtown Bar Harbor, take a sunset kayak tour, and swim at Echo Lake. Eat at Jordan Pond House and Thurston's Lobster Pound.

IF YOU HAVE 2 WEEKS ...

All the above, plus visit the Bass Harbor Head Lighthouse, hike the Wonderland and Ship Harbor trails, and take a whale-watching tour or a boat cruise with Diver Ed. Rent bikes, and tour the carriage roads. Visit the Mount Desert Oceanarium, and eat at the Take A Break Cafe at the College of the Atlantic. Walk out to Bar Island on the land bridge during low tide.

IF YOU HAVE 3 WEEKS ...

All the above, plus take a trek to visit the wild and beautiful Schoodic Peninsula, the only area of Acadia National Park located on the mainland of Maine. Watch the lumberjacks cross-cut saw at Timber Tina's Great Maine Lumberjack Show. Challenge yourself by hiking the Beehive Trail, the Dorr Mountain Trail, or the Precipice Trail. Go shopping in Northeast Harbor and Southwest Harbor.

NORTHEAST

white mountains, new hampshire

The White Mountains are a hiker's paradise, with the most rugged landscape in New England. The area also is home to affordable, family friendly theme parks. The combination makes the region perfect for solo travelers, couples, and families.

HIGHLIGHTS

★ Experience the white-knuckle drive up the **Mount Washington Auto Road.**

★ Ride the tram to the top of **Cannon Mountain** in Franconia Notch State Park.

★ Hike out to the 140-foot (43m) **Arethusa Falls** in Crawford Notch State Park.

BEST TIME TO GO

The weather is perfect in high summer, with warm days and cool nights. Fall is a popular season for viewing foliage.

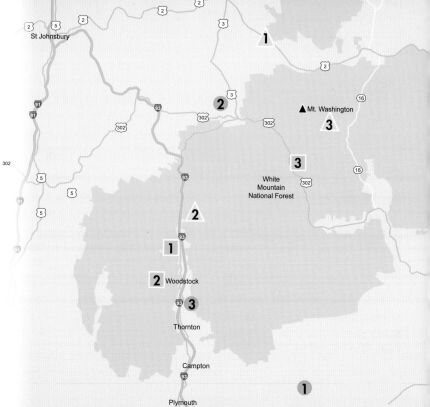

NORTHEAST

CAMPGROUNDS

1 DANFORTH BAY CAMPING AND RV RESORT

👪 👪 ♿ ⚓ 🚿 ✂ 🚚 📶

196 Shawtown Road, Freedom, NH 03836. danforthbay.com; reservations@danforthbay .com; 603-539-2069. $44 to $80. Pools, tennis, volleyball, fishing, game room, playgrounds.

This campground is halfway between the Lakes Region and the White Mountains and offers resort-style amenities. For those who love swimming, kayaking, and fishing—and also don't mind driving into the White Mountains for day trips—this might be the perfect option for you.

Danforth Bay has two large heated pools and an additional kiddie pool. The jam-packed activities schedule keeps you busy when you're not exploring the mountains.

MANY THEME PARKS ARE LOCATED NEAR THE WHITE MOUNTAINS.

2 MOUNTAIN LAKE CAMPGROUND, RV PARK, AND LOG CABINS

👪 👪 ♿ ⚓ 🚿 ✂ 🚚 📶

485 Prospect Street, Lancaster, NH 03584. mtnlakecampground.com; mtnlake@ne.rr.com; 603-788-4509. May 15 to October 15. $49 to $62. Heated pool, fishing, boating, playground, game room.

Family friendly Mountain Lake Campground is a Good Sam RV Park complete with waterslides and a large pool. Reviews consistently applaud its cleanliness and fantastic customer service. Kids will enjoy the playground and pirate ship. Adults will enjoy fresh-baked muffins and Green Mountain coffee, available each morning. The whole family will enjoy kayaking, canoeing, and paddle boating on the 30-acre (12ha) lake.

Book early and spend a few dollars more to enjoy full-hookup, waterfront sites. Check the schedule for special themed weekends, such as the Halloween Extravaganza.

Mountain Lake Campground is just 10 minutes from Santa's Village and 40 minutes from Story Land. Also within driving distance are Clark's Trading Post and the Mount Washington Cog Railway. Be sure to visit Fuller's Sugarhouse for local maple syrup.

THE TRAM AT CANNON MOUNTAIN.

3 LINCOLN/WOODSTOCK KOA

👪 👪 ♿ ⚓ 🚿 ✂ 🚚 📶

1000 East Side Road, Woodstock, NH 03293. koa.com/camp/woodstock; bbkoa1@ roadrunner.com; 603-745-8008. May 1 to October 18. $39 to $85. Pool, inflatable jump pad, game room, mini-golf, playground.

This campground is centrally located near many White Mountain attractions. It offers a variety of sites surrounding a large field for playing ball, running relay races, or flying kites. Scheduled activities are held during the summer, including bingo, face painting, and tractor rides, and it's packed with kid-friendly amenities.

Owners Rob and Darlene are longtime area residents and happy to recommend the best hiking, food, and activities around. With detailed instructions, you can drop your kayak in the Pemigewasset River behind the campground and paddle through the gorgeous scenery.

> The White Mountains include 48 peaks higher than 4,000 feet (1,200m) in elevation.

NORTHEAST

RESTAURANTS

1 SUNNY DAY DINER

Route 3, Lincoln, NH 03251. 603-745-4833. Wednesday to Monday 7 A.M. to 2 A.M.; dinner Friday and Saturday 4:30 P.M. to 8 P.M. $8 to $10. American.

Located right across the street from Clark's Trading Post, everything about this diner is picture-perfect, from the shiny silver exterior to the crispy hash browns served inside.

The food is all made from scratch, and you might find yourself tempted to lick the plate or at least order another round of eggs Benedict. No matter what time of day you visit, always leave room for a slice of homemade pie or any of the scrumptious baked goods prepared daily.

According to the *Guinness Book of Records*, Chutters has the longest candy counter in the world.

2 WOODSTOCK INN STATION AND BREWERY

135 Main Street, North Woodstock, NH 03262. woodstockinnnh.com; 603-745-3951. Monday to Sunday 7 A.M. to 1 A.M. $11 to $30. American.

Woodstock Inn provides the cozy, publike dinner you might crave after kayaking or swimming in the chilly waters of the White Mountains.

Located in the quaint town of Woodstock, the restaurant offers popular appetizers like hot wings, nachos, and onion blossoms that complement the beers on tap from its own brewery. Burgers and steaks are a good bet for a main course, and the fajitas and quesadillas are winners as well. Ribs are another favorite.

The service is friendly and efficient, but it gets busy, so call ahead for reservations.

DRIVE THE KANCAMAGUS HIGHWAY, WHICH PASSES BY SABBADAY FALLS.

3 AMC HIGHLAND CENTER LODGE AT CRAWFORD NOTCH

Route 302, Bretton Woods, NH 03575. outdoors.org/lodging/lodges/highland; 603-278-4453. Breakfast 6:30 A.M. to 10 A.M.; lunch 11 A.M. to 4 P.M.; dinner 6 P.M. to 9 P.M. $5 to $12. American.

After hiking the Elephant Rock or Arethusa Falls trails in Crawford Notch, experience an amazing meal at this cafeteria tucked inside the AMC Highland Center.

The homemade food is healthy and hearty. Sit outside to enjoy the panoramic mountain views. The adventure playground will keep kids occupied for hours while you relax.

THE FLUME GORGE IN FRANCONIA NOTCH STATE PARK.

ATTRACTIONS

1 SANTA'S VILLAGE

528 Presidential Highway, Jefferson, NH 03583. **santasvillage.com**; santa@ santasvillage.com; 603-586-4445. Hours vary by season; summer hours: daily 9:30 A.M. to 6 P.M. Adults $30; children $30; 3 and under free.

Santa's Village offers a Disneylike experience for a fraction of the cost. Tons of rides are available for little ones, and older kids will have a blast, too. Meet Santa in his summerhouse, ride on roller coasters, and splash around in the water park.

Purchase your ticket after 3 P.M., and you can visit the following day as well.

2 THE FLUME GORGE AND CANNON MOUNTAIN AERIAL TRAMWAY

Flume Gorge, Webster Highway, Lincoln, NH 03251. **nhstateparks.org/explore/state-parks/ franconia-notch-state-park.aspx**; nhparks@ dred.nh.gov; 603-745-8391. 10 A.M. to 5 P.M. Adults $16; children 6 to 12 $13; 5 and under free; Discovery Pass option: adults $29; children 6 to 12 $23; 5 and under free.

The price tag might seem steep, but there's logic behind the cost. The attractions are self-sustaining, with no contribution of public funds. If you buy the Discovery Pass, it includes entrance to the Flume Gorge and a ride on the Cannon Mountain Aerial Tramway.

Arrive at the Flume Gorge early to beat the crowds of tourists who visit during the summer, and be sure to wear comfortable walking shoes. After your hike, eat at the café in the visitor center, where you'll be pleasantly surprised at how delicious the food is.

For stunning views, ride the tram to the top of Cannon Mountain, and walk the short ridge trail.

3 MOUNT WASHINGTON AUTO ROAD

1 Mount Washington Auto Road, Gorham, NH 03581. **mtwashingtonautoroad.com**; 603-466-3988. Hours vary based on weather and season. Vehicle and driver $28; each additional adult $8; children 5 to 12 $6; 4 and under free.

You can take a van or a train to the top of Mount Washington, but then you'd miss out on one of the scariest driving experiences ever. The Auto Road claims to be America's oldest manmade attraction, and it's a stunning work of engineering. It winds up at the highest point east of the Mississippi, where you'll need to bundle up to get your picture taken at Mount Washington's peak.

The ticket price includes a CD audio tour you can listen to as you climb. Turnoffs are scattered along the road where you can cool your RV's brakes, calm your nerves, and enjoy the spectacular views.

ITINERARIES

IF YOU HAVE 1 WEEK ...

Explore Mount Washington, Franconia Notch State Park, Flume Gorge, and Cannon Mountain. Hike the Basin Trail, and swim at Echo Lake Beach. If you've been good, ask for an early Christmas present at Santa's Village.

IF YOU HAVE 2 WEEKS ...

All the above, plus explore Crawford's Notch. Hike to Arethusa Falls and Elephant Rock. Eat lunch at the AMC Highland Center. Visit Clark's Trading Post. Reserve a time to ride on the Cafe Lafayette Dinner Train, and enjoy a world-class culinary experience while touring scenic White Mountains.

IF YOU HAVE 3 WEEKS ...

All the above, plus explore Pinkham Notch and hike the Lost Pond Trail. Visit the towns of Littleton and Conway. Ride more coasters at Story Land. Venture into the Lakes Region of New Hampshire, and take a ride on the Winnipesaukee Scenic Railroad or tour the Castle in the Clouds.

vermont
fall foliage

People return year after year to marvel at the breathtaking beauty of Vermont's fall foliage. It's tricky to nail down the perfect timing for peak viewing, as every year is different. But regardless of whether the season is lush and colorful, there's nothing like New England in autumn.

HIGHLIGHTS

★ Drive from Stowe to Jeffersonville through Smugglers' Notch, and enjoy the **corkscrewlike turns.**

★ Ride in a **gondola** to the top of Killington, Vermont's highest peak.

★ Pick up fall produce and baked goods at one of Vermont's more than 100 **farmers' markets.**

BEST TIME TO GO

Visiting during the first full week of October is your best chance for seeing Vermont fall foliage at its peak.

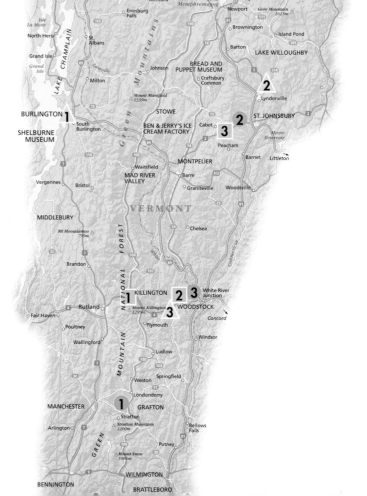

CAMPGROUNDS

① JAMAICA STATE PARK CAMPGROUND

48 Salmon Hole Lane, Jamaica, VT 05343. vtstateparks.com/htm/jamaica.htm; 802-874-4600. May to October. $18 to $22. Bath houses, nature center, swimming hole.

If you want a rustic, backwoods camping experience while visiting Vermont, this state park is the best place to stay. There are no hookups, but the bathhouses do offer hot showers. Many of the sites don't accommodate rigs longer than 20 feet. The online reservation system has a column indicating what size rig fits on each site, so be sure you book a site that will fit your RV.

Interpretative programs are available at the Nature Center, and a playground, horseshoe pit, and volleyball court are nearby. Hiking trails, a picnic area, and a swimming hole make this a lovely camping retreat.

> You'll be rewarded for being an early riser. Foliage is most vivid when it's covered with morning dew.

OTTAUQUECHEE RIVER.

② SUGAR RIDGE RV PARK AND CAMPGROUND

4 Old Stage Coach Road, Danville, VT 05828. sugarridgervpark.com; sugarridgerv@myfairpoint.net; 802-684-2550. May 10 to October 20. $40 to $42. Heated pool, recreation hall, playground, mini-golf.

Sugar Ridge is a family campground with amenities to please every guest. Nestled in the Northeast Kingdom, its location enables you to enjoy the natural beauty of the area.

Kids will love the 18-hole mini-golf course, horse-drawn wagon rides, playground, arcade, and daily organized activities. Adults will appreciate the heated pool, volleyball courts, horseshoes, and rec room.

The campground offers a wide range of sites, so be sure you specify what you'd prefer when making a reservation. Some are open and allow for panoramic views of the mountains; others are more wooded and quiet.

③ QUECHEE/PINE VALLEY KOA

3700 Woodstock Road, White River Junction, VT 05001. koa.com/campgrounds/quechee; quecheekoa@comcast.net; 802-296-6711. May 1 to October 20. $35 to $70. Heated pool, playground, bike rentals, pavilion.

This charming KOA's tall pine trees make it feel like an enchanted storybook forest. Deluxe sites with grills, outdoor furniture, stone fire pits, and paver patios are sought after and worth the price. The campground has two sections connected by a walking path. The playground has a pirate ship for the kids, and the pool is heated during the summer.

The campground's location is delightful: hike down to the Quechee Gorge; watch the artisans work at the Simon Pearce glassblowing studio; go shopping in Woodstock Village; and get up close to eagles, falcons, and owls at the Vermont Institute of Natural Science.

Foliage photographers recommend including white churches and covered bridges in your foliage photos to make them pop.

RESTAURANTS

1 PEAK LODGE

👫 ♿

4763 Killington Road, Killington, VT 05751. killington.com; info@killington.com; 800-621-6867. 10 A.M. to 5 P.M. $11 to $30. American.

During summer and fall months, the Killington ski resort operates an enclosed gondola that takes you to the top of Killington Peak. From there, it's a short walk to the Peak Lodge, where you have a bird's-eye view of the Green Mountains.

The restaurant uses locally sourced ingredients for many of its offerings, so the menu changes seasonally. Keep it simple by ordering a cheeseburger, or be a bit bolder and try the smoked salmon BLT.

YankeeFoliage.com offers live foliage updates and interactive maps during leaf-peeping season.

2 THE SIMON PEARCE RESTAURANT AT THE MILL

👫 ♿

1760 Main Street, Quechee, VT 05059. simonpearce.com; 802-295-2711. Monday to Saturday 11:30 A.M. to 2:30 P.M.; Monday to Sunday 5:30 P.M. to 9 P.M.; Sunday 11 A.M. to 2:30 P.M. $25 to $50. New American.

The Simon Pearce glassblowing studio should be a stop on the itinerary of every visitor passing through Quechee. And if you don't eat at the restaurant after watching artisans blow glass vases, you've missed the opportunity for an amazing culinary experience.

Like so many restaurants in Vermont, this one sources many ingredients from nearby farms and aims to make local specialties shine brightly. The combination of fine dining presentation with comfort food offerings strikes just the right tone. The shepherd's pie and meatloaf are prime examples.

The service is friendly and efficient. The views of the waterfall, covered bridge, and mountains make this one of the most romantic places to dine in the region. Reservations are recommended.

KILLINGTON SKI AREA.

3 THE CREAMERY RESTAURANT

👫 👫

46 Hill Street, Danville, VT 05828. 802-684-3616. Tuesday to Saturday 3 P.M. to 8 P.M. $11 to $30. Pub fare.

If you're looking for a dark, cozy pub on a chilly New England evening, this is it. The downstairs dining room is the more comfortable option.

Homemade soups and seasonal salads are traditional with a hint of creativity. Entrées such as seared scallops and steaks are seasoned and cooked well.

ATTRACTIONS

1 TRAIN FOLIAGE TOURS: GREEN MOUNTAIN FLYER

1 Railway Lane, Burlington, VT 05401. **rails-vt.com**; railtour@vrs.us.com; 800-707-3530. 3 round-trips each day—check train schedule for station stops. Adults $25; children 3 to 12 $20.

Take a break from driving and board the Green Mountain Flyer, which runs three round-trips each day during September and October. The tour sets off from Chester and meanders through miles of countryside, arriving in Ludlow and Rockingham before circling back. This is one of the most relaxing foliage experiences you'll have.

2 BIKING FOLIAGE TOURS: KINGDOM TRAILS

468 VT Route 114, East Burke, VT 05832. **kingdomtrails.org**; info@kingdomtrails.org; 802-626-0737. Saturday to Thursday 8 A.M. to 5 P.M.; Friday 8 A.M. to 6 P.M.

Biking seems to set the perfect leaf-viewing pace for many people visiting Vermont during foliage season. The Kingdom Trail Association maintains miles of trails far away from the trafficked roads and highways you can travel at your leisure.

If you stop in at the Kingdom Trails Welcome Center, they'll be happy to help you plan a bike tour that's the perfect length and difficulty. They'll also recommend nearby bike rental

shops. Some of these, such as Village Sport Shop, run guided tours of the bike paths.

The Lamoille Valley Rail Trail is a work in progress, but dozens of miles of its beautiful bike path are currently open to enjoy.

3 HIKING FOLIAGE TOURS: MARSH-BILLINGS-ROCKEFELLER NATIONAL HISTORICAL PARK

54 Elm Street, Woodstock, VT 05091. **nps.gov/mabi**; 802-457-3368. 10 A.M. to 5 P.M. Adults $8; seniors $4; 15 and under free.

Woodstock, Vermont, is the quintessential New England town, and the covered bridges and quaint streets are particularly spectacular during the height of fall foliage. This National Historical Park is located just a few blocks from restaurants and shopping, with nearly 20 miles (32km) of carriage roads and trails.

During October, the park offers a 2-hour ranger-led walk that allows visitors to take in the park's many vibrant maples while also learning the story of the Mount Tom Forest.

If you prefer to go it alone, stop in at the visitor's center, where the rangers will be happy to help you pick the best trail for fall foliage viewing. You have many different ways to get up to Mount Tom, where you can enjoy the sweeping and stunning views.

ITINERARIES

IF YOU HAVE 1 WEEK ...

Visit the Northeast Kingdom, riding bikes along the Lamoille Valley Rail Trail and attending the Colors of the Kingdom Autumn Festival. Take the Green Mountain Flyer train tour. Get lost in the Great Vermont Corn Maze.

IF YOU HAVE 2 WEEKS ...

All the above, plus visit downtown Woodstock and the Marsh-Billings-Rockefeller National Historical Park, taking a guided tour of Mount Tom. Visit the Simon Pearce glassblowing studio. Hike at the Quechee Gorge, and wander the grounds of Vermont Institute of Natural Science. Take a driving tour of the covered bridges in Windsor County.

IF YOU HAVE 3 WEEKS ...

All the above, plus bike the Kingdom Trails in East Burke. Take a gondola or ski lift ride up a mountain. Kayak or canoe on the Champlain River. Drive through Stowe Hollow. Visit the Stowe Foliage Arts Festival or the Burke Fall Foliage Festival. Check the schedules for Oktoberfests.

cape cod,
massachusetts

With the National Seashore on one side and a pristine bay on the other, Cape Cod is truly a classic summer destination. A variety of campground options plus beaches, seafood, shopping, and outdoor recreation make this the perfect vacation destination.

HIGHLIGHTS

★ Explore the wide-ranging beauty of the cape by riding its **famous bike trails.**

★ Catch a free game and some chowder at the wooden-bat **Cape Cod Baseball League.**

★ Learn about the fascinating maritime history of the cape on the free **Nauset Lighthouse tour.**

BEST TIME TO GO

Go in mid-June, before schools are out, or in late August, when the crowds have died down.

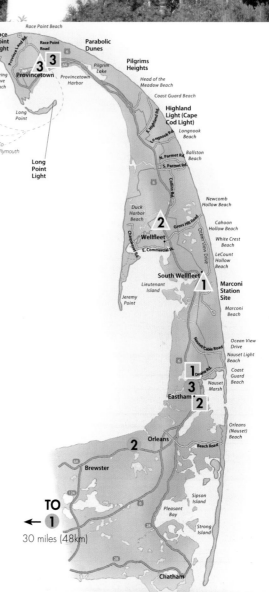

CAMPGROUNDS

❶ CAPE COD CAMPRESORT AND CABINS

176 Thomas B. Landers Road, East Falmouth, MA 02536. **capecampresort.com;** camp@ capecampresort.com; 508-548-1458. $39 to $95. Heated pool, spa, boating, game room, playground.

If you want a resort camping experience while visiting Cape Cod, this is the campground for you. Situated on the western end of the cape, the location is perfect if you want to take a day trip to Boston or Plymouth Rock. It's also near the ferries for Martha's Vineyard and Nantucket Island.

The campground boasts multiple pools and a spa, as well as an adult clubhouse if you want to relax.

❷ NICKERSON STATE PARK CAMPGROUNDS

3488 Main Street, Brewster, MA 02631. **mass.gov/dcr;** nickerson.park@state.ma.us; 508-896-3491. $15 to $17. Bicycle paths, boat rentals, camp store, bathhouses, interpretative programs.

Nickerson State Park has 418 campsites on 1,900 acres (770ha) of deeply wooded pine and oak forest. If you want to experience the natural beauty of the cape without traffic and crowds, you'll love this campground.

The park offers dry camping on spacious and private sites, many of which overlook one of the park's eight freshwater kettle ponds. Bring your own kayak, or rent a canoe on-site.

The park has its own 8-mile (13km) bike path that connects to the Cape Cod Rail Trail. It also has miles of hiking paths, plenty of bird-watching, and lots of spots for catch-and-release fishing.

CLIFF POND AT NICKERSON STATE PARK.

❸ ATLANTIC OAKS CAMPGROUND

3700 State Highway, Eastham, MA 02642. **atlanticoaks.com;** atlanticoaks3700@ capecamping.com; 508-255-1437. $47 to $66. Recreation room, game room, playground, outdoor games.

Located in Eastham, Atlantic Oaks boasts a near-perfect location with direct access to the Cape Cod Rail Trail. The campground has spacious pull-through sites with full hookups.

The grounds and bathhouses are impeccably clean, and the management and staff are friendly and well informed. A stocked camp store, comfortable recreation room, and game room make this campground feel like a home away from home.

You can walk or bike to bay beaches or use the bike path to reach the National Seashore. You'll find several great seafood shacks, ice-cream shops, mini-golf, and a drive-in movie theater, all within walking distance.

CAPE COD NATIONAL SEASHORE.

RESTAURANTS

1 HOLE IN ONE BAKERY AND COFFEE SHOP

4295 US 6, Eastham, MA 02642. **thehole capecod.com**; 508-255-9446. 5 A.M. to 4 P.M. $2 to $10. Baked goods.

The Hole in One Donut Shop in Eastham has been a local tradition for more than 20 years. It serves fresh, hand-cut doughnuts, cupcakes, biscotti, and other pastries, but avoid the distraction and load up on a baker's dozen of donuts. Get in line early for treats that are sinfully delicious and worth the splurge.

For the perfect morning pairing, head to the nearby Beanstock Coffee Roasters for free coffee samples and a bag of freshly roasted beans.

2 ARNOLD'S LOBSTER AND CLAM BAR

3580 Route 6, Eastham, MA 02642. **arnolds restaurant.com**; info@arnoldsrestaurant .com; 508-255-2575. 11:30 A.M. to 9 P.M. $11 to $30. Seafood.

This cash-only lobster shack might be the most famous restaurant on the cape, and for good reason. Try to visit on a weekday or during off hours to avoid the lines that can stretch out the door.

Do you like your lobster roll hot or cold? Try one of each at Arnold's, and order a cold beer as the perfect complement. The fried clam strips and coleslaw are excellent as well. If you have any room left for dessert, Arnold's serves more than 30 flavors of gourmet ice cream from Richardson's Dairy.

Feeling ambitious after your classic Cape Cod seafood feast? Play a round of mini-golf at Arnold's own 18-hole course.

3 THE MEWS RESTAURANT AND CAFE

3429 Commercial Street, Provincetown, MA 02657. **mews.com**; 508-487-1500. 6 P.M. to 8:30 P.M. $21 to $38. American.

If you're looking for a fabulous dinner with great views, make reservations at this restaurant, popular among locals and visiting celebrities. (Ringo Starr and George Harrison were once spotted here.)

Stick with the seafood theme, and order the lobster risotto or lobster vindaloo. Mews also boasts a varied wine menu, a cocktail list, and a delicious Sunday brunch.

More than 300 freshwater kettle ponds are on Cape Cod. Formed by retreating glaciers, they're great for fishing, swimming, canoeing, and kayaking.

President John F. Kennedy signed a bill establishing the Cape Cod National Seashore in 1961. It might not be a coincidence that the area is special to his family, and they vacationed there often.

CAPE COD NATIONAL SEASHORE.

ATTRACTIONS

1 CAPE COD NATIONAL SEASHORE

99 Marconi Station Road, Wellfleet, MA 02667. **nps.gov/caco;** 508-771-2144. 6 A.M. to 12 A.M. Daily vehicle pass $20; pedestrians and bicyclists $3.

Start your day at the Salt Pond Visitor Center, where you'll find orientation videos, a museum, and a bookstore and gift shop.

The rangers here can help you plan the best itinerary for your trip. The seashore has enough wind-swept beaches, lighthouses, bike trails, hikes, and educational programs to keep you busy for weeks on end.

2 WELLFLEET BAY WILDLIFE SANCTUARY

291 State Highway Route 6, South Wellfleet, MA 02663. **massaudubon.org;** wellfleet@ massaudubon.org; 508-349-2615. 8:30 A.M. to 5 P.M. Adults $5; seniors $3; children $3.

Do not skip visiting this tucked-away treasure located on Wellfleet Bay. The extensive system of trails and an award-winning nature center enable you to experience the stunning variety of Cape Cod landscape and wildlife.

Time your visit with low tide so you can hike the boardwalk trail all the way out to the bay. You'll be able to watch fiddler crabs, turtles, and fish scurry and swim around in the tide pools.

The nature center offers a glimpse of a rare blue lobster, and it offers a great scavenger hunt booklet to keep kids engaged and entertained on your salt marsh exploration.

3 PROVINCETOWN

Chamber of Commerce, 307 Commercial Street, Provincetown, MA 02657. **ptownchamber.com;** info@ptownchamber.com; 508-487-3424. 9 A.M. to 6 P.M.

Provincetown has inspired writers and artists for more than 100 years with its unique urban culture in a coastal setting. A wide variety of galleries, bookstores, and boutiques are here, but be sure you also visit the historic public library. This popular tourist destination boasts a half-scale model of a schooner, and the children's library, complete with puppets and dress-up clothes, is a local treasure.

Take a walk out on MacMillan Pier to see all the local fishing boats in action. Many whale-watching tours leave from this location.

Commercial Street runs the length of the city and offers the best people-watching in this fun and funky place. Grab a signed copy of Michael Cunningham's *Land's End: A Walk in Provincetown* for more inspiration.

ITINERARIES

IF YOU HAVE 1 WEEK ...

Visit the Cape Cod National Seashore, and take a lighthouse tour. Swim at a beautiful bay beach, hike at Wellfleet Bay Wildlife Sanctuary, spend the day in Provincetown, and head to the ballpark catch a baseball game.

IF YOU HAVE 2 WEEKS ...

All the above, plus bike the entire 22-mile (35km) Cape Cod Rail Trail, kayak at Nickerson State Park, swim at Race Point Beach, and sign up for one of the many ranger-guided nature programs at the National Seashore. Book a whale-watching trip, too. These leave from various locations along the cape.

IF YOU HAVE 3 WEEKS ...

All the above, plus plan some excursions off the cape. Take a trip into Boston, and walk the historic Freedom Trail. Visit Plymouth Rock, and tour the colony. Take the ferry to Martha's Vineyard, and rent bikes to explore the island. Escape to the quiet island of Nantucket.

lake george
and the adirondacks, new york

A trip to this region offers all the outdoor recreational opportunities you'd hope for among seemingly endless mountains, lakes, and streams.

HIGHLIGHTS

★ Take in the views from the top of the **Lake Placid Olympic Jumping Complex.**

★ Learn about the history of the French in this region on a guided tour at **Fort Ticonderoga.**

★ Hike the short but challenging trail to the top of **Mount Jo,** and get a great view of **Mount Marcy** and **Heart Lake.**

BEST TIME TO GO

The weather is warm and beautiful from May to August, but the crowds disperse in September and the foliage starts to pop.

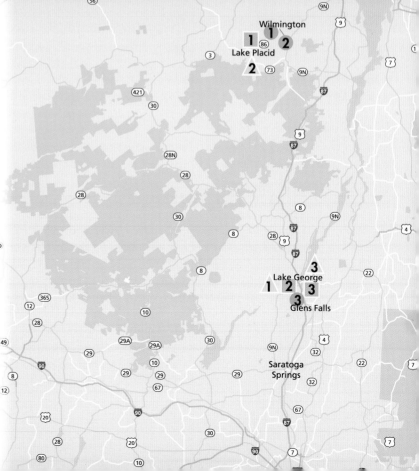

NORTHEAST

CAMPGROUNDS

① NORTH POLE RESORTS

👪 👪 ♿ 🚿 🧺 ✂ 🚚 📶

5644 NY 86 Scenic, Wilmington, NY 12997. northpoleresorts.com; info@northpoleresorts .com; 518-946-7733. May 1 to October 31. $45 to $54. Pools, playgrounds, game room, picnic area.

This campground is made of two sections, so be sure you reserve a site in the area that suits your tastes. The Resort Section has open, sunny sites and runs along the banks of the Ausable River. The 100 Acre Woods Section runs along the side of a mountain and hosts wooded, private sites.

No matter which area you stay in, you have access to the campground's pools, playgrounds, and picnic areas.

② LAKE PLACID/WHITEFACE MOUNTAIN KOA

👪 👪 ♿ 🧺 🚿 ✂ 🚚 📶

77 Fox Farm Road, Wilmington, NY 12997. koa.com/campgrounds/lake-placid; lakeplacid@koa.net; 518-946-7878. $46 to $52. Pool, fishing, snack bar.

If you're looking to be close to downtown Lake Placid and the Olympic Village, this is a great place to park your RV. Many on-site activities are available, such as hayrides and ice-cream socials during the summer, and you also can enjoy the pool, mini-golf, fishing, bike rentals, and the snack bar.

The Lake Placid KOA recently began staying open all year so guests can enjoy the popular winter sports season in the area. The RV sites offer electric only during this part of the year (water is still available in the bathhouses), but if you're willing to rough it a little, this is a phenomenal way to visit one of the most popular ski destinations in the east.

At more than 6 million acres (2.4 million ha), the Adirondack Park is the largest publicly protected area in America.

THE ADIRONDACK HIGH PEAKS.

③ LAKE GEORGE RV PARK

👪 👪 ♿ 🧺 🚿 ✂ 🚚 📶

74 NY 149, Lake George, NY 12845. lakegeorgervpark.com; info@lakegeorgervpark .com; 518-792-3775. May 1 to October 12. $62 to $95. Indoor heated pool, playground, game room, recreation room.

The Lake George RV Park is a favorite for families who return to this region year after year. Large pull-thrus and paved sites are very big rig friendly. Indoor and outdoor heated pools are available for fun regardless of the weather, and a wading pool is great for little ones. Nonstop recreational opportunities are available, with tennis, volleyball, basketball, shuffleboard, and bocce ball courts. Four playgrounds are spaced throughout the park. Hiking and biking trails can be accessed directly from the property, and there are two ponds for fishing and paddleboating.

The Bark Park is nice for those traveling with a dog. It features 2 acres (.8ha) of off-leash property.

LAKE PLACID OLYMPIC VILLAGE.

The Adirondack chair was invented in 1903 by Thomas Lee while visiting a house on Lake Champlain.

RESTAURANTS

1 TOP OF THE PARK

👫 ♿

2407 Main Street, Lake Placid, NY 12946. **topofthepark.bar;** info@topofthepark.bar; 518-523-3632. Monday to Friday 3 P.M. to 12 A.M.; Saturday and Sunday 12 P.M. to 12 A.M. $10 to $30. Tapas.

When you're vacationing in a region known for its stunning topography, you want good food with a fabulous view. Top of the Park offers both.

The focus here is on wine and spirits, but the small-plates menu highlights fresh ingredients and classic flavors, with offerings such as roast quail and smoked salmon. Marinated olives and the cheese plate make the perfect accompaniment to a poached Grey Goose martini.

The Adirondack Forty-Sixers club is open to anyone who has climbed all 46 mountain peaks over 4,000 feet (1,200m).

2 ADIRONDACK BREWERY AND PUB

👪 👫 ♿

33 Canada Street, Lake George, NY 12845. **adkpub.com;** 518-668-0002. Monday to Thursday and Sunday 12 P.M. to 9 P.M.; Friday and Saturday 12 P.M. to 10 P.M. $10 to $25. American.

Although the food here is good, the real star of the show is the beer. Five brews are available year round, including the award-winning Bear Naked Ale, Dirty Blond Ale, and Beaver Tail Brown Ale. You'll find seasonal offerings like Rock the Boat Ale in the summer and an Octoberfest in the fall.

Before you eat, take a tour of the brewery, which operates year round. Then settle in at a cozy pub table to enjoy a pint with your meal. Seating on the outdoor patio is also nice.

Bar and grill favorites like the nachos, chicken wings, or spinach and artichoke dip are solid choices. Or venture out of the box and order the eggplant fries.

3 LONE BULL PANCAKE AND STEAK HOUSE

👪 👫 ♿

3502 Lake Shore Drive, Lake George, NY 12845. 518-668-5703. Monday to Sunday 7:30 A.M. to 1 P.M. $9 to $20. Breakfast.

This is a favorite breakfast joint for Lake George visitors as well as locals. Meals are big and hearty, and the prices are reasonable. You might find a wait on the weekends, but service is friendly and efficient, and the food arrives promptly.

Order the breakfast version of pigs in a blanket and a side of corned beef.

THE WATERS OF LAKE PLACID.

ATTRACTIONS

1 LAKE GEORGE STEAMBOAT COMPANY

👪 👫 ♿

57 Beach Road, Lake George, NY 12845. lakegeorgesteamboat.com; info@ lakegeorgesteamboat.com; 518-668-5777. Hours vary according to cruise schedule. $7 to $46.

This company has been in operation since 1817 and is the classic way to tour Lake George. Two-hour lunch and dinner cruises run daily. There's also a Sunday champagne brunch option.

One-hour cruises depart seven times a day and are perfect for families looking for a short cruise around the lake.

2 LAKE PLACID OLYMPIC MUSEUM AND OLYMPIC CENTER

👪 👫

2634 Main Street, Lake Placid, NY 12946. lpom.org; 518-302-5326. Monday to Sunday 10 A.M. to 5 P.M. Adults $7; juniors $5; 6 and under free; Olympic Sites Passport $32.

Lake Placid hosted North America's first Winter Olympics in 1932 and won another bid in 1980. Start your visit at the museum, where you can learn all about the history of the bobsled, skeleton, and luge and enjoy an exhibit on the hometown heroes Lake Placid has sent to other Olympics around the world.

The Olympic Sites Passport gives you access to both the museum and the entire Olympic venue. Take a ride on the Cloudsplitter Gondola, play a round of disc golf, tour the Olympic Sports Complex, and ride the elevator to the top of the 120-meter ski jump tower.

3 HIKING IN THE ADIRONDACK MOUNTAINS

👪 👫

Lake George Visitor Center. lakegeorgeguide .com; 518-668-4887. Monday to Sunday 9 A.M. to 4 P.M.

With so many amazing hiking trails in the Adirondack Mountains, it can be hard to decide which to explore. Visit the Lake George Visitor Center in the Lake George Village, and someone at the information center can help you plan your hikes. Another great resource is VisitAdirondacks.com, which offers free brochures, hiking maps, and downloadable trail guides.

Start your hiking adventures with the trail to Shelving Rock Falls, an easy scenic hike that delights all ages. Walk 1.6 miles (2.6km) out to the falls, and bring a change of clothes for after you're done splashing.

Another favorite is Mount Jo, where 2.3 miles (3.7km) leads you along an interpretative trail and gives you spectacular views of the High Peaks Wilderness Area.

ITINERARIES

IF YOU HAVE 1 WEEK ...

Visit the Olympic Center and the Olympic Museum. Take a ride with the Lake George Steamboat Company. Hike the trail to Shelving Rock Falls and Mount Jo. Kayak on one of the lakes.

IF YOU HAVE 2 WEEKS ...

All the above, plus visit Santa's Workshop. Tour Fort Ticonderoga. Raft or tube through Ausable Chasm, the "Grand Canyon of the Adirondacks." Spend at least a morning with the animals at the Wild Center. Hike Cascade Mountain and Beaver Meadow Falls. Bike the 9-mile (14.5km) wooded Warren County Bikeway.

IF YOU HAVE 3 WEEKS ...

All the above, plus try mountain biking one of the introductory trails around Lake George. Rent stand-up paddleboards at Mirror Lake Boat Rental. Hike at Paul Smith's College Visitor Interpretive Center and Whiteface Landing. Attend the Painted Pony Rodeo and indulge in barbecue before the show.

niagara
falls

Niagara Falls is full of tourists, for very good reason. The falls are a spectacular sight, and everyone should visit at least once in his or her life. Some say the Canadian side offers more attractions, but the view from either side really is phenomenal.

HIGHLIGHTS

★ Sail on the **Maid of the Mist,** staying dry under your souvenir rain poncho.

★ Tour **Old Fort Niagara,** and learn about the longest-operating fort in North America.

★ Travel 775 feet (236m) above the falls to the **Skylon Tower observation deck.**

BEST TIME TO GO

June and September are the best times to go for warm weather without the crowds. Spring flowers are lovely at this time, too.

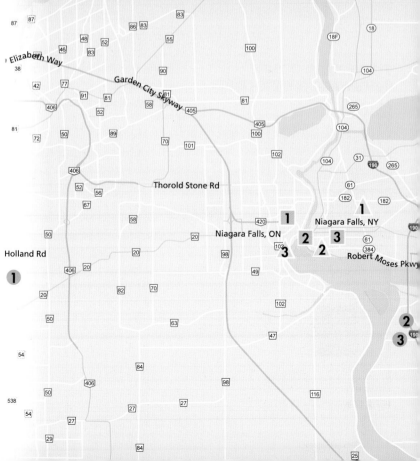

CAMPGROUNDS

1 BISSELL'S HIDEAWAY RESORT

👫 👬 ♿ 🧴 🚿 🔧 🚐 📶

205 Metler Road, R.R. 1, Ridgeville, ON LOS 1MO, Canada. **bissellshideaway.com**; bissellshideway@aol.com; +1 905-892-5706. $40 to $90. Swimming pool, splash pad, fishing, paddleboats, bike rentals.

Located on the Canadian side of Niagara Falls, Bissell's Hideaway is the ultimate camping resort, pairing spacious and private campsites with amazing amenities and regular planned activities. A 1-acre (.4ha) swimming pool, splash pad, and huge water slide delight kids, while fishing, paddleboats, bike rentals, tennis, and shuffleboard courts entertain adults.

A well-stocked camp store, snack bar, and restaurant make this campground a perfect place to relax after exploring the falls.

POPULAR BOAT TOURS OF THE FALLS.

2 NIAGARA FALLS/GRAND ISLAND KOA

👫 👬 🧴 🚿 🔧 🚐 📶

2570 Grand Island Boulevard, Grand Island, NY 14072. **koa.com/campgrounds/niagara-falls-new-york**; niagarany@koa.net; 716-773-7583. $78 to $110. Pool, fishing.

Two pools, playgrounds, a game room, a pet playground, and catch-and-release ponds are at this KOA, and canoe and paddleboat rentals are available. Grand Island also offers two state parks with great bike trails.

With easy access from major highways, Grand Island is only 7 miles (11km) from Niagara Falls State Park and offers tour packages that depart from the campground. The campground is located right near Martin's Fantasy Island, a water/amusement park, and you can take a short train ride to enjoy the rides.

This is a great place to stay if you're planning on driving into Buffalo and enjoying the sights, such as Silo City and Buffalo and Erie County Naval and Military Park. Several casinos also are nearby.

Although they're not the world's largest waterfalls, Niagara Falls are the fastest-moving waterfalls on Earth.

SPANISH AERO CAR.

3 BRANCHES OF NIAGARA CAMPGROUND AND RESORT

👫 👬 ♿ 🧴 🚿 🔧 🚐 📶

2659 Whitehaven Road, Grand Island, NY 14072. **branchesofniagara.com**; info@branchesofniagara.com; 716-773-7600. $44 to $101. Pool, zip lines, canoe and kayak rentals, fishing, playground.

Branches of Niagara is your best bet for a resort campground on the American side of the falls. It offers 80 sites spread out through wooded areas and meadows. In the heat of the summer, ask for a shaded site.

This is a newer campground, and the owners are continually adding amenities and improving the grounds. There's a heated swimming pool, a playground, a stocked lake with swimming area, and a zip line that runs over the water. You can rent canoes and kayaks to enjoy a peaceful paddle. There's a busy schedule of activities, and the arts, crafts, and games create a summer camp atmosphere for kids. Certain activities require an extra fee, but you can purchase a recreation pass if you want.

RESTAURANTS

1 WINDOWS BY JAMIE KENNEDY

5875 Falls Avenue, Niagara Falls, ON L2G 3K7, Canada. **windowsbyjamiekennedy.com**; +1 905-374-4445. 6 P.M. to 10 P.M. $31 to $60. Farm to table.

If you want a special night out, visit this restaurant owned by celebrity chef Jamie Kennedy, who focuses on promoting local cuisine and featuring the best food the Niagara region has to offer. Your server can recommend local wines to accompany your meal.

The view over the falls is stunning, as is the fantastic service and food. The menu is always changing, but you can't go wrong with the Chef's Inspiration, a three-course prix fixe menu option.

> Annie Edson Taylor was the first person to go over the falls in a barrel, on October 24, 1901, her 63rd birthday. She survived the trip with only minor injuries. Stunters are discouraged of repeating her journey today; hefty fines are levied to those who try it.

2 SAVOR

28 Old Falls Street, Niagara Falls, NY 14303. **nfculinary.org/savor**; 716-210-2580. Lunch Tuesday to Saturday 11:30 A.M. to 2 P.M.; dinner Tuesday to Thursday 5 P.M. to 9 P.M., Friday and Saturday 5 P.M. to 10 P.M. Lunch $7 to $20; dinner $15 to $39. Fine American.

At this unique restaurant, students at Niagara Falls Culinary Institute practice their art and showcase their talents. With an open kitchen and wood-stone oven, part of the experience here is watching your food be prepared by chefs-in-training.

The cuisine is classically prepared with a modern twist, and much of the food comes from local farmers. The menu changes throughout the year and is designed to showcase the best seasonal ingredients from the area. Try to taste a variety of items, including the wood-oven pizza and pastas with classic sauces like carbonara. A creative kids' menu is available for the little ones.

No matter what you order, definitely save room for dessert!

SKYLON TOWER AND FALLS AVENUE ATTRACTIONS.

3 ZAIKA INDIAN CUISINE

421 3rd Street, Niagara Falls, NY 14301. **anindianzaika.com**; info@anindianzaika.com; 716-804-0444. Sunday to Thursday 11:30 A.M. to 10 P.M.; Friday and Saturday 11:30 to 11 P.M. $11 to $30. Indian.

You have many Indian restaurants to choose from in Niagara Falls, but Zaika is one of the best. It offers a lunch and dinner buffet, full menu and bar, and many vegetarian options. You can't go wrong with the classics here, so try any of the curries or the chicken tikka with an order of naan.

> Established in 1885, Niagara Falls State Park is the oldest state park in the United States. The park spans 400 acres (162ha)—nearly 140 acres (56.5ha) under water.

ATTRACTIONS

1 NIAGARA WINE TRAIL

Niagara Falls, NY 14303. **niagarawinetrail .org;** contact@niagarawinetrail.org. Hours and pricing vary according to individual winery.

The Niagara region is home to a unique microclimate and soil that makes it perfect for growing grapes. In addition to more than 20 wineries, the surrounding area is full of breweries, farm markets, and charming shops.

The Niagara Wine Trail organization can help you plan your own drive around the countryside, or you can join one of the organized wine tours available.

2 NIAGARA FALLS STATE PARK

24 Buffalo Avenue, Niagara Falls, NY 14303. **niagarafallsstatepark.com;** mmay@dncinc.com; 716-278-1796. Park open 24 hours/7 days a week, but each attraction has its own schedule. Discovery Pass: adults $38; youth $31; 5 and under free.

When you arrive at Niagara State Park, you'll most definitely want to have a good, long look at the falls. Then you can explore all the other attractions. The Discovery Pass is the best value if you're interested in the most popular park attractions. It includes admission to the Niagara Falls Adventure Theater, Aquarium of Niagara, Cave of the Winds, Niagara Gorge Discovery Center, and *Maid of the Mist.*

Arrive early and get right in line for the *Maid of the Mist* and Cave of the Winds because they get very crowded later in the day. Bring a picnic lunch, and dine with a view.

3 NIAGARA FALLS, CANADA

5400 Robinson Street, Niagara Falls, Ontario L2G 2A6. **niagarafallstourism.com;** 800-563-2557. Falls are open for viewing 24 hours a day/7 days a week. Free to view the falls; price varies by attraction.

Many people argue that the Canadian side of the falls offers a much better view than the American side. Access to see all three falls— Horseshoe Falls, the American Falls, and the Bridal Veil Falls—is free, but you pay for all the attractions separately.

Visit the Table Rock Welcome Centre for help planning your day. You can purchase a Classic Adventure Pass there, which grants you access to Journey Behind the Falls and Niagara's Fury, two popular activities for visitors. Skylon Tower and the Niagara SkyWheel are two more ways to get a great bird's-eye view of the falls.

If you're camping on the American side of the falls, you can park and walk across the bridge. Don't forget your passport.

ITINERARIES

IF YOU HAVE 1 WEEK ...

Spend your time exploring Niagara Falls on both the American side and the Canadian side. Ride the *Maid of the Mist,* and visit the Cave of the Winds and Journey Behind the Falls.

IF YOU HAVE 2 WEEKS ...

All the above, plus tour historic Old Fort Niagara. Then venture out to explore the beautiful surrounding countryside. Visit local wineries, breweries, and farm markets. Take in some of the campy touristy fun on the Canadian side and ride the SkyWheel. Enjoy a dinner at the Hard Rock Cafe.

IF YOU HAVE 3 WEEKS ...

All the above, plus explore the city of Buffalo. Tour the ships and submarines at the Buffalo and Erie County Naval and Military Park. If you're staying on the American side, visit the state parks on Grand Island, and ride the bicycle trails.

NORTHEAST

new york
city

It's possible to visit New York City in an RV; you just have to stay outside the city limits and use public transportation whenever possible. If this is your first trip, don't be afraid to stick to the iconic highlights. They won't disappoint.

HIGHLIGHTS

★ Climb all 1,860 steps of the **Empire State Building** on a clear morning.

★ Explore the offbeat boutiques, galleries, cafés, and bars of the **West Village.**

★ **Walk the Highline** with coffee from Blue Bottle after eating lunch at Chelsea Market.

BEST TIME TO GO

Fall, winter, and spring each have their own unique attractions, but if you can stand the heat, summer is much less crowded.

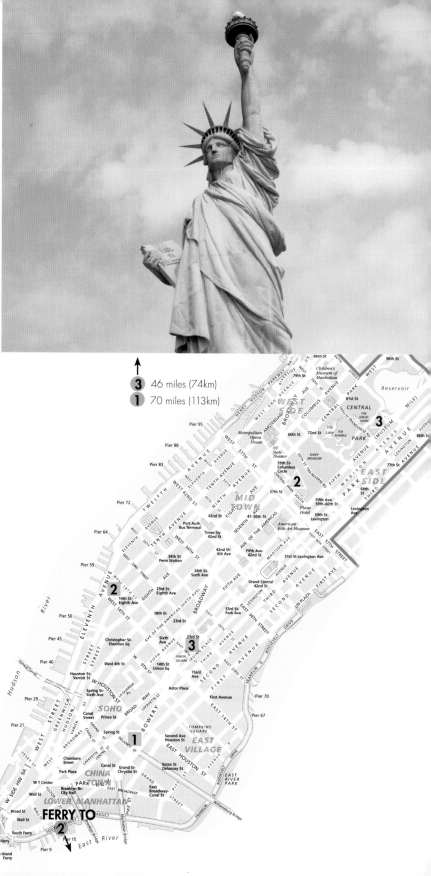

3 46 miles (74km)
1 70 miles (113km)

CAMPGROUNDS

1 NEW YORK CITY NORTH/ NEWBURGH KOA

119 Freetown Highway, Plattekill, NY 12568. koa.com/campgrounds/newburgh; newyorkcitykoa@racpack.com; 845-564-2836. March 27 to November 1. $55 to $70. Pool, snack bar, pavilion, tour shuttle.

Located 70 miles (113km) outside Manhattan, this campground offers the countryside scenery you might be craving after hanging out in the city. The KOA runs fully guided tours of the Big Apple from mid-May to mid-October, stopping at attractions such as Battery Park, Grand Central Terminal, and the Empire State Building. Your tour guide will also walk you through Rockefeller Center.

Amenities at the campground include a pool, mini-golf, fishing, and bike rentals.

30 ROCK.

2 LIBERTY HARBOR RV PARK

11 Luis Munoz Marin Boulevard, Jersey City, NJ 07302. libertyharborrv.com; info@liberty harborrv.com; 201-516-7500. $80. Honey wagon service, daily bus tours.

Liberty Harbor RV Park offers the easiest access to Manhattan compared to any other camping option available. The NY Waterway Ferry leaves right from the park, and it's just a short walk to the subway. It also offers daily bus tours to the city. Guests can see the Manhattan skyline and the Statue of Liberty from their sites.

There's 24-hour security and on-site management, and the office offers good Wi-Fi, a fax machine, and great help planning your itinerary.

Apart from a restaurant and bar, this campground offers virtually no other amenities or activities. But as an urban camping location, it's the most convenient spot to park your RV while exploring the Big Apple.

> You can watch the sunset from Top of the Rock Observation Deck at 30 Rockefeller Center.

EMPIRE STATE BUILDING.

3 BLACK BEAR CAMPGROUND

197 Wheeler Road, Florida, NY 10921. blackbearcampground.com; info@ blackbearcampground.com; 845-651-7717. $50 to $60. Pool, playground, outdoor recreation, fishing pond.

This is the nearest full-service campground to New York City, located in Orange County, 46 miles (74km) northwest of Times Square. This big-rig friendly Good Sam RV Park has long pull-thrus, spacious back-ins, and a parklike setting. Mini-golf, basketball, shuffleboard, volleyball, badminton, a pool table, and arcade are offered, as are a pool and playground. You'll also find a fishing pond and nature trails.

Multiple tour options depart from the campground and visit popular NYC attractions. Plenty of other attractions are close to this campground, too. The Brotherhood Winery, the oldest in America, is only 10 miles (16km) away. Orange County Choppers and West Point also are within driving distance.

NORTHEAST

RESTAURANTS

1 LOMBARDI'S PIZZA

32 Spring Street, New York, NY 10012. firstpizza.com; 212-941-7994. Sunday to Thursday 11:30 A.M. to 11 P.M.; Friday and Saturday 11:30 A.M. to 12 A.M. $11 to $30. Italian.

Serving classic New York–style thin-crust pizza, Lombardi's has been in business for more than 100 years and is often called the oldest pizzeria in America.

You can stick with the basics, a margherita pizza and meatballs, and walk away pretty content. Or you can order one of the many specialty pizzas. Love seafood? Try the clam pizza. Landlubber? Pile on the pancetta. Whatever you eventually order, be prepared to wait in line and bring cash.

2 CHELSEA MARKET

75 9th Avenue, New York, NY 10011. chelseamarket.com; 212-652-2110. Monday through Saturday 7 A.M. to 9 P.M.; Sunday 8 A.M. to 8 P.M. $5 to $30. Seafood, sandwiches, pastries.

Arrive at Chelsea Market prepared to eat and shop. Whether you're in the mood for sushi, tacos, Cambodian sandwiches, lobster rolls, or frozen yogurt, you'll find it here. Be sure to buy some fresh-baked bread, wine, and herbs to take back to the RV.

Chelsea Market is home to many famous restaurants, and it'll be hard to choose just one place to eat. Some visitors enjoy sampling specialties from a variety of places. Eleni's is an iconic dessert shop that perfected the art of specialty cookies before they appeared on every New York City corner. The Lobster Place has been in residence for decades, selling fresh Maine lobster and other well-priced fresh seafood.

3 GRAMERCY TAVERN

42 E. 20th Street, New York, NY 10003. gramercytavern.com; info@gramercytavern .com; 212-477-0777. Sunday to Thursday 12 P.M. to 11 P.M.; Friday and Saturday 12 P.M. to 12 A.M. $65 to $90. New American.

You must experience one transcendent dining experience while in New York City. Hip restaurants come and go, but Gramercy Tavern never disappoints.

The Tavern, unlike the dining room, is open continuously throughout the day, offering an à la carte menu. Try the lamb flatbread and grilled duck leg.

New York City has a higher population than 39 of the 50 U.S. states.

In 1884, P. T. Barnum marched 21 elephants over the Brooklyn Bridge to prove it was safe.

THE ICONIC BROOKLYN BRIDGE.

ATTRACTIONS

1 STATUE OF LIBERTY AND ELLIS ISLAND

Liberty Island–Ellis Island, New York, NY 10004. **nps.gov/stli**; 212-363-3200. Open every day except December 25; ferries run 8:30 A.M. to 5 P.M. Adults 13+ $18; seniors $14; children 4 to 12 $9; 3 and under free; additional $3 fee for crown access.

Visiting the Statue of Liberty and Ellis Island in person is guaranteed to be an emotional experience.

You have to take a ferry over to the island; they depart from either Battery Park in lower Manhattan or Liberty State Park on the New Jersey side. Pay the extra fee for access to the crown.

2 CENTRAL PARK

14 E. 60th Street, New York, NY, 10022. **centralparknyc.org**; 212-310-6600. 6 A.M. to 1 A.M. Price varies by attraction.

With so many things to do in Central Park, you definitely have to pick and choose or risk spending your whole vacation there.

The Conservatory Garden offers English, French, and Italian-style areas with meandering pathways and fountains. The Central Park Zoo is a popular destination for tourists and locals alike. Check the schedule before you visit to catch the animal feedings. Climb to the top of

Belvedere Castle, and be sure to snap a photo on the romantic Bow Bridge. Visit Strawberry Fields to pay homage to John Lennon.

Or simply lounge around on the grass like the locals. Pick up a delicious lunch at Zabar's, and eat alfresco in the park.

3 METROPOLITAN MUSEUM OF ART

1000 5th Avenue, New York, NY 10028. **metmuseum.org**; 212-535-7710. Sunday to Thursday 10 A.M. to 5:30 P.M.; Friday and Saturday 10 A.M. to 9 P.M. Adults $25; seniors $17; students $12; 11 and under free.

If you only have time to visit one of New York's museums, make it the Met. The scope of history represented here is breathtaking, and in one visit, you can see Egyptian mummies and abstract expressionist work by Jackson Pollock. Some of the most popular exhibits are the Asian Art galleries, the Greek and Roman Art galleries, and the Egyptian galleries, where you'll find the Temple of Dendur. Don't miss the collections of Vincent van Gogh, Johannes Vermeer, or Edgar Degas.

The Met is on the Upper East Side of Manhattan and borders Central Park. Spend part of your day at the museum and then head to the park.

ITINERARIES

IF YOU HAVE 1 WEEK ...

Tour the Statue of Liberty, the Empire State Building, and Rockefeller Center. Visit the Metropolitan Museum of Art, the National September 11 Memorial and Museum, and Central Park. See a Broadway show. Walk the Highline.

IF YOU HAVE 2 WEEKS ...

All the above, plus tour Grand Central Terminal, Battery Park, and the Cloisters at the Met. Visit the Museum of Modern Art, Chinatown, and St. Patrick's Cathedral. Walk over the Brooklyn Bridge, and hang out at Bryant Park. Visit the TKTS booth in Times Square for discount tickets for another Broadway show.

IF YOU HAVE 3 WEEKS ...

All the above, plus take a train to Coney Island and return by way of Williamsburg, Brooklyn, for some funky shops. Visit the Guggenheim Museum, and take in a game at Yankee Stadium. Window-shop on 5th Avenue. Listen to live music at South Street Seaport.

pennsylvania
dutch
country

Located in southeastern Pennsylvania, this unique region celebrates many of the cultural characteristics of its early Pennsylvania Dutch settlers. It's also home to America's oldest Amish settlement. The result is a fascinating blend of history, food, and shopping that delights visitors.

HIGHLIGHTS

★ Eat at a traditional **Dutch Country smorgasbord** and sample a whoopie pie.

★ Take a trip on the **Strasburg Rail Road,** enjoying one of the many themed trips.

★ **Tour an Amish farm,** learning about Amish history and contemporary life in Pennsylvania.

BEST TIME TO GO

Dutch Country comes to life in the fall, when you can find pumpkin patches and harvest celebrations around every corner.

CAMPGROUNDS

1 YOGI BEAR'S JELLYSTONE PARK CAMP-RESORT IN QUARRYVILLE

340 Blackburn Road, Quarryville, PA 17566. jellystonepa.com; rangersmith@jellystonepa .com; 717-786-3458. April 16 to November 1. $44 to $110. Pools, waterslides, splash pad, mini-golf, inflatable jump pillow.

If you're looking for a campground with a fast-paced activity schedule and great amenities, this is it. With large waterslides and a full splash pad, you could spend most of your vacation on the campground and simply dip your toes into the surrounding countryside.

When you need a break from all the action, explore the 100-acre (40.5ha) state park just next door. Check the campground schedule for themed weeks such as Christmas in July.

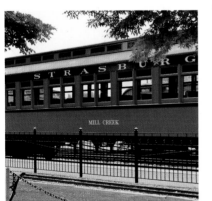

STRASBURG RAIL ROAD.

2 OLD MILL STREAM CAMPGROUND

2249 Lincoln Highway E, Lancaster, PA 17602. oldmillstreamcampground.com; 717-299-2314. $35 to $65. Playground, game room, half basketball court, horseshoes.

This campground is located right next to Dutch Wonderland Family Amusement Park, which makes it an attractive choice for families with children. The convenient location and quiet, peaceful setting make it a great option for everyone else as well. Old Mill Stream runs right along the boundary, and pretty farmland dotted with grazing cows is on the other side.

Friendly customer service and immaculate bathrooms and facilities win rave reviews. Some sites can be tricky to navigate in big rigs, however.

The campground doesn't have a pool, but you can easily enjoy the water park and water rides at nearby Dutch Wonderland. Don't miss buying the cream cheese sticky buns from the Amish bakery wagon that pulls in on weekend mornings.

Handcrafted furniture is one of the biggest draws for shoppers visiting Pennsylvania Dutch Country.

A WORKING AMISH FARM.

3 LAKE-IN-WOOD CAMPING RESORT

576 Yellow Hill Road, Narvon, PA 17555. lakeinwoodcampground.com; lakeinwood@ suncommunities.com; 717-445-5525. May 21 to November 1. $44 to $70. Indoor and outdoor pools, hot tub, playgrounds, mini-golf, café, camp store.

With immaculate landscaping and spacious, private sites, Lake-in-Wood provides all the amenities of a resort.

The indoor and outdoor pool complex has an adult-only hot tub, kiddie pool, and splash pad. There's also a swim-up bar for slushies and ice cream. Picnic tables and umbrellas make it easy to spend an entire day at the pool.

But there's so much more: play mini-golf, rent paddleboats, sign up for free laser tag, and paint ceramics. Ride bikes through the campgrounds, or hunt for all the hidden gnomes in nooks and crannies throughout the area. Enjoy a delicious, affordable breakfast or lunch at the Gnome Café.

NORTHEAST

RESTAURANTS

1 LANCASTER BREWING COMPANY

302 N. Plum Street, Lancaster, PA 17602. lancasterbrewing.com; 717-391-6258. Monday to Sunday 11 A.M. to 10 P.M. $11 to $30. American.

The Lancaster area had a thriving brewery culture before World War I, and Prohibition effectively wiped it out. Lancaster Brewing Company has revived the art and offers stouts, lagers, IPAs, and amber ales crafted with local ingredients.

You also can enjoy some great food while you sample the brews. Partnering with many family farms in Lancaster, this restaurant serves homemade sausages, local cheeses, and house-smoked meats. Be sure to try the hop buggy battered fish and chips.

2 GOOD 'N PLENTY RESTAURANT

150 Eastbrook Road, Smoketown, PA 17576. goodnplenty.com; 717-394-7111. Monday to Saturday 11:30 A.M. to 8 P.M.; Sunday (seasonally) 11:30 A.M. to 5 P.M. $11 to $30. Pennsylvania Dutch cuisine.

If you want to enjoy the best this restaurant has to offer, skip the à la carte menu and embrace the family style buffet. Fried chicken, brown-butter noodles, sweet corn, and homemade mashed potatoes are favorites among the heaping dishes of food served on big platters to long, community-seated tables of guests. Offerings change throughout the week, so check the online menu or call to see what's being served during your visit.

Save room for shoo fly pie and cracker pudding, or buy dessert to go from the on-site bakery, where you can find freshly made sticky buns, breads, whoopie pies, and more. Be sure to check out the gift shop, too.

Pennsylvania is home to the oldest Amish settlement in America.

3 LANCASTER CENTRAL MARKET

23 N. Market Street, Lancaster, PA 17608. centralmarketlancaster.com; 717-735-6890. Tuesday and Friday 6 a.m. to 4 p.m.; Saturday 6 a.m. to 2 p.m. $6 to $25. Farmers' market.

This is the country's oldest farmers' market, and it's a pleasure to stroll through, sampling the cheeses, meats, and baked goods. You can purchase prepared sandwiches, shepherd's pies, and pizzas to go, or you can pick up fresh, delicious ingredients to prepare your own feast back at your campsite.

FAMOUS DUTCH COUNTRY TREATS.

The whoopie pie got its name from children shouting "Whoopie!" when finding the treat in their lunchboxes.

NORTHEAST

ATTRACTIONS

1 HERSHEYPARK

100 W. Hersheypark Drive, Hershey, PA 17033. hersheypark.com; 800-437-7439. Hours vary by season. Regular admission (ages 9 to 54) $61.95; seniors $38.95; children 3 to 8 $38.95; 2 and under free. Combo tickets with Dutch Wonderland available.

This is one of the premier theme parks on the East Coast, with huge roller coasters, concerts, characters, and rides for kids of all sizes.

Admission to the water park is included in your ticket price, and many visitors recommend grabbing a locker for your suits and towels when you first arrive. Buy tickets online to save time.

2 THE AMISH FARM AND HOUSE

B2395 Lincoln Highway East, Lancaster, PA 17602. amishfarmandhouse.com; info@ amishfarmandhouse.com; 717-394-6185. Sunday to Saturday 9 A.M. to 6 P.M. Adults $9.25; seniors $8.25; children $6.25; 4 and under free.

If you're curious about Amish history and way of life, this is a wonderful place to learn about these fascinating people. You can take a guided tour of a 200-year-old Amish farmhouse and learn about Amish education, food, and dress customs. Tours run continuously throughout the day, and you don't need reservations. There's

also an Amish schoolhouse and 15-acre (6ha) farm to explore. Pack a lunch to eat in the picnic area.

For an additional cost, the Amish Farm and House also offers 90-minute guided bus tours and dinner tours.

3 STRASBURG RAIL ROAD

301 Gap Road, Ronks, PA 17572. strasburgrailroad.com; 866-725-9666. Schedule changes daily. Price changes according to event.

The regular excursions on the Strasburg Rail Road last for 45 minutes and wind through scenic Lancaster County farmland.

You can choose from different train cars, taking in the scenery in the open air, riding in a traditional coach, or going upscale in the First-Class Parlor or President's Car. In the dining coach, you can purchase a ticket that includes lunch and a newly introduced Pinball Pendolino car. Special Wine and Cheese trains roll out of the station on many evenings.

This railroad offers many seasonal events and families love the Day Out With Thomas, which takes place every fall. Other popular events include the Great Train Robbery, Vintage Base Ball Day, and the Rolling Antique Auto Event.

ITINERARIES

IF YOU HAVE 1 WEEK ...

Take a tour of an Amish farmhouse, and roll through the countryside aboard the Strasburg Rail Road. Ride the coasters at Hersheypark. Shop for antiques, and eat at a smorgasbord.

IF YOU HAVE 2 WEEKS ...

All the above, plus shop for fabulous fruits, vegetables, and prepared foods at the Lancaster Central Market. Take a tour of the Lancaster Brewing Company. Visit Dutch Wonderland. Take a walking tour of downtown with Lancaster County Historical Society. Squeeze in a little outlet shopping.

IF YOU HAVE 3 WEEKS ...

All the above, plus explore the covered bridges. Or better yet, hop in a horse and buggy to experience a more traditional form of transportation in this region. Tap into the religious heritage here by enjoying a biblical show at Sight and Sound Theaters.

washington, **d.c.**

Visiting Washington, D.C., is awe-inspiring, whether you're seeing it for the first or the fifteenth time. With so many captivating monuments, museums, buildings, and gardens, you could return again and again and see something new each time.

HIGHLIGHTS

★ See the nation's capital from the top of the **Washington Monument.**

★ Visit the grand dinosaur exhibit at the **National Museum of Natural History.**

★ Read the Gettysburg Address and Lincoln's second inaugural speech on the walls of the **Lincoln Memorial.**

BEST TIME TO GO

Go in early spring, when the cherry blossoms are in bloom. Early autumn is also nice.

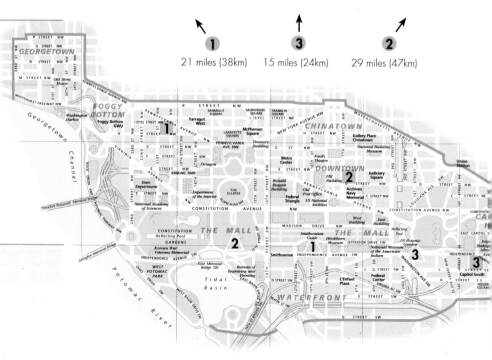

1 21 miles (38km)   **3** 15 miles (24km)   **2** 29 miles (47km)

CAMPGROUNDS

① LAKE FAIRFAX PARK CAMPGROUNDS

1400 Lake Fairfax Drive, Reston, VA 20190. fairfaxcounty.gov; 703-471-5414. $45 to $50. Fishing, swimming hole, boat rentals, picnic areas, hiking trails.

The campground at this state park is quiet and pretty, offering water and electric hookups. A dump station also is on-site.

The campground itself doesn't have many amenities, but the rest of the park has plenty of recreation options, including the Water Mine Family Swimmin' Hole with tubing along the Rattlesnake River. There's also a skate park, trails, and fishing (state fishing license required).

② WASHINGTON, D.C./CAPITOL KOA

768 Cecil Avenue N., Millersville, MD 21108. capitolkoa.com; 410-923-3709. March 1 to November 23. $49 to $77. Pool, basketball court, inflatable jump pillow, playground, outdoor billiards, table tennis.

This well-managed KOA is conveniently located between Washington, D.C., and Annapolis. A shuttle runs to major tourist destinations in the capital between April 1 and September 30.

Although located near a major highway, many parts of the campground are rustic and wooded. The sites in front of the camp store are spacious and big-rig friendly. The sites behind the store offer more privacy. The campground offers many options for outdoor recreation, including a guarded pool, playground, inflatable jump pillow, giant chess set, and outdoor billiards and table tennis. A nature trail is next to the property, and there's an on-site pet playground.

The staff is very friendly and willing to help you plan an itinerary for your visit in the area.

> Due to lack of funds and the Civil War, it took more than 40 years to build the Washington Monument.

THE WHITE HOUSE.

③ CHERRY HILL PARK

9800 Cherry Hill Road, College Park, MD 20740. cherryhillpark.com; info@cherryhillpark.com; 301-937-7116. $63 to $73. Heated pool, spa, fishing, game room, playground.

This highly rated family owned Good Sam RV Park is the closest campground to Washington, D.C., and is only 40 minutes to Baltimore and Annapolis. You can leave your RV at the campground and take advantage of the guided tours and shuttle service.

The spacious sites are known to be big-rig friendly, and the price offers an especially good value for the location and amenities. The café serves breakfast, lunch, and dinner with indoor and outdoor seating. Hand-dipped ice cream is available for dessert. After a day of exploring the nation's capital, relax in the beautiful pools, hot tub, and sauna. It's a perfect place to reenergize for your next day of sightseeing.

CHERRY BLOSSOMS IN BLOOM.

NORTHEAST

> The Library of Congress is the largest library in the world, housing more than 160,000,000 objects.

RESTAURANTS

1 FOUNDING FARMERS

1924 Pennsylvania Avenue NW, Washington, DC 20006. **wearefoundingfarmers.com**; reserveffdc@farmersrestaurantgroup.com; 202-822-8783. Monday to Friday 7 A.M. to 12 A.M.; Saturday 9 A.M. to 12 A.M.; Sunday 9 A.M. to 10 P.M. $11 to $35. American.

Serving breakfast, lunch, and dinner, Founding Farmers is very popular, and the wait time can be long. But many customers are happy to stand in line to eat traditional American classics served with a twist in a beautiful farmhouse atmosphere.

The menu has a diner feel to it, offering lots of options, including fried green tomatoes, deviled eggs, pot roast, burgers, salmon, pastas, and risotto. Chicken potpie is a favorite here.

2 JALEO

480 7th Street NW, Washington, DC 20004. **jaleo.com/dc**; downtown@jaleo.com; 202-628-7949. Sunday 11 A.M. to 10 P.M.; Monday 11:30 A.M. to 10 P.M.; Tuesday to Thursday 11:30 A.M. to 11 P.M.; Friday 11:30 A.M. to 12:30 A.M.; Saturday 11 A.M. to 12:30 A.M. $11 to $30. Spanish.

This tapas restaurant owned by José Andrés has something for everyone. The trendy atmosphere combined with a casual clientele make this the perfect place for a lunch date, drinks and appetizers, a family dinner, or a late-night snack.

The best time to visit is late afternoon, after you're worn out from exploring the monuments and museums on the Mall. The place will be calm and quiet at this time of day, and you can enjoy some flatbreads, cured meats, and raw cheeses. Tasting menus start at 4 P.M. and are served until closing. These are a great option if you want to sample Jaleo's favorites.

3 GOOD STUFF EATERY

303 Pennsylvania Avenue SE, Washington, DC 20003. **goodstuffeatery.com**; 202-543-8222. Monday to Saturday 11 A.M. to 10 P.M. $5 to $15. Burgers.

This is celebrity chef Spike Mendelsohn's popular burger joint in the heart of the Capital.

Service is quick, and prices are reasonable. You'll definitely want to stick to the winning formula of burger, fries, and a shake. Try the toasted marshmallow milkshake, and you won't even miss the s'mores later that night back at your campground.

THE SMITHSONIAN "CASTLE."

> The famous cherry trees lining the Tidal Basin were a gift from Tokyo Mayor Yukio Ozaki in 1912.

IN THIS TEMPLE AS IN THE HEARTS OF THE PEOP FOR WHOM HE SAVED THE UNIC THE MEMORY OF ABRAHAM LINCC IS ENSHRINED FOREVER

LINCOLN MEMORIAL.

ATTRACTIONS

1 SMITHSONIAN MUSEUMS AND ZOO

👪 👫 ♿

1000 Jefferson Drive SW, Washington, DC. **si.edu;** info@si.edu; 202-633-1000. Open every day of the year except December 25; hours vary according to museum and season. Free admission to Smithsonian museums and galleries.

The Smithsonian Institution includes 19 museums and galleries, plus the National Zoo. Entry to all the museums and galleries is free, so you can experience the highlights at each location without a great cost.

Start your visit at the Castle, where employees can help you plan out your itinerary.

2 NATIONAL MALL AND MEMORIAL PARKS

👪 👫 ♿

Between Constitution Avenue NW and Independence Avenue SW. **nps.gov/nama;** national_mall@nps.gov; 202-426-6841. Open 24 hours a day; rangers available 9 A.M. to 10 P.M. Free admission to the monuments; however, there is a service charge for reserving Washington Monument tickets in advance.

If you want to go to the top of the Washington Monument, reserve a timed ticket online before you travel. Otherwise, you'll have to line up very early, and your chances of climbing are slim during peak visiting times.

Plenty of free parking is available around the reflecting pool and up by the Lincoln Memorial, if you arrive early before the tour buses show up. At the ranger booth at the base of the Lincoln Memorial, you can get a map and plan your visit. For many, highlights include the Lincoln Memorial, the Roosevelt Memorial, the Martin Luther King Jr. Memorial, and the Jefferson Memorial. The DC Circulator buses run a loop around the National Mall, and the fare is $1.

3 UNITED STATES BOTANIC GARDEN

👪 👫 ♿

100 Maryland Avenue SW, Washington, DC 20024. **usbg.gov;** 202-225-8333. 10 A.M. to 5 P.M.

These gardens surprise and delight visitors and offer a wonderful respite from the crowds that gather at the museums and monuments. Tour the different climate zones, and discover plants from the jungle and deserts. The gardens house orchids, endangered species, and a collection of medicinal plants. Explore the rose garden, butterfly garden, and conservatory, too.

If you're visiting with kids, pick up a Plant Explorer's Field Journal so they can record observations and complete activities as you travel the gardens. The children's garden offers an outdoor play space as well.

Forty-five-minute guided tours are available on most days at no cost. You also can take an audio tour using your cell phone.

ITINERARIES

IF YOU HAVE 1 WEEK ...

Visit the Washington Monument, Lincoln Memorial, Jefferson Memorial, and White House. Explore the Smithsonian National Air and Space Museum and the National Museum of Natural History. Wander around the Botanic Garden. Shop in Georgetown.

IF YOU HAVE 2 WEEKS ...

All the above, plus visit the Franklin Delano Roosevelt Memorial and the Martin Luther King Jr. Memorial, and tour the Capitol Building. Explore the National Portrait Gallery, the National Zoo, and the National Museum of the American Indian. Drive into Annapolis and take a guided tour of the Naval Academy. Then enjoy the many great shops and eateries.

IF YOU HAVE 3 WEEKS ...

All the above, plus visit the National World War II Memorial and the Holocaust Memorial Museum. Explore the National Museum of African American History and Culture and the Freer Gallery of Art. Tour the Library of Congress and the Washington National Cathedral. Take a day trip to Mount Vernon, home of George Washington.

SOUTH

civil war
battlefield tour

This tour of historic Civil War battlefields centers around Gettysburg, Pennsylvania, to the north; Fredericksburg, Virginia, to the south; and Harpers Ferry, West Virginia, in the middle. Use any location as a base, or plan stops in each town.

HIGHLIGHTS

✴ Visit the **Chancellorsville Battlefield,** where Stonewall Jackson was mortally wounded.

✴ Hike up to **Maryland Heights** in Harpers Ferry for the view of the rivers.

✴ View the 344-foot-long (105m) **Gettysburg Cyclorama** of the battle at the museum.

BEST TIME TO GO

Many of the most popular reenactments take place during the summer months, including the Battle of Gettysburg, which is held over the Forth of July weekend.

SOUTH

CAMPGROUNDS

① FREDERICKSBURG, VIRGINIA/ WASHINGTON, D.C., SOUTH KOA

👫 👫 ♿ ⚓ 🚿 ✂ 🚐 📶

7400 Brookside Lane, Fredericksburg, VA 22408-8856. koa.com/camp/fredericksburg-washington-dc; susan@fredericksburgkoa.com; 540-898-7252. $40 to $70. Pool, bike rentals, snack bar.

This cozy campground is shady and deeply wooded, and conveniently close to I-95. Site sizes are generous, and deluxe patio sites are excellent. The playground is outdated and the pool is unimpressive, but the scheduled weekend activities are a hit with families.

Civil War buffs love the campground's proximity to major battlefields and the Stonewall Jackson Shrine. Downtown Fredericksburg and the James Monroe Museum and Memorial Library are nearby, and Washington, D.C., is within reach.

② HARPERS FERRY/CIVIL WAR BATTLEFIELDS KOA

👫 👫 ♿ ⚓ 🚿 ✂ 🚐 📶

343 Campground Road, Harpers Ferry, WV 25425. koa.com/camp/harpers-ferry; harpersferrykoa@racpack.com; 304-535-6895. Heated pool, inflatable jump pillow, mini-golf.

The Harpers Ferry KOA could use some updating, but it's still a fun and convenient campground for families and Civil War buffs who want to be close to the action—some of which takes place on-site.

Visit the Civil War Living History Museum, cannon firings, and sites next to a trench where soldiers battled to the death. The Grapes and Grinds store serves specialty coffee in the morning and wine during evening tastings. Kids will love the heated pool, giant chess set, game room, and inflatable slides, and everyone can enjoy the nearby historical sites. There's also kayaking and whitewater rafting nearby on the Potomac and Shenandoah rivers.

HALLOWED GROUND AT GETTYSBURG.

③ GETTYSBURG CAMPGROUND

👫 👫 ♿ ⚓

2030 Fairfield Road, Gettysburg, PA 17325. gettysburgcampground.com; camp@ gettysburgcampground.com; 717-334-3304. April 1 to November 22. $37 to $66. Pool, shuffleboard, playground.

Gettysburg is home to many good options for RV travelers, but the Gettysburg Campground is the best, particularly if you can get a premium site along Marsh Creek. The sound of rolling water will put you to sleep at night, and the misty creek will greet you in the morning.

The campground is close to the battlefield and downtown. And if you need to have work done to your RV, the campground has an on-site repair service.

The amenities are nice. The country-style store sells books and Civil War collectibles, and the snack bar is a popular stop for lunch. End your day with hand-scooped Hershey's ice cream from the ice-cream parlor.

FREDERICKSBURG.

> Harpers Ferry was very difficult to defend and changed hands numerous times between 1861 and 1865.

RESTAURANTS

1 COLONIAL TAVERN, HOME TO THE IRISH BRIGADE

👫 👬 ♿

406 Lafayette Boulevard, Fredericksburg, VA 22401. **irishbrigadetavern.com;** thecoltav@aol.com; 540-373-1313. Monday to Saturday 11:30 A.M. to 2 A.M.; Sunday 11:30 A.M. to 12 A.M. $12 to $25. American Irish.

After you've toured the battlefields around Fredericksburg all day, this pub offers comforting, hearty food and a great draft. The menu has plenty of options for traditional Irish fare, such as the corned beef and cabbage or fish and chips. The homemade shepherd's pie is served with mashed potatoes, as is the Guinness beef stew.

A great variety of beers are on tap, and the selection of hard cider is good. Live entertainment plays on many nights

> The Battle of Gettysburg was not the largest of the war, but it was the costliest, with more than 30,000 dead or wounded.

2 CANAL HOUSE CAFE

👫 👬 ♿

1226 W. Washington Street, Harpers Ferry, WV 25425. **canalhousecafe.com;** laura@canalhousecafe.com; 304-535-2880. Thursday to Tuesday 12 P.M. to 9 P.M.; closed Wednesday. $15 to $25. Farm to table.

Canal House Cafe offers the rare opportunity to experience a modern culinary trend in a historically significant location. The Canal House was built around 1800 and features the original six fireplaces, exposed brick, and 2-feet-thick (.6m) stone walls. The hand-dug stone well is still used to supply water year round, and food is served out of the original kitchen.

This restaurant prides itself on locally and sustainably sourced ingredients used in food preparation. A list of partner farms in West Virginia, Virginia, and Maryland is proudly displayed on the dining room wall. The ploughman's starter allows you to sample local cheeses and meats paired with homemade bread. Order "the general" for your entrée, and you might find a new favorite meatloaf sandwich.

3 DOBBIN HOUSE TAVERN

👫 👬 ♿

89 Steinwehr Avenue, Gettysburg, PA 17325. **dobbinhouse.com;** info@dobbinhouse.com; 717-334-2100. 11:30 A.M. to 9 P.M. $12 to $35. Traditional American.

Stick with the historical theme of the area, and dine at the oldest home in Gettysburg, which now operates as an inn and restaurant.

The Springhouse Tavern offers casual fare like French onion soup, spinach salad, and crab cake sandwiches. For fine dining, try the Alexander Dobbin Dining Rooms, which offers shrimp cocktail and prime rib.

Free historical tours are available.

HARPERS FERRY NATIONAL HISTORIC PARK.

ATTRACTIONS

1 FREDERICKSBURG AND SPOTSYLVANIA NATIONAL MILITARY PARK

👪 🚻 ♿

120 Chatham Drive, Fredericksburg, VA 22405. nps.gov/frsp; 540-693-3200. 9 A.M. to 5 P.M. Free admission to park and building.

Daily walking tours are offered at each of the four major battlefields in this park: Fredericksburg, Chancellorsville, Wilderness, and Spotsylvania Court House. You'll get so much more out of your visit if you plan in advance around these guided tour times.

Another option is renting or purchasing a self-guided driving tour CD available at the visitor centers.

2 HARPERS FERRY NATIONAL HISTORICAL PARK

👪 🚻 ♿

171 Shoreline Drive, Harpers Ferry, WV 25425. nps.gov/hafe; 304-535-6029. 9 A.M. to 5 P.M. Vehicle pass $10.

Harpers Ferry is a historic town located at the confluence of the Potomac and Shenandoah rivers. The battle of Harpers Ferry took place here in September 1862.

This is a fantastic hiking park, offering both sublime natural beauty and historical interest. Pick up a map at the visitor center, and walk the easy, scenic trail down to the Lower Town area, or hike the challenging

Maryland Heights trail to see Civil War artilleries and forts.

Ranger-led programs include guided walking tours. For the best historical insight, hire a park guide from the visitor center for a 2.5-hour private tour.

3 GETTYSBURG NATIONAL MILITARY PARK

👪 🚻 ♿

1195 Baltimore Pike, Gettysburg, PA. nps.gov/gett; 717-338-1243. November to March 8 A.M. to 5 P.M.; April to October 8 A.M. to 6 P.M. Free admission to park; museum: adults $12.50; seniors $11.50; children 6 to 12 $8.50; 5 and under free.

For many visitors, the Gettysburg Battlefield ends up being a real educational experience. The key to this historic site is enjoying the many exhibits and tours offered by the National Park Service. Begin your day at the visitor center, touring relics from the war, interactive exhibits, and multimedia presentations. Watch the *A New Birth of Freedom* film, and view the enormous Gettysburg Cyclorama.

During the summer, ranger-led tours operate throughout the day. Listen to talks about specific battles, or join a 2-hour battle walk tour. For the most immersive experience, hire one of the Licensed Battlefield Guides available at the visitor center. For a reasonable fee, this private guide jumps in your vehicle and make history come alive as you tour.

ITINERARIES

IF YOU HAVE 1 WEEK …

In Fredericksburg, rent an audio tour and visit the four major battlefields. In Harpers Ferry, take a horse-and-wagon guided tour. In Gettysburg,  visit the museum and hire a Licensed Battlefield Guide.

IF YOU HAVE 2 WEEKS …

All the above, plus visit the Wilderness Battlefield, tour Ellwood Manor, and hike the Gordon Flank Attack Trail in Fredericksburg. In Harpers Ferry take the ranger-led walking tour "Charles Town and John Brown: The Rest of the Story." Visit the Soldiers' National Cemetery in Gettysburg.

IF YOU HAVE 3 WEEKS …

All the above, plus in Fredericksburg visit the Stonewall Jackson Shrine, and stand in the room where he died. Tour the Old Salem Church, which still has scars from the war. In Harpers Ferry, attend a Living History Workshop. Visit the Shriver House Museum in Gettysburg.

SOUTH

shenandoah national park, virginia

Shenandoah National Park is long and skinny, stretching 105 miles (169km) from Front Royal to Rockfish Gap. Exploring the whole park means a lot of driving. If you set up base camp in the Luray area, you can drive in for shorter day trips.

Pinnacles Overlook

Big Meadows

White Oak Canyon

Bearfence Mountain

Rapidan Camp

Lewis Mountain

3

SKYLINE DRIVE
Skyline Drive runs along the backbone of the park's Blue Ridge Mountains.

HIGHLIGHTS

✴ Pack a picnic lunch and meander down **Skyline Drive,** enjoying the spectacular vistas.

✴ Look for bear, deer, and other wildlife at **Big Meadows** at dawn or dusk.

✴ Descend into the **Luray Caverns,** and see the stalactites and stalagmites.

BEST TIME TO GO

Spring flowers and fall foliage are stunning in Shenandoah. You'll grapple with heat in the summer, so stay cool with water activities.

CAMPGROUNDS

1 SHENANDOAH RIVER STATE PARK CAMPGROUND

350 Daughter of Stars Drive, Bentonville, VA 22610. dcr.virginia.gov/state-parks/shenandoah-river.shtml; shenandoahriver@dcr.virginia.gov; 540-622-6840. $24 to $41. Restrooms, laundry, café/snack bar.

This campground offers 61 sites within a state park that has 5.2 miles (8.4km) of shoreline along the Shenandoah River. You also can see Shenandoah National Park to the east. The park has 24 miles (39km) of trails, horseback riding, zip-lining, and fishing. Boat and canoe launches are also available.

Shenandoah River State Park is the perfect choice for RV travelers looking for pristine beauty with a budget price tag. Book far in advance to get a site here.

THE AMAZING CAVERNS AT LURAY.

2 LURAY KOA

3402 Kimball Road, Luray, VA 22835. koa.com/campgrounds/luray; camp@luraykoa.com; 540-743-7222. March 13 to November 15. $44 to $69. Pool, snack bar, pavilion, camping kitchen.

The Luray KOA features large, pull-thru sites and deluxe patio sites overlooking a large green. Return customers rave that this European-style park is one of the cleanest campgrounds you'll ever visit. Surrounded by rolling hills and farmland, the quiet and romantic campground is perfect for couples. The small pool and playground help entertain little campers, and the billiard room and outdoor table tennis keep older kids busy.

In addition to being near the Thornton Gap Entrance Station, the campground is near several famous Civil War battle sites as well.

Arrive prepared with your own supplies because there's no traditional camp store. On the weekends, you can enjoy homemade pizza from the on-site wood-fired brick oven.

> The Shenandoah National Park is home to 101 miles (163km) of the Appalachian Trail.

DARK HOLLOW FALLS.

3 YOGI BEAR'S JELLYSTONE PARK CAMP-RESORT LURAY

2250 US 211, Luray, VA 22835. campluray.com; yogi@campluray.com; 540-318-7337. March 20 to November 30. $40 to $106. Pool, waterslide, mini-golf, fishing, paddleboats, snack bar, arcade.

There's no better option for families traveling with kids than Jellystone Luray, renowned for its friendly and efficient staff. Craft sessions, tie-dye, story time, hayrides, and counselor-led games and relay races make it impossible for anyone to be bored while staying here.

The theme park–size slide, spray ground, pools, laser tag, and outdoor theater ensure the campground is a destination in its own right. Many other activities are included, such as mini-golf, catch-and-release fishing, and character photo opportunities. Kids will love beginning every day by saying the Pledge of Allegiance with Yogi Bear, Cindy, and Boo-Boo. Adults will enjoy the panoramic views of the mountains.

President Herbert Hoover built Rapidan Camp in Shenandoah National Park. He and his wife summered there during his presidency.

RESTAURANTS

1 GATHERING GROUNDS PÂTISSERIE AND CAFÉ

24 E. Main Street, Luray, VA 22835. **ggrounds .com**; 540-743-1121. Monday to Thursday 7 A.M. to 6 P.M.; Friday and Saturday 8 A.M. to 8 P.M.; Sunday 11 A.M. to 3 P.M. $7 to $15. Bakery and café.

This is a wonderful place to go for delicious and healthy meals that keep you energized for your outdoor activities in Shenandoah. The breakfast burritos, quiche, soups, sandwiches, and specialty coffees might have you coming back a few times during your stay. The desserts and pastries are homemade and top notch.

We suggest ordering a picnic to go, driving up to Big Meadows, and enjoying your scrumptious meal with a view.

2 SPELUNKER'S DRIVE-THRU

116 South Street, Front Royal, VA 22630. **spelunkerscustard.com**; feedback@ spelunkerscustard.com; 540-631-0300. 11 A.M. to 10 P.M. $4 to $8. Burgers.

Whitewater rafting, tubing, or hiking can leave you in the mood for a great burger and shake. Spelunker's is the perfect place to satisfy that craving.

Fresh burger patties are juicy and delicious on their own or topped with cheese, bacon, and other fixings. Cheesesteaks, fish and chips, hotdogs, and Italian sausages also are on the menu. The homemade french fries are fantastic, and there's even malt vinegar on the tables to top them off.

Leave room for dessert because the ice cream, custard, and gelati are specialties. The flavor of the day is always creative and fun, but even a simple dish of vanilla custard with a little chocolate syrup on top is delicious.

3 TRIPLE CROWN BBQ

1079 US 211, Luray, VA 22835. 540-743-5311. Friday to Sunday 11:30 A.M. to 6:30 P.M. $8 to $15. American barbecue.

Triple Crown serves heavenly pulled pork. All the meat here is perfectly cooked and never oversauced. This is road food at its best, with a walk-up window to place your order and picnic tables to sit and enjoy the bounty.

At least 500 mountain families were displaced when Shenandoah National Park was created in the 1930s.

THE SUMMIT OF STONY MAN MOUNTAIN.

ATTRACTIONS

1 SHENANDOAH RIVER OUTFITTERS

👪 👫

6502 S. Page Valley Road, Luray, VA 22835. shenandoah-river.com; 504-743-4159. Hours vary by season and activity. $22 to $90.

This company has been in business for decades, and it knows how to help you experience the Shenandoah River tubing, canoeing, kayaking, or rafting. Multiday excursions are available, as are shorter trips for beginners.

Advance reservations are highly recommended, and if you can visit during the week, you most definitely should.

2 LURAY CAVERNS

👪 👫

101 Cave Hill Road, Luray, VA 22835. luraycaverns.com; 540-743-6551. Tours begin at 9 A.M. Adults $26; seniors $23; children $14; additional fees for other activities.

Even if you've seen pictures of this natural phenomenon, the beauty of this underground world is astonishing. Wear a sweater for your tour, because no matter the temperature above ground, the Luray Caverns are a chilly 54°F (12°C).

The caverns can be seen only by guided tour, which takes you over paved paths for about 1.25 miles (2km). The lines for tours can get

long, so get there right when the caverns open. The tour ends in the Stalacpipe Organ room, where you'll hear the instrument played by an automated system.

Extend your visit by enjoying the Garden Maze, the Rope Adventure Park, and the Luray Valley Museum.

3 SKYLINE DRIVE

👪 👫 ♿ 🐕

Shenandoah National Park. nps.gov/shen; 540-999-3500. Open year round; 24 hours a day. 7-day vehicle pass $20.

Skyline Drive is more than 100 miles (161km) long, with amazing vistas and hundreds of miles of hiking trails shooting off from various stops.

One of the most popular sections of the drive is the Central District, miles 31.5 through 61.5. To see this area, enter at Thornton Gap and exit at Swift Run Gap. The famous Pinnacles and Stony Man overlooks are in this section, as well as Skyland and Big Meadows. The Byrd Visitor Center has regularly scheduled ranger presentations and a fascinating exhibit on the history of the park. Visit Rapidan Camp to see President Herbert Hoover's summer retreat. The Story of the Forest hike right near the visitor center is great for young children. Dark Hollow Falls offers more of a challenge.

ITINERARIES

IF YOU HAVE 1 WEEK ...

Explore the Central District of Shenandoah National Park, taking Skyline Drive from Thornton Gap to Swift Run Gap. Hike the Stony Man Trail. Tour Luray Caverns. Raft or tube the Shenandoah River.

IF YOU HAVE 2 WEEKS ...

All the above, plus explore the North District of Shenandoah National Park. Visit the Dickey Ridge Visitor Center, and hike the Fox Hollow/ Dickey Ridge Trail. Pack lunch to eat at Elkwallow Picnic Area. Spend an afternoon shopping in Front Royal, exploring all the boutiques and gift shops.

IF YOU HAVE 3 WEEKS ...

All the above, plus explore the South District of Shenandoah National Park from Swift Run Gap to Rockfish Gap. Hike to the Jones Run falls. Stop at the dozens of overlooks along the southern part of Skyline Drive. Spend some time on the Shenandoah Valley Wine Trail.

kentucky
bourbon
trail

The Bourbon Trail, established in 1999, is a roughly 60-mile (97km) journey that stretches from Louisville to Lexington and then down to Bardstown. Grab your official passport, start your journey at one of the many "trailheads," and visit all nine distilleries if you can.

HIGHLIGHTS

✳ Learn how to smell bourbon by taking a lesson at the **Maker's Mark Distillery.**

✳ Watch employees bottle and label cases of Blanton's by hand at **Buffalo Trace Distillery.**

✳ Choose your two tasting bourbons, regardless of price point, at the **Jim Beam Distillery.**

BEST TIME TO GO

Visit during the spring or fall because most distilleries reduce or shut down production in the summer.

Kentucky Bourbon Trail

❶ Bulleit Frontier Whiskey Experience
❷ Evan Williams Bourbon Experience
❸ Four Roses Distillery
❹ Heaven Hill Distilleries
❺ The Jim Beam American Stillhouse
❻ Maker's Mark Distillery
❼ Town Branch Distillery
❽ Wild Turkey Distillery
❾ Woodford Reserve Distillery

CAMPGROUNDS

1 KENTUCKY HORSE PARK CAMPGROUND

♔ ♿ 🏕 🚿 ⚡ 🛜

4089 Iron Works Parkway, Lexington, KY 40511. kyhorsepark.com/visit/park-info-resources/khp-campground; 859-259-4200. $25 to $35. Pool, volleyball, tennis and basketball courts, walking and bike trails.

Just 9 miles (14.5km) from downtown Lexington, this campground is a great option if you want to tour the bourbon trail and visit the Kentucky Horse Park, where you get free parking and a discounted admission rate when staying on-site.

All sites are spacious, paved, and furnished with a picnic table and fire ring. There are no pull-thrus. Plenty of outdoor recreation activities are available, including multiple recreational courts, a walking trail, and a bike trail.

KENTUCKY BOURBON.

2 MY OLD KENTUCKY HOME STATE PARK

♔ ♿ 🏕 🚿 ⚡ 🛜

501 E. Stephen Foster Avenue, Bardstown, KY 40004. parks.ky.gov/parks/recreationparks/old-ky-home; 502-348-3502. April 1 to October 31. $20 to $24. Picnic area, historical sites.

This state park campground only has 39 sites, so book as early as you can. The area is well maintained and clean, offering full hookups and access for larger rigs. No extra amenities are offered on the campground, but My Old Kentucky Home State Park provides plenty of recreational and educational opportunities. The grounds are beautiful, and you'll want to spend a fair amount of time walking and biking the trails.

Take a guided tour of the historic Rowan Estate memorialized by Stephen Foster, America's great composer, who wrote classics like "Oh! Susannah" and "Camptown Races." If possible, attend a performance of *The Stephen Foster Story* live at the park amphitheater on scheduled dates throughout the summer.

Each of the nine distilleries on the trail have individual tour policies, so check every location for pricing.

LOUISVILLE, GATEWAY TO THE BOURBON TRAIL.

3 LOUISVILLE SOUTH KOA

♔ ♔ ♿ 🏕 🚿 ⚡ 🚐 🛜

2433 Highway 44 E., Shepherdsville, KY 40165. koa.com/campgrounds/louisville-south; louisvillesouth@koa.net; 502-543-8942. $56 to $81. Pool, hot tub, mini-golf, fishing.

This KOA is just minutes from downtown Louisville and is a great place to stay when exploring the Urban Bourbon Trail and other visitor attractions in the area, such as the Louisville Slugger Museum and Factory, Churchill Downs, and the Muhammed Ali Center.

Large pull-thrus make this campground big-rig friendly, and the staff gets consistent high marks for customer service. Although the facilities are kept clean, they're a bit older and in some need of updating. The pool is open Memorial Day through Labor Day, along with an adults-only hot tub. Many activities are available for kids on the weekends throughout the summer, such as tie-dye, outdoor movies, and organized games.

SOUTH

The official Bourbon Trail website, kybourbontrail.com, offers helpful planning tools and distillery information.

RESTAURANTS

1 ST. CHARLES EXCHANGE

113 S. 7th Street, Louisville, KY 40202. stcharlesexchange.com; 502-618-1917. Monday to Friday 11:30 A.M. to 2 P.M.; Monday to Saturday 5 P.M. to 10:30 P.M.; closed Sunday. $15 to $40. New American.

This restaurant is located in a historic downtown building, where the swanky atmosphere, classic cocktails, and classy service transport you back in time. Where else can you get a daily deviled-egg special? Or an appetizer called "Elvis on horseback" that includes bacon, peanut butter, dates, and bourbon?

Whether you order the salmon prepared with pork belly or the vegetarian-friendly beet risotto, be sure to include some family style sides with your meal.

2 MAMMY'S KITCHEN

116 W. Stephen Foster Avenue, Bardstown, KY 40004. btownmammys.com; 502-350-1097. Monday to Saturday 6:30 A.M. to 9 P.M.; Sunday 8 A.M. to 5 P.M. $15 to $30. American.

Mammy's serves breakfast, lunch, and dinner—and does them all well. If you want to fill up in the morning before heading out to the distilleries, try the hot brown sandwich, a Kentucky original invented in Louisville. If you're stopping in for lunch, order the bourbon dog or bourbon burger with crispy fried onion straws. The supper menu offers all the family style favorites, such as fried catfish, Southern-fried steak, and country ham. Also try the bourbon chops and bourbon chicken.

3 HOLLY HILL INN

426 N. Winter Street, Midway, KY 40347. hollyhillinn.com; hollyhillmidway@aol.com; 859-846-4732. Wednesday to Saturday 5:30 P.M. to close; Sunday brunch 11 A.M. to 2 P.M. $31 to $60. New American.

A foodie's paradise, Holly Hill Inn prides itself on using local agricultural products to create dishes that highlight this Kentucky region.

This restaurant is regularly featured in newspaper and magazine articles, so you definitely need to make reservations. This is a fine dining experience you won't soon forget.

Bourbon can only be produced in America, and 95 percent of America's bourbon comes from Kentucky.

KENTUCKY HORSE PARK.

ATTRACTIONS

1 LOUISVILLE, KENTUCKY

Louisville Visitor Center, 301 S. Fourth Street, Louisville, KY 40202. gotolouisville.com; info@ gotolouisville.com; 888-568-4784. Monday to Saturday 10 A.M. to 5 P.M.; Sunday 12 P.M. to 5 P.M.

Often referred to as the Official Gateway of the Kentucky Bourbon Trail, Louisville is the perfect place to start your trip. Pick up your passport and start your bourbon education at the Bulleit Frontier Whiskey Experience. Then head to Evan Williams, located on the historic Whiskey Row in downtown Louisville, where you can watch whiskey being made. A $10 tour gives you a great introduction to American whiskey produced in this region.

2 BARDSTOWN, KENTUCKY

One Court Square, Bardstown, KY 40004. visitbardstown.com; info@bardstowntourism .com; 800-638-4877. 9 A.M. to 5 P.M.

In 2012, *USA Today* called Bardstown "America's Most Beautiful Small Town." You'll want to spend some time meandering down the picture-perfect streets lined with interesting shops and boutiques.

The Kentucky Bourbon Marketplace isn't officially on the trail, but it offers a great tasting experience. On the outskirts of town is the Bourbon Heritage Center, the largest family-owned producer of bourbon. A short drive away is the Jim Beam American Stillhouse, offering one of the most unique tours full of interactive multimedia exhibits. A highlight in this area of the trail is the Maker's Mark Distillery. The beautiful property and warm family welcome are legendary.

3 LEXINGTON, KENTUCKY

Lexington Visitor Center, 401 W. Main Street, Lexington, KY 40507. visitlex.com; vacation@ visitlex.com; 800-845-3959. April to October. Monday to Friday 9 A.M. to 5 P.M.; Saturday 10 A.M. to 5 P.M.; Sunday 12 P.M. to 5 P.M.

Start in downtown Lexington with a visit to Town Branch Distillery, the only distillery built in Lexington in more than 100 years. It also brews beer, and your tour ticket includes sampling four of its five beers and three spirits. Then it's off to the Woodford Reserve, the oldest and smallest distillery in Kentucky. Basic tickets are $10 for a tour and tasting. Enjoy beautiful scenery as you drive to the Wild Turkey Distillery, set against the backdrop of the Kentucky River. Master distiller Jimmy Russell has been crafting bourbon here for more than 60 years and still poses for pictures. Many people particularly enjoy their time at the Four Roses Distillery, soaking in the Spanish mission-style architecture and gardens of sweet-smelling roses.

ITINERARIES

IF YOU HAVE 1 WEEK ...

Use Bardstown as your launching point, and visit the Kentucky Bourbon Marketplace, Bourbon Heritage Center, and the Oscar Getz Museum of Whiskey History. Tour Jim Beam and Maker's Mark distilleries. Eat at Talbott Tavern.

IF YOU HAVE 2 WEEKS ...

Consider staying in two different campgrounds to explore different locations along the Bourbon Trail. Louisville and Bardstown make good base camps. Do all the above, plus tour the Bulleit Frontier Whiskey Experience and the Evan Williams Bourbon Experience. Take in the Urban Bourbon Trail in downtown Louisville. Visit the Kentucky Derby Museum.

IF YOU HAVE 3 WEEKS ...

Consider spending a week in each main area, Louisville, Bardstown, and Lexington, so you can fully explore each distinct area of the bourbon trail. Do all the above, plus visit all nine distilleries on the trail and receive a free T-shirt when you hand in your fully stamped passport. Then you can begin your Kentucky Bourbon Trail Craft Tour.

SOUTH

mammoth cave national park, kentucky

Under the rolling Kentucky hills lies the world's longest known cave system, with 365 miles (587km) of mapped caves and more being discovered all the time.

HIGHLIGHTS

✳ Learn about the **geological and social history** of the caves on the Historic Tour.

✳ Belly-crawl in the dark through tight spaces on the **Wild Cave Tour.**

✳ **Kayak the Green River,** or fish for bass, catfish, and perch.

BEST TIME TO GO

The weather in the caves is the same year round, so this is the perfect park to explore off-season, between November and April.

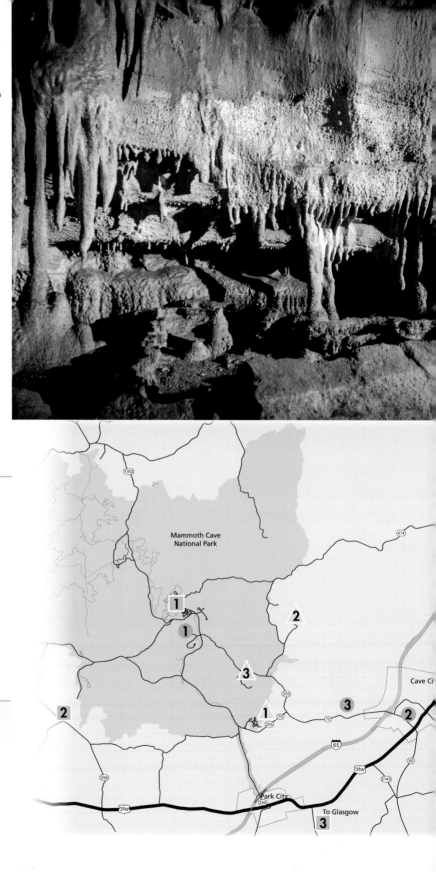

CAMPGROUNDS

1 MAMMOTH CAVE NATIONAL PARK CAMPGROUND

Mammoth Cave Campground, Mammoth Cave, KY 42259. nps.gov/maca/planyourvisit/camping.htm; 270-758-2424. March 1 to November 30. $17. Paved pads, picnic tables, fire rings, restrooms.

If you're willing to boondock, and you want to save a few bucks, this wooded campground is a great pick. Reservations are not accepted, and although there are no amenities, each site is spacious and features a paved parking area, a picnic table, and a fire ring. Those who love to hike, bike, kayak, and ride horses won't miss a pool and playground.

It's also a short ¼ mile (.4km) from the park's visitor center.

2 CAVE COUNTRY RV CAMPGROUND

216 Gaunce Drive, Cave City, KY 42127. cavecountryrv.com; office@cavecountryrv.com; 270-773-4678. $38 to $40. Lounge area, fitness room, camp store.

This Good Sam RV Park wins rave reviews for its cleanliness, relaxing atmosphere, and excellent customer service. The knowledgeable and friendly staff make you feel at home and can help you plan your stay.

The campground is only 5 miles (8km) from the entrance to Mammoth Cave National Park. The pull-thru sites all have full hookups and are big-rig friendly. Many restaurants are nearby. There is no pool, and amenities are limited. If you're traveling with kids, this might not be for you.

Prices are more than reasonable, making this an obvious pick for those traveling on a budget but still desiring full hookups.

3 YOGI BEAR'S JELLYSTONE PARK CAMP-RESORT MAMMOTH CAVE

1002 Mammoth Cave Road, Cave City, KY 42127. jellystonemammothcave.com; frontdesk@jellystonemammothcave.com; 270-773-3840. $42 to $89. Pool with waterslide, inflatable jump pillow, splash pad, playground, mini-golf.

If you're traveling to Mammoth Cave with kids, this campground is ideal. After a morning cave tour, your family will appreciate time spent above ground cooling off in the pool, racing down the large waterslide, running through the splash pad, hopping on the inflatable jump pillow, playing a game of horseshoes, or fishing at the pond. Hungry? Grab some Carolina barbecue or a corn dog at the Pic-A-Nic Basket snack bar. The amenities here are first class.

A wide variety of full-hookup sites can accommodate everything from a pop-up camper to a big rig.

This campground offers many themed weekends, from Boo-Boo's Birthday Bash to Family Olympics. Check the calendar for a preview.

RANGER-LED TOURS OF THE CAVES.

Geologists believe Mammoth Cave began forming 10 million years ago and will eventually erode into canyons.

In 1842, Mammoth Cave housed an underground tuberculosis hospital. The experimental facility failed after a few short months when patients began to die from the lack of ventilation.

RESTAURANTS

1 TRAVERTINE RESTAURANT

👪 👫 ♿

Mammoth Cave National Park, Mammoth Cave, KY 42259. **mammothcavehotel.com**; 270-758-2225. Breakfast 7 A.M. to 10 A.M.; lunch 11 A.M. to 4 P.M.; dinner 5 P.M. to 8 P.M. $11 to $30. American.

Mammoth Cave National Park is home to three restaurants, and this is by far the best place for a nice lunch or dinner. You'll find typical grill food like hamburgers and hotdogs, but you also can order a sirloin steak or trout.

Prices are a bit high for most people's liking. Few other options are nearby, though, so if you want a hearty meal after a cave tour, this is the spot.

2 PORKY PIG DINER

👪 👫 ♿

125 National Park Boundary Road, Smiths Grove, KY 42171. 270-597-2422. Sunday 7 A.M. to 3 P.M.; Monday to Thursday 6 A.M. to 7 P.M.; Friday and Saturday 6 A.M. to 8 P.M. $6 to $15. Diner fare.

This diner will satisfy your search for downhome flavors in the heart of Kentucky. Here, pig decorations abound, and the pork sandwiches are a big hit. The fact that the park rangers eat here says everything.

Catfish sandwiches, onion rings, and coleslaw serve as the perfect posthike lunch.

3 A LITTLE TASTE OF TEXAS

👪 👫 ♿

303 S. Broadway, Glasgow, KY 42141. **glasgow-ky.com/littletastoftexas.com**; 270-659-2441. Monday to Friday 11 A.M. to 2 P.M.; Monday to Thursday 4:30 P.M. to 8:30 P.M.; Friday and Saturday 4:30 P.M. to 9 P.M. $30 to $55. Steak.

This area is full of chain restaurants, so A Little Taste of Texas stands out for being independently owned and a local favorite.

This is a steak house, and you should order as such. The sirloin steaks are big and perfectly seasoned, and the prime rib cuts like butter. Salads are cold, crunchy, and topped with creamy dressings, and large baked potatoes and coleslaw are served on the side. Other popular menu options include chicken fried steak, which is definitely big enough to share. For starters, order the fried mushrooms or pickles.

As with many restaurants in this dry county, beer, wine, and spirits are not served. Order the sweet tea instead.

AMAZING MAMMOTH CAVE.

ATTRACTIONS

1 MAMMOTH CAVE CANOE AND KAYAK

1240 Old Mammoth Cave Road, Cave City, KY 42127. mammothcavecanoe-k.com; 877-592-2663. Memorial Day to Labor Day 8 A.M. to 2 P.M.; Labor Day to October 9 A.M. to 2 P.M. Call ahead for reservations. $45 to $85 depending on trip package.

Mammoth Cave Canoe and Kayak is one of the few outfitters licensed to operate within the park. You can schedule half-day, full-day, or multi-day trips. The staff drops you off at the Green River dam, sending you downriver, and picks you up at a designated location. Along the way, you enjoy beautiful scenery and abundant wildlife.

2 MAMMOTH CAVE ADVENTURES

1994 Roy Hunter Road, Cave City, KY 42127. mammothcave-adventures.com; 270-773-6087. Monday to Thursday 9 A.M. to 4 P.M.; Friday and Sunday 9 A.M. to 5 P.M.; Saturday 9 A.M. to 8 P.M. $25 to $60, depending on course.

If you're looking for an adrenaline rush, Mammoth Cave Adventures has you covered, with multiple zip-lining courses, a Giant Super Swing, and a Drop Tower. Horseback riding is also available if you prefer a less-extreme adventure.

The primary zip-lining course has five zips up to 950 feet (290m) long.

A smaller course is available for children. The Giant Super Swing sends you flying out over a ridge and 40 feet (12m) above the ground. The Drop Tower is a 70-foot (21m) controlled free fall. The horseback riding tour is an easy, 1-hour ride through the Mammoth Cave hills.

3 NATIONAL PARK SERVICE CAVE TOURS

nps.gov/maca. Summer 8 A.M. to 6:30 P.M.; fall 8:30 A.M. to 5:15 P.M. Tour schedules vary by season. $4 to $50 depending on tour.

The park service offers many options for exploring Mammoth Cave. Detailed descriptions of each tour are available on the website, along with current schedules. Reservations aren't required, but they're recommended, as you're unlikely to find a tour open during the summer season. Book online as far in advance as possible to guarantee your spot.

A popular pick for first-time visitors is the Frozen Niagara Tour, which is perfect for small children and folks who might not enjoy spending lengthy time in confined spaces. The family friendly Historic Tour leads you past all the famous landmarks of the caves. Feeling daring? Try the Wild Cave Tour and climb and crawl through the caves in the dark, accompanied by experienced guides.

ITINERARIES

IF YOU HAVE 1 WEEK ...

Take the Historic Tour and the Domes and Dripstones Tour in the park. Hike the River Styx Spring Trail. Zip-line at Mammoth Cave Adventures. Rent kayaks and paddle down the Green River.

IF YOU HAVE 2 WEEKS ...

All the above, plus take the Violet City Lantern Tour and the Gothic Avenue Tour in the park. Hike the Cedar Sink Trail. Enjoy a guided horseback riding tour in the park. Rent bikes and explore the Mammoth Cave Railroad Bike and Hike Trail. Visit Dinosaur World.

IF YOU HAVE 3 WEEKS ...

All the above, plus take a risk and sign up for the Wild Cave Tour and Tall Man's Misery. Hike the Echo River Trail. Fish for bass on the Green River. Visit Kentucky Action Park. Take a day trip to the Abraham Lincoln Birthplace National Historical Park in Hodgenville.

memphis
and
graceland

Located on the Mississippi River, Memphis, Tennessee, is a thriving commercial city with world-class medical and educational centers. But most visitors arrive for two major reasons: to soak in the thriving music scene and to tour some of the most important historical sites in American history.

HIGHLIGHTS

☀ Tour **Sun Studio,** a small place with a big history where Elvis Presley got his start.

☀ Visit the **Jungle Room** at Graceland, decorated with animal print and shag carpeting.

☀ Reflect on the civil rights struggle at the **Lorraine Motel,** where Martin Luther King Jr. was assassinated.

BEST TIME TO GO

To avoid the heat and crowds, visit in either April and May or October and November, when it's as temperate as Memphis gets.

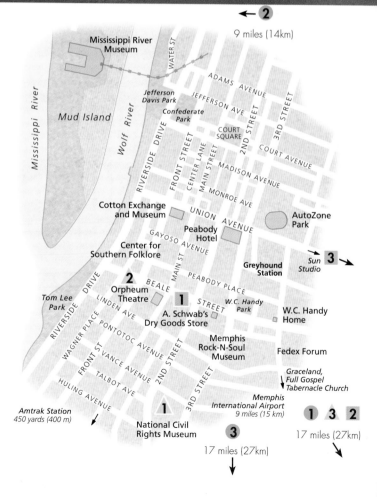

CAMPGROUNDS

1 GRACELAND RV PARK AND CAMPGROUND

3691 Elvis Presley Boulevard, Memphis, TN 38116. **memphisgracelandrvpark.com**; gracelandrvpark@graceland.com; 866-571-9236. $36 to $41. Pool, playground, horseshoes.

The Graceland RV Park and Campground is all about location. Elvis's colonial revival–style mansion is directly across the street, and you can walk there in about 2 minutes, even if you're wearing blue suede shoes.

The park itself lacks the kitschy glamour of Graceland, but it earns solid reviews for being clean and affordable. The campground offers a swimming pool and a camp store that sells Elvis memorabilia, and Beale Street and downtown Memphis are also nearby.

2 TOM SAWYER'S RV PARK

1286 S. 8th Street, West Memphis, AR 73201. **tomsawyersrvpark.com**; tomsawyerrvpark@gmail.com; 870-735-9770. $27 to $40. Fishing, outdoor games.

Tom Sawyer's RV Park is located directly on the Mississippi River in West Memphis, Arkansas. It's just 15 minutes from downtown Memphis and 25 minutes from Graceland.

Three dozen concrete pull-thru sites are here; some are shaded, and others are located directly on the river. A special riverfront section is available just for motor homes, and another section is designed to allow fifth wheels to back in for spectacular rear-window views of the mighty Mississippi. After spending the day touring Memphis, you can kick back under your awning and watch the barges go by as you dine alfresco.

The park has friendly, hospitable managers and camp workers who can escort you to your site and make you feel at home.

3 YOGI BEAR'S JELLYSTONE PARK CAMP-RESORT MEMPHIS

1400 Audubon Point Drive, Horn Lake, MS 38637. **memphisjellystone.com**; reservations@memphisjellystone.com; 662-280-8282. $45 to $55. Inflatable waterslide, swimming pools, inflatable jump pillow, exercise room.

This park is almost universally well reviewed and wins high marks for its cleanliness, immaculate landscaping, and warm Southern hospitality. If you're traveling to Memphis with kids, you'd be hard-pressed to find a better campground. The action-packed schedule of events, such as pool bingo and water balloon games, allow you to relax while your kids have a blast. The park is full of kid-friendly amenities such as the inflatable waterslide, volleyball court, multiple pools, and playground. Mom and Dad will appreciate the exercise room, and those traveling with dogs will enjoy the enclosed bark park.

Book a big-rig friendly premium site with a large concrete patio, Adirondack chairs, and a wrought-iron fire table for an experience that borders on "glamping." Major attractions are all a short drive away.

HISTORIC BEALE STREET.

President George W. Bush met with Japanese Prime Minister Junichiro Koizumi, a huge Elvis fan, at Graceland in 2006.

> When he was assassinated in 1968, Martin Luther King Jr. was in Memphis to support a workers' strike.

RESTAURANTS

1 BB KING'S BLUES CLUB

143 Beale Street, Memphis, TN 38103. **bbkings.com/memphis**; memphissales@ bbkingclubs.com; 901-524-5464. Monday to Thursday and Sunday 11 A.M. to 12:30 A.M.; Friday and Saturday 11 A.M. to 2 A.M. $15 to $32. Southern barbecue.

The house band at BB King's Blues Club is as good as it gets in a city full of amazing music. This is a restaurant where it all comes together for the first-time visitor, showcasing solid Southern cuisine against a backdrop of live jazz, blues, and rock 'n' roll.

You can stick with the classics here and walk away pleased. The ribs are tender, the shrimp and grits are buttery, and the fried green tomatoes are crisp-tender.

The first Piggly Wiggly opened in Memphis in 1916, ushering in the era of the modern grocery store. You can tour a replica at the Pink Palace Museum.

2 MARLOWE'S RIBS AND RESTAURANT

4381 Elvis Presley Boulevard, Memphis, TN 38116. **marlowesmemphis.com**; 901-332-4159. 12 P.M. to 3 A.M. $11 to $30. Southern barbecue.

Featured on Food Network's *Diners, Drive-Ins and Dives*, Marlowe's stands out for offering a fabulously kitschy experience along with fantastic food. Close to Graceland and a perfect follow-up to your visit, Marlowe's offers much better fare than you'll find at the mansion.

Huge portions of barbecue chicken, brisket, and ribs are served with cornbread, coleslaw, and fried okra. Call ahead to arrange for a free ride to the restaurant in a pink limo.

3 FOLK'S FOLLY PRIME STEAK HOUSE

551 S. Mendenhall Road, Memphis, TN 38116. **folksfolly.com**; 901-762-8200. Monday to Thursday 5:30 P.M. to 10 P.M.; Friday and Saturday 5:30 P.M. to 11 P.M.; Sunday 5:30 P.M. to 9 P.M. $35 to $80. American.

An institution in Memphis, this restaurant offers everything you want in a classic steakhouse: perfect cuts of meat and lobster tails paired with creamed spinach, garlic mashed potatoes, and asparagus with hollandaise sauce.

The service is impeccable, and the atmosphere classy. For any special occasion, or just a special night on the town, this is a perfect choice.

GRACELAND.

ATTRACTIONS

1 NATIONAL CIVIL RIGHTS MUSEUM AT THE LORRAINE MOTEL

450 Mulberry Street, Memphis, TN 38103. civilrightsmuseum.org; cdyson@civilrights museum.org; 901-521-9699. Monday and Wednesday to Saturday 9 A.M. to 5 P.M.; Sunday 1 P.M. to 5 P.M.; closed Tuesday. Adults $15; seniors $14; children 4 to 17 $12; 3 and under free.

A visit to this museum is an educational and emotional experience you're not likely to forget.

Located in the Lorraine Motel, where Martin Luther King Jr. was assassinated, the exhibits take you through five centuries of history, beginning with periods of slave resistance and moving through the bus boycotts and sit-ins of the twentieth century.

2 BEALE STREET HISTORIC DISTRICT

Beale Street, Memphis, TN 38103.

Beale Street is the center of the Memphis food and music scene, so you'll want to spend a good deal of time eating, drinking, shopping, and sightseeing your way down this road that was declared a National Historic Landmark in 1966.

During the day, explore legendary attractions such as the WC Handy House and the Orpheum Theatre. Shop at the A. Schwab Dry Goods Store and other funky vendors that line the street.

At night, the place comes alive with a party atmosphere, and music and people spill out into the street. To truly appreciate the magic of this place, get off the rowdy street and dive into one of the long-established clubs, like Mr. Handy's Blues Hall.

3 GRACELAND

3734 Elvis Presley Boulevard, Memphis, TN 38116. graceland.com; graceland@graceland. com; 901-332-3322. Monday to Saturday 9 A.M. to 5 P.M.; Sunday 9 A.M. to 4 P.M. Standard ticket prices (upgrades available): adults $36; seniors $32.40; children 7 to 12 $16; 6 and under free.

It would be unthinkable to visit Memphis without stopping in to pay respects to the king of rock 'n' roll. When you purchase the basic mansion tour ticket at Graceland, you get an interactive iPad that provides a narrated multimedia experience.

A few ticket upgrades are available, but the best deal is the Platinum Tour, which offers access to special exhibits and the airplanes for only a few more dollars. Skip the VIP Ticket, which is almost double the price without adding much value to the experience.

ITINERARIES

IF YOU HAVE 1 WEEK ...

Visit Graceland, touring the mansion and Memorial Gardens. Shop Beale Street during the day, and return at night for live music at BB King's. Explore the National Civil Rights Museum, and tour Sun Studio.

IF YOU HAVE 2 WEEKS ...

All the above, plus visit the exhibits at the Stax Museum of American Soul Music. Listen to a show at the Rum Boogie Cafe. Catch a Memphis Redbirds baseball game at AutoZone Park. Explore the Memphis Zoo and the Memphis Botanic Garden. Shop at the Memphis Pyramid.

IF YOU HAVE 3 WEEKS ...

All the above, plus visit the Memphis Rock 'n' Soul Museum. Catch a show at Earnestine and Hazel's or the Blues Hall Juke Joint. Wander around the Elmwood Cemetery and Mud Island River Park. Shop on Peabody Place in downtown Memphis. Tour the Pink Palace Museum. Take a day trip to the Elvis Presley Birthplace in Tupelo, Mississippi.

SOUTH

great smoky mountains
national park

With its rushing streams, majestic vistas, and diverse wildlife, the Great Smoky Mountains National Park is the most visited national park in the country, drawing more than 10 million visitors every year.

HIGHLIGHTS

✳ Climb the steep half-mile path to **Clingmans Dome,** the highest point in the park.

✳ Ride the **Smoky Mountain Alpine Coaster** in Pigeon Forge.

✳ Drive through Cades Cove, or hike through Elkmont for the best chance of **spotting bear.**

BEST TIME TO GO

Summer is very crowded, so if you're not determined to raft or tube, visit during spring wildflower or fall foliage seasons.

CAMPGROUNDS

1 TOWNSEND/GREAT SMOKIES KOA

8533 State Highway 73, Townsend, TN 37882. koa.com/campgrounds/townsend-great-smokies; townsend@koa.net; 865-448-2241. $26 to $94. Pool, playground, fishing, tubing, bike rental.

Families return to this campground year after year to enjoy its quiet beauty and prime location near the entrance of Cades Cove. You'll need to book early, especially if you want a riverfront site during the summer season.

With a whimsical playground, tubing in the Little River, and scheduled activities in the pavilion, this is the perfect campground for relaxing and unwinding between jaunts into the park. Be sure to sample the fudge in the sweets shop.

TUBING IN THE PARK.

2 ANCHOR DOWN RV RESORT

1703 Highway 139, Dandridge, TN 37764. anchordownrvresort.com; info@anchordownrvresort.com; 877-784-4446. March 5 to December 19. $49 to $139. Paved roads, pool with waterslide, playground, sandy beach and lake swimming.

This newest addition to the many campground options available in the Great Smokies is getting rave reviews and quickly becoming a favorite destination for luxury camping, having already earned a perfect rating in the Good Sam RV Travel Guide.

All sites offer astonishing views of Douglas Lake and the Smoky Mountains. Paved roads and concrete pads make this a great option for those who love to ride bikes. A pool with a large waterslide and a sandy beach with a swimming area also are here. Gorgeous stone fire pits and fireplaces are the centerpiece of every campsite.

Because the campground is new, the landscaping isn't mature and doesn't offer much shade, which might be a consideration in the heat of the summer.

> The Great Smoky Mountains National Park has 16 peaks with an elevation of more than 4,000 feet (1,219m).

RAPIDS AND WATERFALLS ABOUND IN THE SMOKIES.

3 GREAT SMOKY JELLYSTONE

4946 Hooper Highway, Cosby, TN 37722. greatsmokyjellystone.com; 423-487-5534. March 13 to November 30. $33 to $53. Pool, playground, mini-golf, ice-cream shop.

This family owned campground manages to be quiet and relaxing but still offers the kid-centered activities and amenities guests expect at a Jellystone.

Many of the sites are located on a creek that circles the main body of the campground. Book one of these early to ensure you spend hours relaxing to the sound of rushing water while your children splash and play.

Enjoy the heated saltwater pool after hiking in the mountains, or play a round of mini-golf. The camp store contains a charming ice-cream parlor. Order a mountain mud sundae, and eat it while watching a movie shown every evening in the outdoor theater. The spacious recreation room features air hockey, pool table, and more.

> The Great Smoky Mountains National Park receives almost double the number of visitors each year as the Grand Canyon.

RESTAURANTS

1 BENNETT'S PIT BAR-B-QUE

714 River Road, Gatlinburg, TN 37738. **bennetts-bbq.com;** 865-436-2400. Sunday to Thursday 11 A.M. to 10 P.M.; Friday and Saturday 11 A.M. to 11 P.M.; hours subject to change based on season. $9 to $35. Barbecue.

Eating in Gatlinburg can mean long lines, high prices, and lackluster food. Bennett's is a welcome relief, offering very good food and friendly, efficient service. If you're traveling with family or friends, this is the perfect restaurant because it features long tables with plenty of elbowroom.

Start with the deep-fried pickles and the brisket-stuffed mushrooms. The ribs are good, but the Ultimate Super Duper Brisket Burger is unbelievable.

Approximately 1,500 black bears live in the Great Smoky Mountains National Park.

2 THE OLD MILL

164 Old Mill Avenue, Pigeon Forge, TN 37863. **old-mill.com;** guestservices@old-mill.com; 865-429-3463. 8 A.M. to 9 P.M. $10 to $30. Southern cuisine.

This restaurant is open all day and is perfect for a satisfying breakfast before your big day at Dollywood or a relaxing dinner afterward.

As with all favorites in this area, it does get crowded, but fast service means you usually won't wait long. The restaurant is located in a complex with a bakery, candy store, and general store so you can shop while you wait for your table to become available.

Breakfast offerings include country favorites like biscuits and gravy, sausage, pancakes, and ham. Or go in a lighter direction with options like oatmeal, fruit, and quiche. Lunch and dinner feature fried catfish, meatloaf, chicken potpie, and grilled pork chops. The corn chowder and corn fritters, served with every dinner, are particularly popular.

3 CARVER'S APPLEHOUSE RESTAURANT

3460 Cosby Highway, Cosby, TN 37722. 423-487-2710. 8 A.M. to 8 P.M. $8 to $20. American homestyle.

The view here is picture perfect, with orchards and rolling meadows leading to mountains in the distance.

Your meal starts with complementary warm apple fritters served with apple butter and a glass of apple cider. From there, head directly to the chicken fried steak. Be sure to shop at the produce market before heading home.

DOLLYWOOD.

ATTRACTIONS

1 DOLLYWOOD

2700 Dollywood Parks Boulevard, Pigeon Forge, TN 37863. dollywood.com; 800-365-5996. 10 A.M. to 10 P.M.; limited hours in the off-season. Adults $62; seniors $57; children 4 to 11 $49; 3 and under free.

Dollywood isn't cheap, but it's worth every penny. The theme park has rides for the littlest visitor as well as scream-inducing roller coasters for thrill-seekers. Music lovers will revel in the foot-stomping fun of the Smoky Mountain String Band and other world-class acts.

Don't leave without touring Dolly Parton's RV!

2 BIG CREEK EXPEDITIONS

3541 Hartford Road, Hartford, TN 37753. bigcreekexpeditions.com; 877-642-7238. Tour times vary. $21.95 to $108.95.

With a variety of options ranging from easy family floating trips to whitewater rafting rides, you can find a river experience here that's just right for you. Stick with full-day rafting, or try out one of the creative and adventurous packages.

The Splash and Zip Combo combines more than 4.5 miles (7.2km) of zip-lining in the morning with whitewater rafting on the Pigeon River in the afternoon. The Paddle and Saddle

Combo takes you for a relaxing 6-mile (9.7km) horseback ride along mountain streams and past a moonshine distillery. Then it's off to raft through Class III and IV rapids in the afternoon.

3 HIKING THE PARK'S STREAMS AND WATERFALLS

107 Park Headquarters Road, Gatlinburg, TN 37738. nps.gov/grsm; 865-436-1200. Visitor centers open 9 A.M. to 7:30 P.M. during summer season.

The definitive Great Smoky Mountain hike features trails that crisscross over mountain streams on rustic wooden bridges and lead you to waterfalls and swimming holes. Many of these hikes are perfect for people with limited trail experience.

The Crosby Nature Trail is only a 1-mile (1.6km) loop but offers a taste of all the best elements of hiking in these mountains. The only paved path in the park is the trail leading to the 80-foot (24.4m) Laurel Falls. You can enjoy the rhododendron and laurel along this 2.6-mile (4.2km) round-trip hike with an easy 300-foot (91m) elevation gain without breaking a sweat. For more of a challenge, try the 5-mile (8km) round-trip hike to Abrams Falls, just off of the Cades Cove Loop Road.

ITINERARIES

IF YOU HAVE 1 WEEK ...

Start at the Sugarlands Visitor Center, drive the Cades Cove Loop Road, and visit Clingmans Dome. Hike to Abrams Falls. Enjoy a picnic lunch at Chimneys. Ride the coasters at Dollywood. Shop in downtown Gatlinburg.

IF YOU HAVE 2 WEEKS ...

All the above, plus drive Roaring Fork Motor Nature Trail, and hike to Grotto Falls. Walk the self-guided Cosby Nature Trail, and drive on the nearby Foothills Parkway. Go on a whitewater rafting adventure. Grab dinner with the locals at Smokies Cuban Cafe in Pigeon Forge.

IF YOU HAVE 3 WEEKS ...

Move your base camp over to the North Carolina side of the Smokies, and stay at the Cherokee/Great Smokies KOA. Visit the Oconaluftee Visitor Center and the Mountain Farm Museum. Hike the Kephart Prong Trail, tube at the Deep Creek Tube Centre and Campground, and tour the Museum of the Cherokee Indian.

driving the **great smokies**

You can experience much of the wild beauty of Great Smoky Mountains National Park from the comfort of your RV. The park is home to 384 miles (618km) of roads, and most are paved and easy to navigate. Visitors have been packing picnic lunches and enjoying auto tours since the 1930s, and these three drives definitely should not be missed.

Newfound Gap Road This iconic drive across Great Smoky Mountains National Park takes you on an almost 4,000-foot (1,219m) climb and pass through misty forests and diverse ecosystems that look more like Canada than the American South.

Whether you start at the Sugarlands Visitor Center in Tennessee or the Oconaluftee Visitor Center in North Carolina, first stop in for a souvenir and a chat with a knowledgeable park ranger. Or bring comfortable shoes and meander into one of the park's numerous and well-marked Quiet Walkways for short but magical walks. Feeling more ambitious? Hike on narrow wooden bridges over rushing water on the Kephart Prong Trail. Hungry? Unpack your picnic lunch at Chimneys Picnic Area, and dip your feet into the cool stream.

Cades Cove A drive on the 11-mile (17.7m), one-way Cades Cove Loop Road transports you deep into the past of a thriving nineteenth-century farming community. Although the inhabitants are long gone, the park service lovingly maintains the cabins, churches, mills, and graveyards.

A drive through Cades Cove at dawn or dusk provides your best opportunity to see one of the park's 1,500 black bears. If you spot one, don't cause a bear jam. Pull over onto the shoulder to get your photo so other traffic can pass.

The first half of the loop is filled with astonishing views of the mountains, so plan on pulling over often to enjoy the fresh air and abundant wildflowers. Stretch your legs and buy a book at the Cable Mill Visitor Center and historic area before heading back to the campground.

Roaring Fork Motor Nature Trail
For a quick and soothing escape from the frenzied pace of Gatlinburg, head directly from town onto the Roaring Fork Motor Nature Trail. The road follows the path of a rushing mountain stream and crosses over it several times on charming wooden bridges.

If you're feeling adventurous, pack your hiking shoes and take the 2.4-mile (3.9km) round-trip hike out to Grotto Falls, where you actually can walk underneath the waterfall. Leave early in the morning to nab a parking spot and enjoy the falls without a crowd.

If you blink, you might miss the Place of a Thousand Drips at marker 15. It's gorgeous, particularly during rainy weather, when dozens of waterfalls cascade over a hodge-podge of mossy rocks.

cape hatteras
national seashore, north carolina

Visitors return to Cape Hatteras year after year for one main reason: the beaches.

HIGHLIGHTS

❋ Surf, bodyboard, or bodysurf in the **world-class waves** of Cape Hatteras.

❋ Eat dinner while enjoying one of the **stunning sunsets** over the sound.

❋ Go parasailing or kiteboarding, and take in the sweeping views of the **Outer Banks.**

BEST TIME TO GO

The best time to visit is in September and October, after the crowds have thinned out but while the water is still warm.

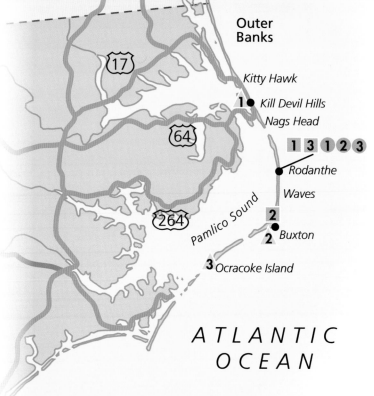

SOUTH

CAMPGROUNDS

① OCEAN WAVES CAMPGROUND

👫 👭 ♿ 🧺 ⛽ ✂ 🚐 📶

25313 Highway 12, Waves, NC 27982. **oceanwavescampground.com;** info@ocean wavescampground.com; 252-987-2556. $44 to $48. Pool, game room, playground.

Ocean Waves Campground offers 64 paved, full-hookup sites on the ocean side of the Outer Banks. The most budget-friendly option on the beach, the campground offers basic amenities such as a pool, a playground, and a game room. There's a fully stocked camp store and laundry facilities, too. Some sites are shaded, so book early if that's important to you.

If you're into surf fishing, you can easily wade into the surf and catch fish from the beach here.

THE BEACHES OF CAPE HATTERAS.

② CAMP HATTERAS RV RESORT AND CAMPGROUND

👫 👭 ♿ 🧺 ⛽ ✂ 🚐 📶

24798 Highway 12, Rodanthe, NC 27968. **camphatteras.com;** camping@camphatteras .com; 252-987-2777. $48 to $102. Cable, Wi-Fi, laundry, heated pool, wading pool, spa, playground, game room.

Camp Hatteras offers both oceanfront and sound-front sites, so if you want the resort camping experience and also love to fish and kayak, this might be the perfect spot for you.

You'll also find an Olympic-size outdoor pool, an indoor heated pool, a kiddie pool, and a hot tub. Other amenities include a game room, mini-golf, shuffleboard, tennis courts, and kayak rentals. Regularly scheduled activities also abound. Paved roads and sites are an added feature not seen at many beachfront campgrounds.

Open year round, Camp Hatteras offers lower off-season rates from September through May. So if you can travel during the shoulder seasons, you can get beautiful weather and great amenities for a lower price.

> The waters off the Outer Banks are infamously known as the "Graveyard of the Atlantic."

WRIGHT BROTHERS NATIONAL MEMORIAL.

③ CAPE HATTERAS KOA

👫 👭 ♿ 🧺 ⛽ ✂ 🚐 📶

25094 Highway 12, Rodanthe, NC 27968. **koa.com/campgrounds/cape-hatteras;** capehatteras@koa.net; 252-987-2307. $50 to $129. Pool, hot tub, Wi-Fi, snack bar, cable, bike rentals.

Completely rebuilt in the last few years, this campground features brand-new, beautiful facilities. The resortlike pool has a zero-entry area that's great for little ones to splash around in. Double water slides, a swimming lane area, and a hot tub make this the perfect place to cool off after a morning on the beach. There's a poolside snack bar and clubroom with decent Wi-Fi.

Many other kid-friendly amenities and activities are offered, such as playgrounds, an inflatable jump pillow, mini-golf, and an outdoor cinema. Summer activities include tie-dye, pirate parades, water wars, and outdoor movies. Kids will love the train, which circles the campground every afternoon. You also can rent paddleboards, kayaks, and banana bikes.

On December 17, 1903, brothers Orville and Wilbur Wright made their first flight on the dunes of the Outer Banks.

RESTAURANTS

1 LISA'S PIZZERIA

👪 👫 ♿

24160 NC Highway 12, Rodanthe, NC 27968. **lisaspizzeria.net**; 252-987-2525. 11 A.M. to 10 P.M. $10 to $22. Italian.

Sometimes a day at the beach is so exhausting, you just can't summon the energy to cook. Lisa's Pizzeria is perfect for the beautiful campground day that ends with you lounging at the pool wondering what you'll eat for dinner.

The food is very good, particularly the specialty pizzas like the vegetarian delight. Subs and sandwiches are also on the menu. The best part might be that you can get delivery right to your campground.

2 BUXTON MUNCH

👪 👫

Osprey Shopping Center, Buxton, NC 27920. **buxtonmunch.com**; 252-995-5502. Monday to Saturday 11 A.M. to 4 P.M. $10 to $15. Sandwiches.

If you want to eat where the locals eat, this is your spot. Buxton Munch offers wraps, sandwiches, and burgers here, but the star of the show is the fish taco. Warm tortillas are served with perfectly seasoned fish and a huge helping of rice, beans, lettuce, tomato, salsa, and sour cream. The smoothies are big, cold, and refreshing on a hot summer day.

Sit inside or outside, but order your food to go if you want to eat out on the porch.

3 GOOD WINDS SEAFOOD AND WINE BAR

👪 👫 ♿

24502 NC Highway 12, Rodanthe, NC 27968. **goodwindsrestaurant.com**; 252-987-1100. 11:30 A.M. to 9 P.M. $11 to $30. Seafood.

Good Winds is the place for date night or a nice family dinner out. The atmosphere is casual, but the food is upscale and creative.

The highlight here is the view over the sound, so be sure you go on a night when a spectacular sunset is expected. Enjoy a glass of wine and watch the kitesurfers soar.

SURFING ON THE SOUND.

According to legend, the pirate Blackbeard settled Ocracoke Island as his outpost in the eighteenth century.

ATTRACTIONS

1 WRIGHT BROTHERS NATIONAL MEMORIAL

1000 N. Croatan Highway, Kill Devil Hills, NC 27948. nps.gov/wrbr; 252-473-2111. 9 A.M. to 5 P.M. Adults $4; children 15 and under free.

This national memorial is something both kids and adults will enjoy. The museum is engaging and educational, and don't miss the ranger presentation.

Walking the distance of the first three flights certainly brings history to life. It gets hot in the summer, though, so visit early in the day or later in the afternoon.

2 CAPE HATTERAS LIGHTHOUSE

46368 Old Lighthouse Road, Buxton, NC 27920. nps.gov/caha; 252-473-2111. 9 A.M. to 5 P.M. Adults $8; seniors $4; children $4.

A trip to the Cape Hatteras Lighthouse is a must for first-time visitors to the Outer Banks. Climbing the 257 steps to the top of the tallest brick lighthouse in North America is a strenuous task, but the view is a great payoff. Children must be at least 42 inches (1m) tall to climb.

At the visitor center, you can learn about the fascinating history of the Outer Banks and the sensitive ecology of the nation's first national seashore. Regular educational activities, programs, and events are also offered, so be sure to check the schedule in advance.

3 OCRACOKE ISLAND

Ocracoke, NC 27960. ocracokevillage.com; info@ocracokevillage.com; 252-928-6711. Check ferry schedule and pricing.

Get an early start if you're planning on spending the day on Ocracoke Island. You'll have to take the Hatteras Ferry to get there, and lines can back up during the busy summer months.

After the short ferry ride, it's a beautiful 14-mile (22.5m) drive to the charming village of Ocracoke, home to the many art galleries, boutique shopping, and small eateries the quiet island has to offer.

You also can stop to visit the Ocracoke ponies, cared for by the National Park Service. Legend has it, these ponies were left by shipwrecked explorers in the sixteenth or seventeenth century. They've played an interesting role in the history of the island ever since.

ITINERARIES

IF YOU HAVE 1 WEEK ...

Bring your chair, umbrella, and a good book to enjoy the best the Outer Banks has to offer ... the beach! Take advantage of campground amenities, and swim, fish, and kayak the week away.

IF YOU HAVE 2 WEEKS ...

In addition to long, lazy days on the beach, visit Cape Hatteras National Seashore and climb the lighthouse. Check the schedule for interesting ranger-led programs. If you're feeling adventurous, sign up for kitesurfing or parasailing, or take a surf lesson.

IF YOU HAVE 3 WEEKS ...

All the above, plus visit the Wright Brothers National Memorial and learn about the fascinating history of flight in America. Spend the day on Ocracoke Island, enjoying a ferry ride, lots of great shopping, and a visit to the ponies cared for by the National Park Service.

myrtle beach,
south
carolina

Myrtle Beach has a great boardwalk and beach scene. But just off the Grand Strand, you'll find a treasure trove of salt marshes, swamps, state parks, and world-class golf courses.

HIGHLIGHTS

✳ Ride the **SkyWheel** for a breathtaking, bird's-eye view of the coastline.

✳ Catch a Pelicans minor league baseball game at beautiful **Pelicans Ballpark.**

✳ Get your heart thumping by zip-lining right over the **boardwalk** toward the ocean.

BEST TIME TO GO

Visit Myrtle Beach in early spring to experience warm weather, blossoming foliage, and minimal crowds.

CAMPGROUNDS

1 MYRTLE BEACH STATE PARK

4401 S Kings Highway, Myrtle Beach, SC 29575. southcarolinaparks.com; mbeachsp@ scprt.com; 843-238-5325. $21 to $42. Camp store, laundry.

This campground has the space and privacy of a state park but with close proximity to all the Myrtle Beach action. The park is beachfront yet still deeply wooded, with shaded playgrounds and nature walks.

The nature center offers daily activities and a small educational area with big learning opportunities. Check the schedule for story hour, crafts, and ranger-led walks. A well-stocked camp store offers all the basics like ice, firewood, and s'mores fixings.

2 HUNTINGTON BEACH STATE PARK

16148 Ocean Highway, Murrells Inlet, SC 29576. southcarolinaparks.com; huntingtonbeach@scprt.com; 843-237-4440. $24 to $62. Boating, fishing, camp store, nature center.

Huntington Beach State Park is a bit south of Myrtle Beach, so if you want to escape the crowds, this might be your best option. The campground has a variety of sites—some shaded, some not. For the best site, call and talk to a ranger if you're going to be visiting in the heat of the summer.

A short walk over the dunes lands you on beautiful, pristine beaches. A variety of other activities are available here as well. Ranger-led walks teach you all about the animals and plants in the coastal region, and guided kayak tours leave right from the nature center, which also has a telescope focused on a bald eagle's nest.

RV-FRIENDLY SOUTH CAROLINA STATE PARKS.

3 MYRTLE BEACH KOA

613 5th Avenue S., Myrtle Beach, SC 29577. koa.com/campgrounds/myrtle-beach; myrtlebeach@koa.net; 843-448-3421. $45 to $90. Pool, cable, fishing, bike rentals.

Although only two blocks from the beach, this campground is a surprisingly quiet, wooded retreat. A great choice for families with children, this KOA boasts two pools, a splash pad, an inflatable jump pillow, and live magic shows. It's also a popular choice for snowbirds who appreciate the friendly atmosphere, attentive staff, and excellent amenities. The large, pull-thru sites can accommodate big rigs and small tent trailers alike.

The friendly staff is happy to recommend a great breakfast joint or help you reserve a tee time at one of the area's golf courses. A shuttle is available to transport you to the beach and pick you up at an agreed-upon time. Rides, mini-golf, and a water park are within walking distance.

SPOTTING ALLIGATORS.

Chicago Cubs manager Joe Maddon brings his RV, named *Cousin Eddie*, to Myrtle Beach for vacation every off-season.

SOUTH

Jimmy Buffet, Michael Jordan, and Johnny Depp all own homes on the Myrtle Beach Intracoastal Waterway.

RESTAURANTS

1 NOIZY OYSTER

👪 👫 ♿

101 S. Kings Highway, Myrtle Beach, SC 29577. 843-444-6100. Tuesday to Sunday 12 P.M. to 10 P.M. $11 to $30. Seafood.

With a seafood buffet on every corner in Myrtle Beach, it can be hard to know where to find fresh and tasty seafood. If you ask the locals, they'll suggest the Noizy Oyster, where casual, friendly service goes hand in hand with perfectly steamed seafood.

Crab seems to be the star of the show here, so try the blue crab legs, crabby mac and cheese, or the crab cake. Key lime pie for dessert is sure to please.

Myrtle Beach has more than 100 public and private golf courses.

2 BISQIT

👪 👫 ♿

10880 Ocean Highway, Pawleys Island, SC 29585. 843-979-2747. Monday to Thursday 8 A.M. to 9 P.M.; Friday and Saturday 8 A.M. to 10 P.M.; Sunday 8 A.M. to 8 P.M. $10 to $30. Burgers, breakfast, and brunch.

This gem is tucked away alongside boutique shops in Pawleys Island. It's the perfect place to stop for breakfast or lunch before visiting nearby Brookgreen Gardens.

bisQit takes the average burger and shake and adds fun and unusual ingredients like bacon jam or braised pork belly. Brioche buns and homemade french fries make every dish feel a little bit more special. If you're very hungry, order the fries with queso and chili. Vegetarians have plenty of options here, too, including a sweet potato burger, delicious guacamole, and specialty vegan dessert options.

A full-service bar is offered, and the Bloody Marys are a wonderful accompaniment to the breakfast tacos.

3 DUFFY STREET SEAFOOD SHACK

👪 👫 ♿

319 Sea Mountain Highway, North Myrtle Beach, SC 29582. duffyst.com; 843-249-7902. 12 P.M. to 10 P.M. $10 to $30. Seafood.

At Duffy's, you can soak in the fun atmosphere of the Grand Strand while eating po'boys, listening to blues, and tossing peanut shells on the ground.

Stick with the standards here: the fried crab cake sandwich, the seafood pot, and steamed shrimp. The happy hour is great, with budget-friendly prices for oysters and beer.

BROOKGREEN GARDENS.

ATTRACTIONS

1 BROOKGREEN GARDENS

1931 Brookgreen Garden Drive, Murrells Inlet, SC 29576. **brookgreen.org;** info@brookgreen.org; 843-235-6000. 9:30 A.M. to 5 P.M. Adults $15; seniors $13; children $7.

This stunning botanical garden is just south of Myrtle Beach, in Murrells Inlet. It's far too much to experience in one day, so thankfully your ticket is good for an entire week.

While there, tour the gardens, visit the zoo, play in the Enchanted Storybook Forest, or ride on a pontoon boat and learn about the local ecology.

2 BLACK RIVER OUTDOORS CENTER

1229 38th Avenue N., Myrtle Beach, SC 29577; **blackriveroutdoors.com;** info@blackriveroutdoors.com; 843-546-4840. Tour schedule varies. $35 to $55.

The Black River Outdoors Center is the best way to explore the rivers, creeks, and marshes of South Carolina's low country. Guided kayak tours are 2, 4, or 6 hours long and led by the friendliest, most knowledgeable staff imaginable. You can choose to tour the Cyprus Swamp or the Salt Marsh—the owner will help you choose one depending on the time of year and weather. Other options include kayak fishing or moonlight tours.

The world of roller coasters and mini-golf nearby will melt away as you experience the romance of coastal Myrtle Beach. You'll want to return again and again during your stay.

3 BROADWAY AT THE BEACH

1325 Celebrity Circle, Myrtle Beach, SC 29577. **broadwayatthebeach.com;** 843-444-3200. 10 A.M. to 11 P.M. Price varies depending on attraction.

This is the big, bold, and bright Myrtle Beach everyone wants to experience at least once. Rides are available for every age, as well as zip-lining, and you can tour Ripley's Believe It or Not! Museum and Aquarium.

WonderWorks is a very popular attraction, combining a children's museum, ropes course, and arcade in one very busy building. Here you'll find simulated space adventures and giant bubble factories. Get there early to avoid long lines, especially on rainy days.

Visit a wax museum, go on a MagiQuest, take a helicopter tour, dress up for an old-timey photo, or go back to the age of dinosaurs. You name the tourist attraction, and it's at Broadway on the Beach.

ITINERARIES

IF YOU HAVE 1 WEEK ...

Put in some quality time at the beach, and play a round of golf, either real or mini. Visit Brookgreen Gardens, and eat a fantastic seafood dinner at sunset.

IF YOU HAVE 2 WEEKS ...

All the above, plus visit Huntington Beach State Park and check out the alligators lounging by the side of the road. Tour Atalaya Castle, and learn about the restoration efforts for this beachfront mansion. Take a guided kayak tour of the swamp or dance to Jimmy Buffet aboard the *Barefoot Princess Riverboat.*

IF YOU HAVE 3 WEEKS ...

All the above, plus catch a Pelicans baseball game. Then take a day trip down to the Center for Birds of Prey in Awendaw, where a guided tour teaches you more about raptors than you ever thought possible. End the day with dinner at SeeWee Restaurant, a road food legend and local favorite.

SOUTH

new orleans

If any place was made for eating, drinking, and making merry, it's the Big Easy. This city is designed for the wandering traveler, so be prepared to go from jazz club to restaurant to bar and back again. There's something to discover around every corner.

HIGHLIGHTS

✶ Catch a performance by the **Preservation Hall Jazz Band.**

✶ Sample **gumbo and mint juleps** from famous restaurants such as Brigtsen's.

✶ Ride the **St. Charles Streetcar** route, and see the Garden District and historic mansions.

BEST TIME TO GO

Most people think Mardi Gras, but to see the city in its true glory, visit during the New Orleans Jazz and Heritage Festival.

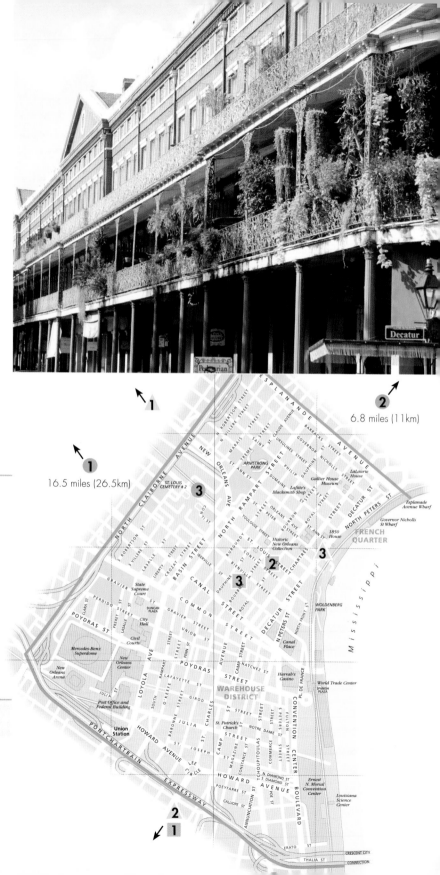

CAMPGROUNDS

① NEW ORLEANS WEST KOA

11129 Jefferson Highway, River Ridge, LA 70123. koa.com/campgrounds/new-orleans; neworleanskoa@bellsouth.net; 504-467-1792. $49 to $89. Pool, shuttle, laundry facilities.

This is a safe, clean KOA located about 20 miles (32km) away from the French Quarter. The owners are area experts and happy to help guests plan vacation itineraries, and a shuttle service can take you into New Orleans. On-site you'll find a pool and dog-walking services.

The campground is well situated to explore the region surrounding New Orleans, so if you want to fish in the Gulf of Mexico or take a steamboat tour, this might be the spot for you.

PARADE IN THE FRENCH QUARTER.

② PONTCHARTRAIN LANDING

6001 France Road, New Orleans, LA 70126. pontchartrainlanding.com; 504-286-8157. $59 to $179. Pool, playground, bar, restaurant, shuttle service.

This waterfront marina resort offers luxurious RV accommodations just 12 minutes from the French Quarter and Bourbon Street, and the price tag definitely reflects that.

Six different types of sites are available with varying features, the most deluxe being the two presidential sites that are extra large and have a private hot tub and gazebo. Or opt for a waterfront sites that offers direct access for your boat or personal watercraft.

Although this is a perfect romantic getaway for couples, the playground and pool make it family friendly as well. The on-site bar and grill offers solid New Orleans classics like gumbo and jambalaya. The RV park operates day and evening shuttles to and from the French Quarter and offers 24-hour gated security.

Only 4,000 residents live in the French Quarter, but more than 15 million people visit every year.

NEW ORLEANS STREET CAR.

③ FRENCH QUARTER RV RESORT

500 N. Claiborne Avenue, New Orleans, LA 70112. fqrv.com; stay@fqrv.com; 504-586-3000. $96; higher pricing for special events. Pool, clubhouse, recreation room, fitness center.

If you want to park your RV in the heart of downtown New Orleans, head to the French Quarter RV Resort. The resort caters to all size rigs, with 52 paved, back-in sites. Each site has full hookups. The RV park says it operates like a luxury hotel, and its prices fluctuate greatly depending on city events.

On-site is an upscale clubhouse with fitness facilities, recreation room, gazebo with bar, pool, and hot tub. The park is fully gated with 24-hour on-site management and security. The trolley runs right past the park, but it's not advised to walk the area after dark. Taxi service is easily accessed in New Orleans.

Traveling with friends or family? A one-bedroom suite is available for rent.

SOUTH

SOUTH

> The St. Charles Streetcar is the oldest continuously operating streetcar in the world.

RESTAURANTS

1 COMMANDER'S PALACE

1403 Washington Avenue, New Orleans, LA 70130. **commanderspalace.com**; 504-899-8221. 6:30 P.M. to 10:30 P.M.; Monday to Friday 11:30 A.M. to 2 P.M.; Saturday 11 A.M. to 1:30 P.M.; Sunday 10:30 A.M. $30 to $60. Creole.

Any meal eaten at this historical New Orleans restaurant is an event, but if you make reservations for the jazz brunch, it'll be even more special.

Located in the Garden District, eating here is the perfect finale to a walking tour and Lafayette Cemetery visit. The 25-cent martini lunch special is legendary. Order the turtle soup, stuffed quail, and bread pudding for tradition's sake.

Dress code is strict, if not strictly enforced.

> Founded in 1853, New Orleans City Park is one of the largest municipal parks in the country.

2 BRENNAN'S

417 Royal Street, New Orleans, LA 70130. **brennansneworleans.com**; 504-525-9711. 8 A.M. to 2 P.M.; 6 P.M. to 10 P.M. $30 to $59. Contemporary creole.

Some people say you haven't truly experienced New Orleans until you've had breakfast at Brennan's. The Old World décor and seriously attentive service always delights guests.

The eggs Benedict, oysters, soft-shell crabs, and rabbit are classic favorites, and the prix fixe menu pleases the budget conscious. The bar serves perfect Bloody Marys, mimosas, and Pimm's cups.

But really, everyone comes here for the bananas Foster, which the owner of Brennan's invented and made popular in the early 1950s. After you enjoy the signature breakfast dessert, prepared right at your table along with a captivating history lesson, you can use the recipe on the website to try to re-create it at home.

3 GALATOIRE'S RESTAURANT

209 Bourbon Street, New Orleans, LA 70130. **galatoires.com**; 504-525-2021. Tuesday to Saturday 11:30 A.M. to 10 P.M.; Sunday 12 P.M. to 10 P.M.; closed Monday. $25 to $60. French creole.

A century-old institution on Bourbon Street, Galatoire's is famous for its Friday lunch tradition, when the locals gather to celebrate the upcoming weekend.

You must be dressed in your Sunday finest (jackets are required) and arrive at 11:30 sharp if you have hopes of getting a table. The shrimp remoulade is a standout favorite.

ANNE RICE'S FORMER GARDEN DISTRICT MANSION.

ATTRACTIONS

1 NEW ORLEANS CITY PARK

👨‍👧 👬 ♿ 🐕

1 Palm Drive, New Orleans, LA 70124. neworleanscitypark.com; info@nocp.org; 504-482-4888. Open 30 minutes before sunrise to 30 minutes after sunset. Price varies according to attraction.

One of the most successful post–Hurricane Katrina revitalization efforts, City Park is the perfect place to take a break from the hectic pace of the French Quarter.

There's something for everyone here—the Museum of Art and Sculpture Garden, Botanical Garden, Carousel Gardens Amusement Park, and City Putt. Kids love Storyland, a playground with 25 larger-than-life storybook sculptures.

2 GUIDED GARDEN DISTRICT WALKING TOUR

👨‍👧 👬 ♿

2613 Laurel Street, New Orleans, LA 70130. freetoursbyfoot.com; nola@freetoursbyfoot.com; 504-222-2967. Hours vary according to tour schedule. You pay what you choose at the end of the tour.

You can tour the beautiful streets of the Garden District on your own, but you'd miss the history and legend that brings the beautiful mansions, gardens, and cemeteries to life.

Many types of tours are available, including bus or bike options, but Free Tours by Foot allows its customers to pay what they want at the end of tour.

The guides seem to work a little harder to get you to open your wallet.

Lafayette Cemetery No. 1 is a particularly popular tour stop, and scenes from many movies have been filmed in this historic, spooky location, including *Interview with the Vampire* and *Double Jeopardy*.

3 FRENCH QUARTER

👨‍👧 👬 ♿

French Quarter Visitor Center, 419 Decatur Street, New Orleans, LA 70116. nps.gov/jela/french-quarter-site.htm; 504-589-2636. Monday to Tuesday 9 A.M. to 7 P.M.; Wednesday to Friday 9 A.M. to 5 P.M.

The highlight of most people's visit to the Big Easy is the French Quarter, which offers countless options for amazing food, delicious drinks, and world-class music.

During the day, you can explore the amazing choices for breakfast and lunch and shop the creative and quirky boutiques and voodoo gift shops. By night, join the bands of revelers who hop from club to club, spilling out into the streets with their drinks.

Stop in at the French Quarter Visitor Center, operated by the National Park Service, at the beginning of your visit. Guides there can help you plan your exploration of the historical attractions in the area. Don't miss a visit to Jackson Square, where the people-watching is at its finest.

ITINERARIES

IF YOU HAVE 1 WEEK …

Walk the historical streets of the French Quarter, visit Jackson Square, and shop on Frenchmen Street. Catch a jazz performance at Preservation Hall. Take a tour of the Garden District.

IF YOU HAVE 2 WEEKS …

All the above, plus spend a day at New Orleans City Park. Ride an entire loop on one of the city's three streetcar lines. Watch a show at The Spotted Cat Music Club. Take a ghost tour at night. Rent bikes, and ride around the Big Easy.

IF YOU HAVE 3 WEEKS …

All the above, plus visit the Audubon Zoo and the National WWII Museum. See a jazz show at Maison Bourbon. Take a culinary tasting tour of the city. Drive along the River Road National Scenic Byway, and tour the historical plantations. Cruise along the Mississippi River on a steamboat.

walt disney world

If you have kids and an RV, Walt Disney World should be on your vacation bucket list. Staying at a campground during your visit cuts down on two huge vacation costs: lodging and food. Plus, low-key campground downtime with your family is priceless.

HIGHLIGHTS

✴ Ride the Seven Dwarfs Mine Train, Disney's newest ride in the **Magic Kingdom.**

✴ Relive your youth on **It's a Small World,** a Disney World staple since 1971.

✴ Watch the amazing **IllumiNations** fireworks and laser light show at **Epcot.**

BEST TIME TO GO

If you can, go whenever school is in session to avoid the crowds. September and October offer the best combination of warm weather and short lines. If you go during school holidays, expect crowds.

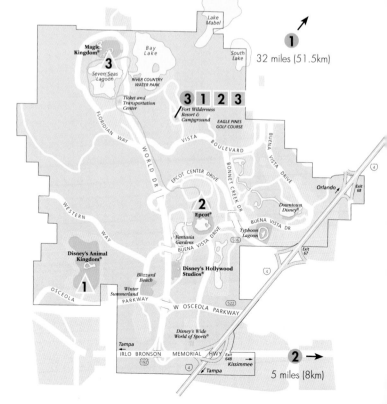

CAMPGROUNDS

① WEKIWA SPRINGS STATE PARK CAMPGROUND

1800 Wekiwa Circle, Apopka, FL 32712. **floridastateparks.org**; 407-884-2009. $24. Biking, horseback riding, concessions, playground, swimming, fishing, birding.

Looking for a natural campground experience that feels far away from the madness of Orlando, but still close enough for Disney-centered day trips? Then plan ahead and reserve one of the 60 wooded sites at the popular Wekiwa Springs State Park. Some have full hookups, and many are big rig accessible.

After a hot day at the theme parks, swim in the cool springs or go for a kayak ride on the peaceful Wekiwa River.

CHINESE THEATRE AT DISNEY'S HOLLYWOOD STUDIOS.

② ORLANDO/KISSIMMEE KOA

2664 Happy Camper Place, Kissimmee, FL 34746. **koa.com/camp/kissimmee**; orlandokiss@koa.net; 407-396-2400. $62 to $81. Pool, hot tub, playground, bike rentals, fitness center.

This KOA wins points for its proximity to Disney, Universal, and LEGOLAND parks, and for its squeaky-clean facilities and friendly management. There's a pool for the kids, but it's uninspiring. Considering the nearby entertainment options, this might not matter. Kids can enjoy the horseshoe pit, the basketball court, and the bike rentals instead.

This park accommodates big rigs with ease. The back-in and pull-thru sites range from good to very good, and the deluxe patio sites with furniture and chimeneas are worth the extra bucks. Adults will appreciate the hot tub, which is open 23 hours a day, and the fitness room, which was recently rebuilt.

If Fort Wilderness is booked, this may be your next best option.

About 800 pounds of ribs are served every night at Fort Wilderness's Hoop-Dee-Doo Musical Revue.

SPACESHIP EARTH AT EPCOT.

③ FORT WILDERNESS

4510 N. Fort Wilderness Trail, Lake Buena Vista, Florida 32830. **disneyworld.disney.go .com**; 407-824-2900. $69 to $85. Pools, hot tub, archery, restaurants.

Fort Wilderness is America's favorite family campground, offering the full magic of Disney at a very reasonable price. Staying here gives you the same perks as staying at a Disney resort.

The full hook-up sites and premium campsites set the standard for an entire industry, and recreation is world class. The Meadow Swimmin' Pool and its 67-foot-long (20m) corkscrew waterslide entertain for hours, the Fort Wilderness Archery Experience makes kids 7 and up feel like they're on a great adventure, and horseback trail rides at the Tri-Circle-D Ranch might prove more memorable than meeting Mickey Mouse. End each night by roasting marshmallows and singing songs with Chip 'n' Dale around a cozy campfire.

SOUTH

> The reservation window for Disney dining opens 180 days in advance of your arrival, and tables fill up fast.

RESTAURANTS

1 TRAIL'S END RESTAURANT

4510 Fort Wilderness Trail, Lake Buena Vista, FL 32830. **disneyworld.disney.go.com**; 407-939-3463. 7:30 A.M. to 2 P.M., 4:30 P.M. to 9:30 P.M. $11 to $20. American.

Although not necessarily an amazing lunch or dinner option, Trail's End is a great place for breakfast, especially if you're camping at Fort Wilderness. Meals are served buffet style, with an à la carte option available for takeout.

The atmosphere stays true to the theme, with big wooden beams and mounted animals on the wall. The buffet is heaped with comfort foods like Mickey waffles and biscuits and gravy. Fill up and then head to the park.

If you have young children, don't spend extra for Park Hopper tickets. Visit one park per day and then chill at the campground.

2 HOOP-DEE-DOO MUSICAL REVUE

4510 Fort Wilderness Trail, Orlando, FL 32830. **disneyworld.disney.go.com**; 407-939-3463. 4 P.M. to 10 P.M. $33 to $68. American.

This dinner show is a hands-down Disney World favorite for almost anyone who attends. The 2-hour musical hootenanny features dancing, singing, and slapstick humor performed by the Pioneer Hall Players. The jokes may be a bit corny, but everyone in your family will appreciate the feel-good fun this show provides. You might even be put on the spot with a little audience interaction.

Between performances, dinner is served family style on platters heaped with fried chicken, barbecue pork ribs, salad, baked beans, and corn bread. Dessert is yummy strawberry shortcake. Unlimited beer, wine, and sangria are also included.

The price tag might seem steep to some, but consider that the ticket cost includes live entertainment, tax, tip, and beverages.

3 MICKEY'S BACKYARD BBQ

4510 N. Fort Wilderness Trail, Orlando, FL 32885. **disneyworld.disney.go.com**; 407-939-5277. March to December. 6:30 P.M. $36 to $60. American.

No visit to Disney World is complete without a character meal, and this is a phenomenal one offered right at Fort Wilderness. Eat hamburgers, hotdogs, and mac and cheese while Mickey, Minnie, Chip 'n' Dale, and Goofy dance along to a country band.

The characters mingle for photographs and also lead the audience in line dances.

GIRAFFES AT DISNEY'S ANIMAL KINGDOM.

ATTRACTIONS

1 ANIMAL KINGDOM

2901 Osceola Parkway, Orlando, FL 32830.
disneyworld.disney.go.com/attractions/animal-kingdom; 407-939-5277. 9 A.M. to 7 P.M.
$91 to $97.

Many visitors consider this the most visually beautiful of all the Disney parks, with the Tree of Life as the show-stopping centerpiece.

The theme here is animal conservation, and most rides, like the Safari, are more experiential. Thrill seekers can get their kicks on Expedition Everest and DINOSAUR. The Affection Section and The Boneyard delight little ones.

2 EPCOT

200 Epcot Center Drive, Lake Buena Vista, Orlando, FL 32092. **disneyworld.disney.go**.com/attractions/epcot; 407-824-4321.
9 A.M. to 9 P.M. $91 to $97.

Even with an entire day scheduled to visit Epcot, it's hard to take in all the sites and attractions. There are two distinct sections of the park, World Showcase and Future World, and you should try to sample both.

Start at Future World upon arrival, as many of those attractions end up with longer wait times. Test Track, Journey into Imagination with Figment, and The Seas with Nemo and Friends are top picks.

The World Showcase, featuring the culture and cuisine from 11 countries, offers the opportunity for a slower pace later in the day. Consider creating your own food tour, snacking as you visit all the regions.

3 MAGIC KINGDOM PARK

3111 World Drive, Orlando, FL 32830.
disneyworld.disney.go.com/destinations/
magic-kingdom; 407-934-7639. 9 A.M. to
9 P.M. $99 to $105.

Because it's the biggest of all the parks and difficult to fully explore in a single day, many people choose to spend 2 days in the Magic Kingdom.

The sheer size of the park means it's crucial that you plan out a loose itinerary before you arrive. Look at the list of attractions online, and note your must-visit picks. This especially helps when navigating the newer FastPass system, which allows you to make a certain number of ride reservations per visit.

Hit Pirates of the Caribbean, Space Mountain, and the Seven Dwarfs Mine Train first thing in the morning or before closing at night. Don't skip taking the boat ride through It's a Small World—it's a Disney rite of passage.

ITINERARIES

IF YOU HAVE 1 WEEK ...

Spend 2 days at the Magic Kingdom, 1 day at Epcot, and 1 day at your choice of Animal Kingdom or Hollywood Studios. Relax at the campground, shop in Downtown Disney, and hang out on the promenade of Disney's Boardwalk.

IF YOU HAVE 2 WEEKS ...

Spend 1 full day at each of the four parks, or consider a 5-day ticket for an additional day at the Magic Kingdom. Explore Downtown Disney and Disney's Boardwalk. Go to Universal Studios and take in the magic at the Wizarding World of Harry Potter. Cool off at Typhoon Lagoon.

IF YOU HAVE 3 WEEKS ...

All the above, plus escape the hectic pace of theme park life and head to Lake Eola Park, a 43-acre (17.4ha) recreational park in downtown Orlando. Visit LEGOLAND, and tour the mini re-creations of New York City and Washington, D.C. Take a trip to the Space Coast beaches, just an hour away.

florida
keys

Visiting the Florida Keys is all about enjoying the crystal-clear ocean, stunning sunsets, and fabulous nightlife. While you're here, you'll want to spend as much time as possible kayaking, birding, and snorkeling around one of the largest coral reefs in the world.

HIGHLIGHTS

✳ Sample Key lime pie at bakeries and restaurants such as **Hobo's Cafe** and **Kermit's Key West Key Lime Shoppe.**

✳ Visit the six-toed cats all named after famous people at the **Ernest Hemingway Home and Museum.**

✳ Take a selfie at the **Southernmost Point** of the United States.

BEST TIME TO GO

The snowbirds have it right—the Florida Keys are most enjoyable when you're escaping the snow and ice of the cold, northern winter months.

CAMPGROUNDS

1 LONG KEY STATE PARK CAMPGROUND

👪 👪 ♿ 🧺 🚿 🔌

PO Box 776, Long Key, FL 33001. floridastateparks.org/park/long-key; 305-664-4815. $36. Picnic area, boardwalk, paved roads, canoe rentals, ranger programs.

This is state park camping at its best. At this campground, you can park your rig just steps away from the Atlantic Ocean, and all 60 campsites have water views. (Many campers love to launch their kayaks right from their sites.) The sites also all have water and electric hookups, a picnic table, and a ground grill. The bathhouses provide hot showers.

The reservations window opens 11 months in advance, and you must book early to secure a spot.

SOUTHERNMOST POINT IN THE UNITED STATES.

2 POINT OF VIEW KEY LARGO RV RESORT

👪 ♿ 🧺 🚿 🔌 🚐 📶

99010 Overseas Highway, Key Largo, FL 33037. pointofviewrvresort.com; 305-451-5578. $65 to $140. Infinity pool, marina with boat ramp, dog run.

Big-rig friendly and located in Key Largo, this is the best resort campground option in the Florida Keys. Only a few years old, the amenities are up to date and focused on creating a great customer experience. A large infinity pool reaches the edge of the bay, and the clubhouse, game room, and tiki hut are contemporary and comfortable. A marina with boat ramp and fishing area are here, and a dog run and dog walk area make this a pet-friendly option.

You can walk to restaurants right from the RV resort, and it's just minutes away from Key Largo's shops, markets, and charter boats. It's also close to Key Largo Community Park, which offers fantastic recreational facilities.

Geographically, Key West is closer to Cuba than it is to Miami.

POPULAR KEY WEST.

3 BAHIA HONDA STATE PARK CAMPGROUND

👪 👪 ♿ 🧺 🚿 🔌

36850 Overseas Highway, Big Pine Key, FL 33043. bahiahondapark.com; info@bahiahondapark.com; 305-872-2353. $36. Beach, kayak rentals, snorkeling tours, snack bar.

Bahia Honda has three different campgrounds. Sandspur and Bayside accommodate only very small popup campers, but Buttonwood has sites suitable for larger RVs. Buttonwood also has some waterfront sites. The campground is simple, but it's surrounded by amenities, programs, and activities offered by the state park. Enjoy traveling the 3.5-mile (5.6km) paved biking path, swimming at one of the three white-sand beaches, birding during low tide on the sand flats, and fishing for snapper or grouper. Or rent ocean kayaks at the concession stand. Ranger-led Campfire Circles are offered exclusively for overnight guests at the amphitheater and address a variety of topics such as local plants, animals, and history.

SOUTH

SOUTH

When made according to locals' standards, Key lime pie is pale yellow, not bright green.

RESTAURANTS

1 HARRIETTE'S RESTAURANT

95710 Overseas Highway, Key Largo, FL 33037. 305-852-8689. 6 A.M. to 3 P.M. $5 to $10. Breakfast and brunch.

This is *the* place to go for breakfast in Key Largo. Everything here is homemade, and the owner, Harriette, loves to personally welcome guests to her decades-old establishment.

Although many menu items are delicious—corned beef hash, hotcakes, and omelets, to name a few—it would be a shame to visit and not try a Key lime muffin, which is huge, warm, and topped with confectioners' sugar. You might return again and again throughout your vacation, just for more muffins.

2 HOGFISH BAR AND GRILL

6810 Front Street, Stock Island, FL 33040. hogfishbar.com; 305-293-4041. Monday to Saturday 11 A.M. to 12 A.M.; Sunday 9 A.M. to 12 A.M. $11 to $30. Seafood.

You can't leave the Keys without experiencing the quintessential seafood shack, and Hogfish is where locals go to eat shrimp and chips served in newspaper and fried grouper with Key lime mustard. The Hogfish taco is a hands-down favorite and always prepared with freshly caught fish.

The chef also will prepare anything you catch yourself.

3 SANTIAGO'S BODEGA

207 Petronia Street, Key West, FL 33040. santiagosbodega.com; info@santiagosbodega .com; 305-296-7691. Monday to Friday 11 A.M. to 2 A.M.; Saturday and Sunday 10 A.M. to 2 A.M. $21 to $40. Spanish tapas.

A pitcher of sangria, a few tapas, and the ambiance of Santiago's Bodega makes for the perfect way to spend an afternoon or evening in Key West.

The menu has options for the sea lover and land lover alike. The tuna ceviche is tangy and flavorful without being chewy, and the tender short ribs are paired with a crisp slaw. Save some room for bread pudding for dessert. It's as decadent and rich as bread pudding should be. If you can't decide, the personable staff will be delighted to help you make your menu selections.

Reservations are strongly recommended if you want to enjoy a meal here without waiting quite a while to do so.

SEVEN MILE BRIDGE IS PART OF THE 113-MILE-LONG (182KM) OVERSEAS HIGHWAY.

The Florida Reef is more than 200 miles (322km) long, making it the third-largest coral barrier reef in the world.

ATTRACTIONS

1 SAIL FISH SCUBA

👪 👫

103100 Overseas Highway #33, Key Largo, FL 33037. **sailfishscuba.com;** info@sailfish scuba.com; 305-453-3446. Sunday 9 A.M. to 1 P.M.; Tuesday to Saturday 8 A.M. to 5 P.M.; closed Monday. Price varies by package.

People dream of exploring the Florida Reef when they visit the Keys. Sail Fish Scuba has a tour or package option for anyone, whether you have zero experience or you have your scuba certification.

It offers reef dives, snorkeling, boat charters, and guided kayak tours. Or try an Adventure Day, in which you combine many different water activities in one tour.

2 ERNEST HEMMINGWAY HOME AND MUSEUM

👫 ♿

907 Whitehead Street, Key West, FL 33040. **hemingwayhome.com;** 305-294-1136. 9 A.M. to 5 P.M. Adults $13; children $6; 4 and under free.

The Florida Keys has attracted many writers and artists during the last century, but none so famous as Ernest Hemingway, who renovated this Spanish colonial in the 1930s with his wife Pauline. If you're a Hemingway fan, the house will automatically be on your itinerary. But even if you've never read one of his books, the guided tour is a fascinating look into the history of Key West and the Lost Generation.

For many guests, the real stars of the show are the polydactyl cats who roam the property. They're descendants of Papa's original one, Snow White, given to him as a gift by a ship's captain.

3 JOHN PENNEKAMP CORAL REEF STATE PARK

👪 👫 ♿

102601 Overseas Highway, Key Largo, FL 33037. **pennekamppark.com;** info@ pennekamppark.com; 305-451-6325. 8 A.M. to 5 P.M. Vehicle admission $8; additional cost for tours and rentals.

This undersea park is particularly special. Starting on land, there's a 30,000-gallon (114,000l) saltwater aquarium in the Environmental Education and Visitor Center, along with interpretive exhibits about the area's ecosystem and history. Guided tours through the mangroves are offered seasonally. The majority of your time at this state park is spent in the water, with many snorkeling and scuba tour options available. The first item on your itinerary should be a ride on the glass-bottom boat, which tours the shallow reefs full of wildlife.

Kayaks, canoes, and paddleboards are available to rent if you want to explore the 50 miles (80.5km) of water trails that meander through the mangrove wilderness. Or rent a powerboat and head to open water.

ITINERARIES

IF YOU HAVE 1 WEEK ...

Head straight for Key West and the Southernmost Point. Visit the Ernest Hemingway Home and Museum, and enjoy a trolley tour of Old Town. Ride the glass-bottom boat at John Pennekamp Coral Reef State Park.

IF YOU HAVE 2 WEEKS ...

All the above, plus snorkel or scuba dive in the reef. Rent kayaks at Curry Hammock State Park, and explore the mangroves. Visit the Dolphin Research Center. Take a sunset dinner cruise. Catch your own fish on a chartered boating trip, and have it prepared at a local restaurant.

IF YOU HAVE 3 WEEKS ...

All the above, plus use all that time to take a scuba diving certification class and spend days exploring the magical world underwater in the Florida Keys. Take a boat or seaplane to Dry Tortugas National Park, located about 70 miles (113km) away from Key West.

SOUTH

hocking hills, ohio

Tucked into the southeastern corner of Ohio, the Hocking Hills area surprises and delights visitors with a landscape drastically different from the rest of the state. This region is best explored by hiking, so come prepared with a good set of walking shoes.

HIGHLIGHTS

✳ Hike the **Rim Trail** along the gorge at Conkles Hollow State Nature Preserve.

✳ Climb inside the **Rock House,** the only true cave in Hocking Hills State Park.

✳ Splash in the cascading waterfalls along the trail at **Old Man's Creek.**

BEST TIME TO GO

The hills and gorges are particularly beautiful when they're showing off the spring wildflowers of May and bright hues of foliage in October.

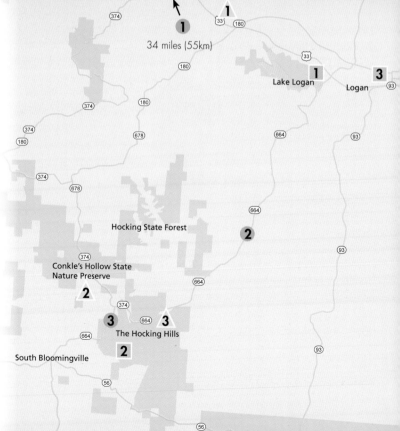

MIDWEST

CAMPGROUNDS

1 BUCKEYE LAKE/COLUMBUS EAST KOA

👪 👫 ♿ 🐾 🚿 ⚡ 🚐 📶

4460 Walnut Road SE, PO Box 972, Buckeye Lake, OH 43008. koa.com/camp/buckeye-lake; info@buckeyelakekoa.com; 740-928-0706. April 1 to October 31. $60 to $95. Heated pool, inflatable jump pillow.

This beautiful and fun campground is an hour away from Hocking Hills State Park, but it serves as a great choice for a family vacation that includes day trips into Columbus and Hocking Hills.

The campground is packed with fun amenities. Test out the inflatable jump pillow before diving into the brand-new pool. Enjoy a day of boating at Buckeye Lake and hitch a ride on an antique fire truck before cozying up around the campfire.

BUTTERFLIES IN HOCKING HILLS STATE PARK.

2 LOGAN/HOCKING HILLS KOA

👪 👫 ♿ 🐾 🚿 ⚡ 🚐 📶

29150 Pattor Road, Logan, OH 43138. koa.com/camp/logan; camp@hockinghillskoa.com; 740-385-4295. April 1 to October 31. $32 to $82. Heated pool, game room, gem mining, playground.

This campground conveniently located just 3 miles (4.8km) from Hocking Hills State Park offers a great combination of fun amenities and gorgeous valley views.

Kids love the large gem-mining sluice and pool. Adults love the spacious, shady sites and campfire cooking demonstrations. Deluxe sites with brick paver patios, log swings, gas grills, and daily newspaper delivery are worth the splurge for those who love to fancy camp. The campground hosts many fun planned activities, including pudding slides, bingo, wet and wild hayrides, guest storytellers, and ghost-hunting tours of the cemetery next door. Dog owners appreciate the fenced, off-leash Kamp K-9, which is large and shady.

The owners and staff are friendly and welcoming and can offer great local recommendations.

> Rock Cave is also known as Robbers' Roost because of the robbers, thieves, and bootleggers who hid out there in the nineteenth century.

HOCKING HILLS TRAILS.

3 HOCKING HILLS STATE PARK CAMPGROUND

👪 👫 ♿ 🐾 ⚡

19852 State Route 664, Logan, OH 43138. parks.ohiodnr.gov/hockinghills; 740-385-6841. $22 to $26. Amphitheater, fishing, game room, hiking trails, pool, naturalist programs, playground.

This campground is central to all the best the park has to offer. The sites, which have electric hookups but not water or sewer, are fairly spacious, and many are private. Some are badly sloped, so choose carefully. A clean and inviting pool is guarded in the summer, and other amenities such as a playground and a recreation room keep kids busy.

The campground is bustling and noisy in the summer, but you can easily escape the crowds by heading off for a hike or bike ride. The campground is close to many excellent trails, including Old Man's Cave, Ash Cave, and Cantwell Cliffs.

Fishing is allowed, but a license is required.

MIDWEST

In the early 1900s, the large rock near the entrance of Ash Cave was used as a pulpit for local preachers.

RESTAURANTS

1 MILLSTONE BBQ

12970 Grey Street, Logan, OH 43138. millstonebbq.com; bbqmillstone@yahoo.com; 740-385-5341. Sunday 10 A.M. to 9 P.M.; Monday to Thursday 11 A.M. to 9 P.M.; Friday and Saturday 11 A.M. to 10:30 P.M. $12 to $25. Barbecue.

From pulled pork to baby back ribs to beef brisket, this Southern-style barbecue joint offers all the favorites, smoked on-site. House-made cornbread and baked beans round out the authentic dining experience.

The menu offers plenty for those not interested in mounds of smoked meat. Traditional pub grub like nachos, potato skins, and quesadillas is plentiful. Try the Sriracha soft tacos or vegetarian stuffed green peppers.

Cedar Falls earned its name when early European settlers misidentified the area hemlock trees as cedars.

2 HOCKING HILLS DINING LODGE

20020 Hocking Hills State Park, Logan, OH 43138. hockinglodge.com; info@ hockinglodge.com; 740-380-0400. Monday to Thursday 11 A.M. to 8 P.M.; Friday 11 A.M. to 9 P.M.; Saturday 8 A.M. to 9 P.M.; Sunday 8 A.M. to 8 P.M. $12 to $30. American.

The only eating establishment in Hocking Hills State Park, this casual dining restaurant offers burgers, pizza, steak, and sandwiches for a reasonable price in a convenient location. Skip the inside dining room, and ask for one of the outdoor tables that offer a view of the hills and a peaceful setting to enjoy a leisurely lunch or dinner after hiking around the park. The service is friendly but can be slow.

The chefs take pride in sourcing ingredients locally and offering beef from the farms at The Ohio State University. All breads and desserts are made from scratch, including the cookies featured in the homemade ice-cream sandwich. Pulled pork and catfish po'boys are house specialties.

3 M & M FAMILY DINER

34 W. Main Street, Logan, OH 43138. 740-380-9181. Monday to Wednesday 7 A.M. to 2 P.M.; Thursday to Saturday 7 A.M. to 3 P.M.; Sunday 8 A.M. to 2 P.M. $6 to $12. Breakfast.

At this family owned breakfast joint, the friendly staff welcomes out-of-town visitors with open arms, happy to share opinions about the best dishes on the menu.

The kitschy décor adds to the mom-and-pop vibe, and hearty servings of sausage and biscuits might tempt you back many mornings during your visit.

HOCKING HILLS FALLS.

ATTRACTIONS

1 HOCKING HILLS CANOPY TOURS

10714 Jackson Street, Rockbridge, OH 43149. **hockinghillscanopytours.com;** info@ zipohio.com; 740-385-9477. Tour times vary; check online schedule. $64 to $109.

Take in the beautiful scenery of the Hocking Hills area on the first zip-line canopy tour in Ohio.

Options are available for both timid and daring souls. The basic canopy tour takes guests zipping between platforms on a 3-hour adventure. The DragonFly tour is for young children, and the SuperZip is for those who need a bit more speed.

2 CONKLES HOLLOW STATE NATURE PRESERVE

24858 Big Pine Road, Rockbridge, OH 43149. **naturepreserves.ohiodnr.gov/ conkleshollow;** 614-265-6565.

This nature preserve is a favorite destination for many visitors because of the easy access to amazing views.

The Lower Gorge Trail is an ADA-accessible 1-mile (1.6km) path that runs along the bottom of the gorge. At the end, you can cool off in the waterfall. There's also the much more challenging Rim Trail, which lives up to its name. This 2.5-mile (4km) hike is steep and a bit precarious at times,

clinging to the edge of the gorge, and offers hikers sweeping views and stunning overlooks as a reward for their efforts.

No dogs are allowed in the preserve. Park rangers enforce this rule very strictly.

3 HOCKING HILLS STATE PARK

19852 State Route 664, South Logan, OH 43138. **parks.ohiodnr.gov/hockinghills;** 740-385-6842. Open dawn to dusk.

In this state park, hiking is necessary to enjoy all the natural beauty. There are six popular hiking areas, all fairly accessible with lots of interesting features.

The trail leading to Ash Cave is paved and accessible for wheelchairs and strollers. Sandstone cliffs and towering hemlocks line the path, which leads to a waterfall. Cedar Falls Trail is about ½ mile (.8km) and takes you to one of the largest waterfalls in the region. Old Man's Cave offers bridges and scenic views, and the 1-mile (1.6km) hike takes you to a recessed cave and waterfalls. The Rock House Trail is about ½ mile (.8km) and leads to the only true geological cave in the park.

The park also offers many interpretative programs.

ITINERARIES

IF YOU HAVE 1 WEEK ...

Start your visit at the Hocking Hills State Park Visitor Center. Hike to Old Man's Cave and Ash Cave. See where bandits hid their loot in Rock House.

IF YOU HAVE 2 WEEKS ...

All the above, plus hike the Cedar Falls Trail and Cantwell Cliffs. Rent mountain bikes, and try out the trails at Hocking Hills State Park or nearby Lake Hope State Park. Take a day trip into the city of Columbus, and take a tour of The Ohio State University.

IF YOU HAVE 3 WEEKS ...

All the above, plus hike Conkles Hollow State Nature Preserve. Rent ATVs, and ride the rugged trails in the region. Take a moonlight kayak tour of the Hocking River. Fish at Lake Logan State Park. Take a ride on the Hocking Valley Scenic Railway. Ride horses through Waterloo State Forest.

sleeping bear dunes

national lakeshore, michigan

MIDWEST

The serene beauty of the giant dunes meeting a seemingly endless lake is a breathtaking experience for many visitors to Sleeping Bear Dunes National Lakeshore.

HIGHLIGHTS

✳ Making it to the top of the 300-foot-tall (91m) dune on the **Dune Climb.**

✳ Standing 450 feet (137m) above the water at #9 overlook on **Pierce Stocking Scenic Drive.**

✳ Kayaking or tubing down the **Platte River** along the edge of the dunes.

BEST TIME TO GO

The weather is glorious at the height of summer, but if you go in late August or early September, you can avoid crowds.

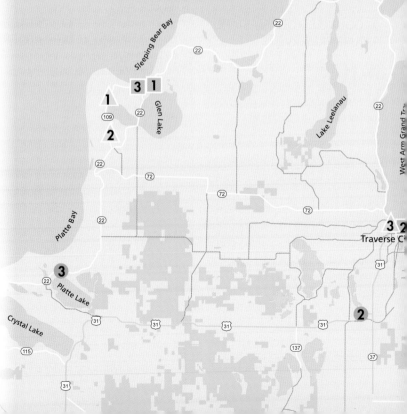

MIDWEST

CAMPGROUNDS

1 TRAVERSE CITY STATE PARK

👫 👫 ♿ 🔥 ⚡

1132 US 31-N, Traverse City, MI 49686.
michigan.gov/dnr; 231-922-5270. Boat
rentals, fishing, biking, concessions, swimming,
hiking, playground.

Traverse City State Park wins high
marks for its prime location on the
Grand Traverse Bay just 2 miles (3km)
away from downtown. Sleeping Bear
Dunes is just a short drive away.

The sites aren't huge, but the park has
a ¼-mile (.4km) stretch of beach. And
those who love to bike will delight in
the bike path that runs along the back
of the park and provides a safe route
right into downtown Traverse City.

> The park features the
> world's largest freshwater
> sand dunes, created by
> wind and glaciers.

2 HOLIDAY PARK CAMPGROUND

👫 👫 ♿ 🔥 ⚡ 🚐 📶

4860 US 31-S, Traverse City, MI 49685.
holidayparktc.com; 231-943-4410. April 25
to October 25. $45 to $60. Lake, dock,
boating, fishing, playground.

Looking for a full-service campground
near the National Lakeshore and
downtown Traverse City? This
generational favorite is located on
Silver Lake just 10 minutes from
downtown Traverse City and 30
minutes from Sleeping Bear Dunes.

Families return here because of the
campground's natural beauty,
convenient location, and warm
customer service. Many of the large,
full-hookup sites have water views and
are surrounded by shady trees. Kids
and adults love swimming and
canoeing in the lake's surprisingly
warm waters. The playground is
unimpressive and there is no pool, but
who needs one when a sparkling lake
is so close by? The campground is
impeccably clean, and the fire pits
are emptied daily.

VIEWS FROM THE PARK'S SCENIC DRIVE.

3 PLATTE RIVER CAMPGROUND IN SLEEPING BEAR DUNES NATIONAL LAKESHORE

👫 👫 ♿ 🔥 ⚡

5685 Lake Michigan Road, Honor, MI 49640.
nps.gov/slbe/planyourvisit/platterivercamp
.htm; 231-326-4700, ext. 5029. $19.
Amphitheater.

The Platte River Campground inside
the National Lakeshore offers
spacious, private sites with electric
hookups at a bargain price. Many
sites are more than 50 feet (15m)
long and can accommodate big rigs.
Plan on booking 6 months early to get
a site during the busy summer months.

Quiet time is strictly enforced, and
generator use is not allowed at night,
making this a peaceful spot to
reconnect with nature. In the summer,
ranger-led interpretive programs are
held at the amphitheater every night.

A canoe launch for the Platte River is
within walking distance, and rentals
are available at Platte River Point.
Many hiking trails are nearby, and the
Lake Michigan shoreline is less than
2 miles (3.2km) away.

THE EXHAUSTING DUNE CLIMB.

MIDWEST

Sleeping Bear Dunes has a 35-mile (56km) stretch of beach on the shore of Lake Michigan.

RESTAURANTS

1 BLU

👫 ♿

5705 S. Lake Street, Glen Arbor, MI 49636. glenarborblu.com; 231-334-2530. Tuesday to Sunday 5 P.M. to 9 P.M. $30 to $60. New American.

The real food scene in this region is located in Traverse City, but if you want to eat close to the park, you have better options in the town of Glen Arbor than in Empire. Be prepared for tourist pricing.

Blu is the perfect option if you want to soak in the beautiful lake views for just a little bit longer after visiting the park. Try the baked crab puffs, the lake trout, and the crème brûlée.

2 CHERRY REPUBLIC GRAND CAFÉ

👫 👫 ♿

6026 Lake Street, Glen Arbor, MI 49636. cherryrepublic.com; 800-206-6949. 8 A.M. to 9 P.M. $11 to $25. Café fare.

Yes, there really is a restaurant devoted to celebrating the cherry. From the cherry-bacon marmalade burger to the chicken-cherry salad sandwich, the menu will definitely surprise you. The best part is that it also will please your taste buds.

Don't leave without purchasing some cherry salsa or chocolate-covered cherries from the gift shop.

3 THE COOKS' HOUSE

👫 ♿

115 Wellington Street, Traverse City, MI 49686. **thecookshouse.net**; 231-946-8700. Tuesday to Saturday 5 P.M. to 12 A.M. $28 $50. Farm to table.

The Cooks' House was opened by two chefs intent on celebrating northern Michigan's local agriculture and artisanal products. As such, the menu is constantly changing and highlights seasonal offerings. The three-, five-, or seven-course tasting menus are an excellent way to truly experience the talent of the kitchen and the culinary specialties of this region. Order the wine pairings along with your tasting menu, and this might be a meal you never forget.

So many amazing restaurants are packed into Traverse City, but this is a favorite. Make reservations because tables fill up well in advance.

PIERCE STOCKING SCENIC DRIVE COVERED BRIDGE.

Michigan has more miles of shoreline than any other of the lower 48 states—more than 3,000 miles (4,800km).

ATTRACTIONS

1 THE DUNE CLIMB

6748 S. Dune Highway, Empire, MI 49630. **nps.gov/slbe**; 231-326-4700. 7-day vehicle pass $10.

Some people make the mistake of running down the dune and then not having the stamina to climb back up. Avoid this common conundrum by heading to the Dune Center at the bottom, where there are restrooms, a picnic area, and a bookstore.

From there, scamper up the sand until you can't go any farther. Relive your youth as you tumble back down.

2 PIERCE STOCKING SCENIC DRIVE

6748 S. Dune Highway, Empire, MI 49630. **nps.gov/slbe**; 231-326-4700. 7-day vehicle pass $10.

This 7.5-mile (12km) scenic drive is the perfect introduction to the park. Begin your trip early in the morning to avoid the mini traffic jams that start to form around popular overlooks later in the day.

Drop by the Philip A. Hart Visitor Center first, and pick up an interpretative tour brochure to help guide you through the 12 sites along the road.

Many visitors take a break from driving and hike the 1.5-mile (2.4km) Cottonwood Trail. At the Lake Michigan overlook, you'll find the popular viewing platform that sits 450 feet (137m) above the water. And Picnic Mountains is the perfect place to enjoy your packed lunch.

3 TRAVERSE CITY

Visitor Center, 101 W. Grandview Parkway, Traverse City, MI 49684. **traversecity.com**; info@traversecity.com; 800-872-8377. Monday to Saturday 9 A.M. to 6 P.M.; Sunday 11 A.M. to 3 P.M.

Small and accessible, yet full of food, art, and shopping, Traverse City is one of Michigan's great treasures. If you can, visit during the National Cherry Festival or the Traverse City Film Festival.

At the visitor center, friendly volunteers give you the local's scoop on all the seasonal events happening during your stay. Interested in microbrewery or wine tours? They'll help you set that up. Looking for gallery recommendations? They have brochures galore.

Eat breakfast at Frenchies Famous, and sample wine at Left Foot Charley. Stroll down Front Street, and shop at the bookstores, clothing boutiques, and specialty stores. The Traverse Area Recreation and Transportation Trails offers a great way to bike through town.

ITINERARIES

IF YOU HAVE 1 WEEK ...

Stop in at the Philip A. Hart Visitor Center, drive the Pierce Stocking Scenic Drive, and try to master the Dune Climb. Bike the Sleeping Bear Heritage Trail. Take a tour of the many craft breweries in Traverse City.

IF YOU HAVE 2 WEEKS ...

All the above, plus visit the park's Maritime Museum, and walk through Glen Haven, the restored lumbering village. Shop at the Glen Haven General Store. Try your luck at the  casinos located right outside of Traverse City. Play a round of golf at one of 17 championship golf courses.

IF YOU HAVE 3 WEEKS ...

All the above, plus enjoy a day on South Manitou Island, and take a tour of the lighthouse. (Check the park schedule for ranger-led programs during your stay.) Tour the local wineries. Canoe or kayak the Platte River. Charter a fishing boat, and catch some bass for dinner.

traverse city **craft brewery tour**

Located on the same parallel as the wine regions of France and Italy (the 45th), Traverse City, Michigan, has hosted a thriving wine industry for decades. But with the recent emergence of 17 microbreweries, brewpubs, and craft brew taprooms, this area is starting to gain a reputation for bold, creative beers as well. The city even hosts a beer week in November.

You can spread your visits to these breweries throughout your stay, picking up a TC Ale Trail guide map at the visitor center. Or let one of the many tour companies take you for a spin. Check out the creative TC Cycle Pub tour, on which you ride from brewery to brewery aboard a pedal-powered beer taxi.

No matter how you arrive, a visit to these breweries will be a highlight of your time spent in Traverse City.

❶ The Filling Station Microbrewery

Sit at outdoor picnic tables alongside the Traverse City Depot, and sample a wide variety of beers, from IPAs to porters, all brewed in small batches. The choices here take you around the globe, from the northwestern United States to the United Kingdom and Germany.

❷ Right Brain Brewery

Lots of IPAs are on tap here, and cherries make a regular appearance in the brews. The atmosphere is loud and hopping, with large, open spaces and regulars who bring board games and cards.

❸ Rare Bird Brewpub

With lots of exposed brick and reclaimed wood, the atmosphere here is German *bier* hall meets hipster. There are options on tap from other breweries as well, and visitors particularly like the variety of beer flights available for tasting.

❹ Jolly Pumpkin Restaurant, Brewery, Distillery

This is a standout favorite for many Ale Trail all-stars. The atmosphere is comfortable and low key, and outside seating offers water views. The sour beer is a love-it-or-hate-it type of thing, but the many tap and flight options provide something for everyone.

❺ The Workshop Brewing Company

The atmosphere here shouts family fun, with pinball and table football and shelves of books. The brews are traditional, though, making them "approachable" to craft beer newcomers. IPAs, blonde ales, stock ales, and porters—they're all done well here.

❻ Mackinaw Brewing Company

This was the first brewery to open in downtown Traverse City back in 1997, and it definitely has more of a traditional bar-and-grill atmosphere than its younger, hipper cousins. The cherry lager is brewed only in season, and you could probably order the oatmeal stout for your entire meal. IPAs and pale ales round out the offerings. Locally brewed ciders and wines also are on the menu.

MIDWEST

mount rushmore and the badlands, south dakota

Visiting Mount Rushmore is a must for many. The monument itself is impressive, but the landscape surrounding it is even more stunning.

HIGHLIGHTS

✷ Successfully squeeze your car through the tunnel on **Needles Highway.**

✷ Take a picture with a T-Rex at **Wall Drug,** the ultimate roadside tourist attraction.

✷ Spot bison, deer, prairie dogs, and wild burros on the **Wildlife Loop Road.**

BEST TIME TO GO

June is the best time to visit, offering warmer weather without the crowds of July. The Sturgis Motorcycle Rally is in August, so plan accordingly.

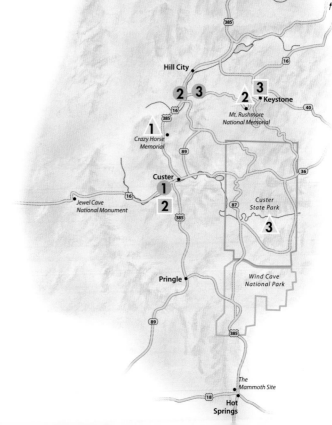

CAMPGROUNDS

① CUSTER STATE PARK (BLUE BELL AND LEGION LAKE)

Custer State Park, 13329 US Highway 16A, Custer, SD 57730. **campsd.com**; 800-710-2267. May to October. $25. Blue Bell: hayrides, chuck wagon cookouts; Legion Lake: fishing, boat rentals.

Looking to reconnect with nature and have no interest in playgrounds or inflatable jump pillows? Then camp at the Blue Bell or Legion Lake campgrounds within Custer State Park.

Bluebell is set in a Ponderosa pine forest and is near French Creek. Looking to do some trout fishing? This is your spot. Legion Lake is located in a mountain valley and provides many wonderful opportunities for wildlife photography.

Both campgrounds accommodate large rigs.

BLACK HILLS.

② RAFTER J BAR RANCH

12325 Rafter J-Bar Road, Hill City, SD 57745. **rafterj.com**; 888-723-8375. May 1 to October 1. $35 to $55. Playground, heated pool, hot tub, snack bar, recreation hall, volleyball and basketball courts.

Rafter J Bar Ranch is conveniently located within 8 miles (13km) of Mount Rushmore, Crazy Horse, and Custer State Park, so it serves as a terrific base camp for exploring the region.

The campground, which has sites in the sun and sites shaded by pine trees, consists of five separate camping areas. The Island and Ranch Camp sections are the best.

After spending the morning touring the area, head back to Rafter J to relax in the heated pool and hot tub. Or if you're craving exercise and fresh air, head out for a bike ride on the adjacent trail or a hike in the national forest that surrounds the campground. Whether you're traveling as a couple or with kids, Rafter J won't disappoint.

> Every year, about 500,000 people attend the Sturgis Motorcycle Rally. It's considered the largest rally in the world.

BISON GRAZING AT CUSTER STATE PARK.

③ MOUNT RUSHMORE KOA AT PALMER GULCH

12620 Highway 244, Hill City, SD 57745. **koa.com/camp/mount-rushmore**; info@palmergulch.com; 605-574-2525. May 1 to October 1. $35 to $115. Heated pools, spas, inflatable jump pillow, mini-golf.

The Mount Rushmore KOA is an obvious choice for families with kids who love action—don't camp here if you're looking for peace and quiet.

This campground was recently rebranded as a KOA "Resort," and it's easy to see why, with two pools, two spas, a splash pad, and an inflatable jump pillow. But you'll also find chuck wagon dinners, guided horseback rides, and self-guided ATV tours. Plan on hitting the pancake tent before a full day's worth of adventures in the Black Hills, and plan on returning to the on-site restaurant for dinner.

The Wi-Fi here is weak. Some campers climb onto large rocks to get a better signal.

> The Mammoth Site at Hot Springs, an active paleontological dig, has the world's largest concentration of mammoth remains.

RESTAURANTS

1 INDEPENDENT ALE HOUSE

👪 👫 ♿

625 St. Joseph Street, Rapid City, SD 57701. independentalehouse.com; 605-718-9492. Monday to Saturday 11 A.M. to close; Sunday 3 P.M. to close. $12 to $25. Pizza and pub fare.

This spot offers excellent beer, very good pizza, a decent wine selection, and a friendly staff. After a day of sightseeing, it's a comfortable place to relax. It has 40 beers on tap that are constantly rotated to offer seasonal and craft brew options.

Try the Althea pizza with sun-dried tomatoes. Or order the three little pigs pizza, piled with pepperoni, sausage, and bacon.

2 RUBY HOUSE RESTAURANT

👪 👫 ♿

124 Winter Street, Keystone, SD 57751. rubyhousekeystone.com; rubyhouse1@hotmail.com; 605-666-4404. 11 A.M. to 9 P.M. $11 to $30. American.

The Mount Rushmore National Memorial is in the town of Keystone, so if you're looking to grab lunch or dinner after your visit, this is your best bet.

The décor is meant to reference the early 1900s, with lots of velvet drapes and ornate sconces. Stick with burgers and prime rib, and you won't be disappointed.

THE BADLANDS.

3 CHUCK WAGON COOKOUT, BLUE BELL LODGE

👪

13329 US Highway 16A East, Custer, SD 57730. custerresorts.com; 605-255-4531. Departure time varies. $45 to $52. Cowboy cuisine.

You'll find many chuck wagon dinner shows in the region, but this one goes far beyond the typical tourist experience. The evening starts with a 45-minute hayride through the beautiful back roads of Custer State Park and includes a sing-along and souvenir cowboy hats and bandannas to set the proper tone. Some guests bring their own drinks for the ride.

When you arrive at the dining ranch, steaks and burgers are served along with all the cowboy fixings, like beans, coleslaw, and watermelon on speckled enameled plates. Seconds are served.

Entertainment continues throughout the meal with audience interaction and participation. Chicken dances and the hokey pokey get everyone up and dancing. After returning to the lodge, an employee can take a picture of your party in front of the chuck wagon (free of charge with your camera).

> Although discouraged by rangers, many visitors bring carrots for the "begging burros" at Custer State Park.

ATTRACTIONS

1 CRAZY HORSE MEMORIAL

2151 Avenue of the Chiefs, Crazy Horse, SD 57730. **crazyhorsememorial.org;** memorial@ crazyhorse.org; 605-673-4681. 7 A.M. to 9 P.M. $11 per person, $5 per motorcyclist, $5 per bicyclist, $28 per car with 3 or more people, 6 and under free.

When the Crazy Horse Memorial is completed, it will be the world's largest mountain sculpture. Korczak Ziolkowski, who had previously worked on Mount Rushmore, began this awe-inspiring project in 1948. He died in 1982, but his dream to honor the legendary leader has been carried on by his wife and children. The short orientation video is rich in human drama.

2 MOUNT RUSHMORE

13000 Highway 244, Keystone, SD 57751. **nps.gov/moru;** 605-574-2523. 5 A.M. to 11 P.M. Vehicle parking $11.

The origins of the Mount Rushmore monument have more to do with commerce than patriotism. A South Dakota historian named Doane Robinson wanted to create a large-scale sculpture that would attract tourism to his beloved state. His plan worked. Almost 3 million people visit Mount Rushmore each year.

If you're an amateur photographer and wanting to get some great shots, arrive at 8 A.M., when the light is best. If you want to walk to the base of the monument, take a 30-minute Ranger Walk on the Presidential Trail. The most popular time to visit is for the evening program, which includes a patriotic film and ends with the lighting of the monument.

3 CUSTER STATE PARK

13329 US Highway 16A, Custer, SD 57730. **gfp.sd.gov/state-parks/directory/custer;** 605-255-4464. Vehicle pass $15.

The first thing many people do when arriving at Custer State Park is drive the Wildlife Loop Road. The park is home to more than 1,300 bison, so you're almost guaranteed to come across a herd taking its sweet time crossing the road. Elk, mountain goats, turkeys, and burros also might make an appearance.

Needles Highway is another spectacular drive with views of granite spires reaching into the sky.

Iron Mountain Road offers what many people consider the best views of Mount Rushmore.

This state park has so much to offer, so it's worth asking a ranger to help map out your visit. Check the schedule for ranger-led programs that share information about wildlife and Native American history in this area.

ITINERARIES

IF YOU HAVE 1 WEEK ...

Take the tour at Mount Rushmore, and prepare to be awed by the sheer size of the Crazy Horse Memorial. Navigate the Wildlife Loop Road and Needles Highway in Custer State Park. Ride the 1880 Train. Shop at Wall Drug.

IF YOU HAVE 2 WEEKS ...

All the above, plus swim at Sylvan Lake and visit the Jewel Cave National Monument. Drive Iron Mountain Road. Hike the Cathedral Spires Trail. Take a day trip to Devils Tower National Monument. Reserve

early to dig for bones at the Mammoth Site. Visit the Prairie Berry Winery.

IF YOU HAVE 3 WEEKS ...

All the above, plus swim at Legions Lake and visit Wind Cave National Park. Rock climb at Spearfish Canyon. Take a day trip to the Badlands, and drive the Badlands Loop Road. Visit the Reptile Gardens, and mine for gold at Deadwood. Tour the beautiful Black Hills Wild Horse Sanctuary.

route 66:
tulsa to oklahoma city

Route 66 starts in Chicago, Illinois, and ends in Santa Monica, California, but its heart and soul is in Oklahoma. The state maintains many historical attractions along the route.

HIGHLIGHTS

✴ Stop at the **Blue Whale of Catoosa,** a roadside attraction since 1972, just before entering Tulsa.

✴ Visit the **Cyrus Avery Centennial Plaza** for a Route 66 photo op where "East meets West."

✴ Discover an urban oasis by visiting the **Myriad Botanical Gardens** and **Crystal Bridge Tropical Conservatory.**

BEST TIME TO GO

October offers lovely weather in Oklahoma, with 70°F (21°C) days and low humidity. Avoid tornado season in spring and the thunderstorms of summer.

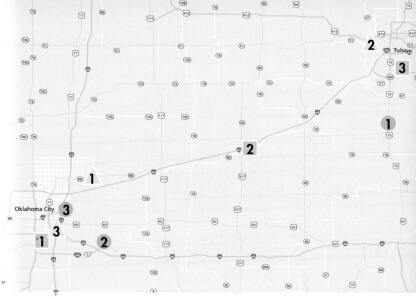

CAMPGROUNDS

1 TULSA RV RANCH

👨‍👩‍👧 👫 ♿ 🧺 🚿 ⚡ 🚐 📶

2538 US 75, Beggs, OK 74421. **tulsarvranch .com**; tulsarvranch1@gmail.com; 918-267-9000. $40. Game room, playground, pool, fishing, horseshoes, pond, recreation room.

Looking for a place to rest and recharge your battery before heading farther west? The Tulsa RV Ranch has a restaurant and saloon on-site where you can enjoy a steak and a cold beer. Then head over to the on-site rodeo arena for a fun night out without having to drive anywhere.

The facilities are clean and new. Light sleepers be forewarned: the park is located directly next to the interstate. Crank up your AC for a good night's sleep.

REMINDERS OF THE PAST.

2 OKLAHOMA CITY EAST KOA

👨‍👩‍👧 👫 ♿ 🧺 🚿 ⚡ 🚐 📶

6200 S. Choctaw Road, Choctaw, OK 73020. **koa.com/camp/oklahoma-city**; camp@oklahomacitykoa.com; 405-391-5000. $40 to $60. Pool, playground, snack bar.

This KOA is clean and quiet but close to all the action in Oklahoma City, just 15 minutes away. The staff is friendly and helpful and can offer recommendations for area dining and activities. Some sites are small, and there are areas where you'll feel packed in, so call in advance and ask for a site with some breathing room.

The campground fills with families on the weekend. Kids enjoy the hayrides and scavenger hunts, the playground, and the pool. Stretch your legs on the 1-mile (1.6km) walking trail to enjoy some peace and quiet.

The owners here are RVers themselves, and they take pride in treating their guests like family.

Tulsa business owner Cyrus Avery was the first to call Route 66 the "Main Street of America."

CATOOSA WHALE.

3 TWIN FOUNTAINS RV RESORT

👨‍👩‍👧 👫 ♿ 🧺 🚿 ⚡ 🚐 📶

2727 NE 63rd Street, Oklahoma City, OK 73111. **twinfountainsrvpark.com**; reservations@ twinfountainsrvpark.com; 405-475-5514. $50. Pool, spa, playground, game room, shuffleboard.

If you plan on exploring Oklahoma City for a few days, you won't find a better base camp than Twin Fountains. RV sites are spacious and attractive, and customer service is tops. The playground is nice, and the pool is lovely and relaxing. All the other shared areas, including the pavilion and recreation room, are clean and comfortable.

Want to burn off all those burgers and shakes you've been eating out on Route 66? Spend some time in the physical fitness center. An on-site masseuse can work on your back if it's stiff from all that driving.

Let them know if you're current or former military, and they'll treat you like a star.

SOUTHWEST

> Route 66 was officially designated in 1926, and the last stretch disappeared off official maps in 1985, replaced with interstate highways.

RESTAURANTS

1 CATTLEMEN'S STEAKHOUSE

1309 S. Agnew Avenue, Oklahoma City, OK 73108. cattlemensrestaurant.com; 405-236-0416. Sunday to Thursday 6 A.M. to 10 P.M.; Friday and Saturday 6 A.M. to 12 A.M. $11 to $35. Steakhouse.

There are other items on the menu, but you really shouldn't dine here unless you're ordering a hearty portion of beef. You won't find any grass-fed steaks; this traditional steakhouse is proud to offer corn-raised meat, slowly aged according to a secret in-house method. The result is tender, perfectly cooked steaks served on a platter with plenty of *au jus*.

Breakfast is served every morning, and if you're craving some calf brain and eggs, stop in for a bite.

The automated parking meter and the shopping cart both were introduced in Oklahoma City in the 1930s.

2 CANCUN INTERNATIONAL RESTAURANT

705 S. Lewis Avenue, Tulsa, OK 74104. eatatcancun.com; customerservice@ eatatcancun.com; 918-583-8089. Monday, Tuesday, Thursday, and Friday 11 A.M. to 9 P.M.; Saturday and Sunday 10 A.M. to 9 P.M.; closed Wednesday. $8 to $15. Mexican.

This restaurant gives travelers what they yearn for: delicious, fresh food with a ridiculously cheap price tag.

You can stay safe and order some beef tacos or enchiladas. Or step out of your comfort zone and try the goat tacos and pork and hominy stew. Either way, you won't be disappointed.

3 ROCK CAFE

114 W. Main Street, Stroud, OK 74079. rockcafert66.com; 918-968-3990. 7 A.M. to 8 P.M. $10 to $15 American.

In 2001, a team from Pixar Animation Studios visited the Rock café, doing research for the animated film *Cars*. After meeting owner Dawn Welch, the Pixar folks left with inspiration for the character of Sally, a car who arrives in a worn-out town along Route 66 and finds it charming enough to open a business and put down roots.

Welch takes her stewardship of the iconic restaurant very seriously and offers visitors a slice of history along with their pie. The original Wolfe grill, which they call Betsy, is still in use even after a devastating fire in 2008. Route 66 memorabilia wallpapers the joint.

Try to visit during off hours, or you might find yourself with a long wait and frazzled service.

ROCK CAFE.

ATTRACTIONS

1 THE ARCADIA ROUND BARN

👪 👫

107 E. Highway 66, Arcadia, OK 73007. arcadiaroundbarn.com; abadavis@sbcglobal.com; 405-396-0824. 10 A.M. to 5 P.M. Free admission.

The Arcadia Round Barn is one of the most photographed buildings along Route 66. Go inside to find lots of "Mother Road" memorabilia and information about unusual barns around the world. There's a gift shop as well.

Also in Arcadia, you can find POPS, a 66-foot-tall (20m) illuminated pop bottle built in 2007.

2 TULSA

👪 👫 ♿

11th Street, Tulsa, OK 74127. riverparks.org; staff@riverparks.org; 918-596-2001. 5 A.M. to 11 P.M.

Start your visit in Tulsa by walking or biking along the trails that have recently been developed near the historic 11th Street Bridge. The Cyrus Avery Centennial Plaza is still under development, but it currently features flags from all eight Route 66 states as well as some great photo ops of the bridge.

You won't want to miss the huge *Praying Hands* sculpture at the entrance of Oral Roberts University measuring 60 feet (18m) tall and weighing 30 tons (27,000kg). Another must-visit site is the Tulsa

Center of the Universe, stunning tourists with a mysterious acoustical effect that causes your voice to strongly reverberate when speaking.

3 OKLAHOMA CITY

👪 👫 ♿

Oklahoma City Visitor Bureau, 123 Park Ave, Oklahoma City, OK 73102. visitokc.com; contact@visitokc.com; 405-297-8912. Monday to Friday 9 A.M. to 6 P.M.

Route 66 traced many different paths through this city over the years, so jump around a bit to see all the cool sites.

The National Cowboy and Western Heritage Museum should be at the top of your list, containing fascinating exhibitions including a replica of a Western town. Another worthwhile stop is the Oklahoma Music Hall of Fame.

The Harn Homestead, in the middle of the city, was built by William Fremont Harn when he moved into the Oklahoma Territory to preside over disputes arising from the Land Rush of 1889. Stick to the historical theme, and tour the governor's mansion if you happen to be in town on a Wednesday.

Ride a train at the Oklahoma Railway Museum, or learn everything you ever wanted to know about vintage telephones at the Oklahoma Museum of Telephone History.

ITINERARIES

IF YOU HAVE 1 WEEK …

See the Will Rogers Memorial; the Blue Whale of Catoosa; the *Golden Driller*, the giant oil worker statue at the Tulsa Fairgrounds; and the 11th Street Bridge in Tulsa. Stop in Stroud, Chandler, and Arcadia, and end your trip in Oklahoma City.

IF YOU HAVE 2 WEEKS …

All the above, plus take a day trip north of Tulsa to Bartlesville, an oil-boom town from the early 1900s. Visit Davenport, where you can spot an old Texaco station and the still-operating Lincoln Motel. Detour to Guthrie, and catch a move at the Beacon Drive-In.

IF YOU HAVE 3 WEEKS …

Consider splitting your time between Tulsa and Oklahoma City to more fully explore each region without so much driving. Embark on full day trips to the towns of Miami and Claremore, north of Tulsa. Use Oklahoma City as a base camp to explore Yukon and Clinton to the west.

top route 66
attractions

If you haven't gotten your fill of roadside diners and kitschy souvenir shops, keep traveling west on Route 66 out of Oklahoma toward the Golden State. Here are some highlights you'll find along the way.

TEXAS

Cadillac Ranch This work of public art isn't located directly on Route 66, but the classic Cadillacs, each half buried and pointed skyward at the same angle as the Great Pyramid of Egypt, have become a must-see for pilgrims traveling on the mother road. Spray painting is allowed, so bring a can and sign your name.

MidPoint Cafe Pilgrims drive Route 66 to capture the spirit of the Old West, but they also come to eat. So why not stop halfway and grab a juicy burger and a slice of ugly pie? This café served as the inspiration for Flo's diner in Pixar's *Cars*, and the owner is an old road aficionado.

NEW MEXICO

Tucumcari The neon signs along Motel Row offer the traveler a satisfying Route 66 tableau, advertising classic overnight stops like the Blue Swallow Motel and Buckaroo Motel. Drop into Tee Pee Curios to expand your growing collection of touristy trinkets. Tour the Mesalands Community College Dinosaur Museum, and eat brisket at Watson's BBQ.

El Rancho Hotel and Motel This joint outclasses all the other motels along the route with its history of hosting Hollywood stars when they were filming movies in the area. The restaurant serves traditional Southwest fare like enchiladas and tamales, but you also can order a satisfying steak or burger. Try a hand-squeezed margarita at the 49er Lounge before dining.

ARIZONA

Meteor Crater Yes, this really is just a large hole in the ground, but Elvis Presley enjoyed it, and so have many other travelers along Route 66. For the entrance fee, you get to watch a film, explore the museum, and take a guided tour around the rim of the crater. The science and history make the site come to life, so don't skip the tour.

Winslow The Eagles sang about standing on a corner in Winslow, Arizona, and many, many travelers have done just that, taking a picture by the intersection of 2nd and Kinsley Streets. After your photo op, walk a few doors down to Dar's Route 66 Diner for a kitschy road-food experience.

CALIFORNIA

Wigwam Motels You still can sleep in a wigwam at this motel, but if you're traveling by RV you'll probably just want to take a picture. You'll also want to snap photos of the vintage automobiles on permanent display around the property. The main office is now a museum that features the various collections of Chester Lewis, original proprietor of this Route 66 gem.

Santa Monica Pier This is where the Main Street of America finally comes to an end, and if you search hard, you'll find a brass plaque commemorating the official spot where Santa Monica Boulevard dead-ends at Ocean Avenue. Walk a few blocks south to the Santa Monica Pier to enjoy a last bit of nostalgia by riding Looff's carousel and the Ferris wheel.

austin
and san
antonio,
texas

These Texas cities attract visitors from all over with a mix of local music, delicious food, and fascinating history. This is urban tourism at its best, providing museums to explore during the day and live music to enjoy at night.

HIGHLIGHTS

✴ Have a drink at **The Esquire Tavern,** the oldest bar on the River Walk.

✴ Catch a live show in the **6th Street District,** the heart of the Austin music scene.

✴ Watch *Alamo: The Price of Freedom* in 3-D at the IMAX theater in **San Antonio.**

BEST TIME TO GO

The weather is best in November and March, but this is the land of festivals, so check city schedules before booking.

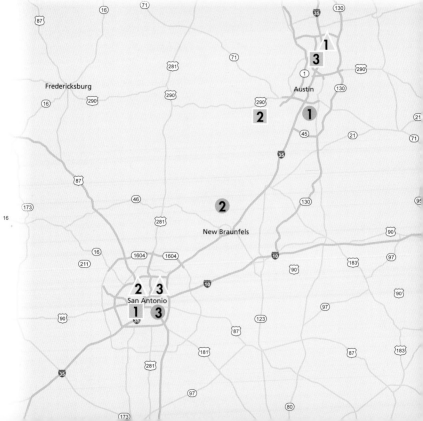

CAMPGROUNDS

① MCKINNEY FALLS STATE PARK

5808 McKinney Falls Parkway, Austin, TX 78744. tpwd.texas.gov/state-parks/mckinney-falls; 512-389-8900. $20 to $24. Picnic tables, restrooms with showers.

This state park has large, private sites in a beautiful natural setting that's only 20 minutes from downtown Austin. The bathrooms need to be renovated, and so do some of the roads and trails, but this is still a terrific option considering its proximity to the city.

You can swim in Onion Creek, and the falls are attractive, if not magnificent, and worth a visit. Kid-friendly ranger-led programs also are offered in the park.

> Countless weddings are held on the River Walk's Marriage Island, a tradition dating to the Mexican Revolution.

② JELLYSTONE PARK HILL COUNTRY

12915 FM 306, Canyon Lake, TX 78132. jellystonehillcountry.com; info@jellystonehillcountry.com; 877-964-3731. $48 to $65. Heated pool, water playground.

For families traveling with young kids, there's no more exciting option than this theme park–like campground. Don't come here for the peace and quiet; come here for the playground, heated pool, laser tag, inflatable jump pillow, and water balloon battle station. Tubing on the nearby Guadalupe River is also a blast. Older kids will enjoy basketball and volleyball, but this Jellystone hits the sweet spot for preteens. This place will wear out your kids so you can enjoy a peaceful night around the campfire.

Deluxe sites near the back of the campground are excellent for big rigs, and offer a bit more peace and quiet. Some sites are small, so call and ask specific questions to get a good one.

DOWNTOWN AUSTIN.

③ SAN ANTONIO KOA

602 Gembler Road, San Antonio, TX 78219. koa.com/camp/san-antonio; info@sanantoniokoa.com; 210-224-9296. $41 to $54. Pool, snack bar, tour shuttle, dog park.

This campground, KOA's 2015 Campground of the Year, is only 10 minutes from downtown San Antonio. If you want to stretch your legs on the River Walk and visit the Alamo, make this your base camp.

Located on 40 shady acres (16ha) in an otherwise urban environment, this campground offers the best of both worlds. The restrooms and showers are incredibly clean. The heated pool is relaxing and nicely landscaped. The K9 Corral dog park is spacious and has lots of toys for pups to play with. Benches are provided so you can relax while your dog plays.

The customer service is excellent. The staff is knowledgeable about the city and can recommend your next favorite restaurant.

MISSION SAN JOSÉ.

A mere 700 people showed up for the first South by Southwest in 1987. In 2015, the attendees numbered closer to 48,000.

RESTAURANTS

1 BOUDRO'S

421 E. Commerce Street, San Antonio, TX 78205. boudros.com; 210-224-8484. Sunday to Thursday 11 A.M. to 11 P.M.; Friday and Saturday 11 A.M. to 12 A.M. $11 to $50. New American.

The River Walk is home to many wonderful local restaurants, so there's no need to frequent the chain joints that have crept into the area.

Boudro's is a picturesque café situated right on the river and offers the perfect spot to sit and soak in the atmosphere while sipping cocktails and watching your guacamole be prepared tableside. Order the chicken-fried rib eye for lunch or the shrimp and grits for dinner.

Riverboat dining is also available, but advance reservations are recommended.

Plans are in place for a Phil Collins museum at the Alamo to honor the British pop star, a loyal patron.

2 HUT'S HAMBURGERS

807 W. 6th Street, Austin, TX 78703. hutsfrankandangies.com; hutsfna@yahoo.com; 512-472-0693. 11 A.M. to 10 P.M. $6 to $15. Burgers.

The vibe in downtown Austin is seriously laid back, and this is the perfect burger joint for a bite to eat before enjoying the live music scene in the 6th Avenue District.

Try the Wolfman Jack, piled high with sour cream, diced green chilies, cheese, and bacon. Fries and a shake will round out your meal nicely.

3 THE SALT LICK

18300 FM 1826, Driftwood, TX 78619. saltlickbbq.com; saltlick@saltlickbbq.com; 512-858-4959. 11 A.M. to 10 P.M. $14 to $35. Barbecue.

The Salt Lick offers the classic Texas barbecue experience. Bring your own beer or wine to complement your meal. Also bring cash because credit cards aren't accepted.

The restaurant is located on a ranch outside Austin amidst rolling hills and towering oaks. The drive there is part of the experience, and the atmosphere of the ranch house is quintessential Texas.

The best bang for your buck is the family style, all-inclusive meal, which gets you platters of brisket, sausage, ribs, and sides. An à la carte menu is offered as well. For dessert, buy a whole pecan pie to enjoy back at the campground.

REMEMBER THE ALAMO.

ATTRACTIONS

1 LYNDON BAINES JOHNSON PRESIDENTIAL LIBRARY

2313 Red River Street, Austin, TX 78705. lbjlibrary.org; johnson.library@nara.gov; 512-721-0200. 9 A.M. to 5 P.M. Adults $8; seniors $5; children $3; 11 and under free; active military free.

Although visiting a presidential library might sound dull to some, the LBJ library always surprises visitors with its dynamic and educational exhibits. The phone recordings alone are enough to keep people captivated for quite a long time.

Children will be particularly interested in LBJ's daughters' account of their time in the White House.

2 SAN ANTONIO RIVER WALK

River Walk, San Antonio, TX 78205. thesanantonioriverwalk.com; nhunt@paseodelrio.com; 210-227-4262.

You'll enjoy strolling up and down the walkway of the San Antonio River Walk, enjoying the shopping and bistro options. Then head to the Museum Reach, which offers gardens, walking paths, and public art displays. Don't miss watching the river barges use the lock and dam system at Brooklyn Street. Also drop in at the Rivercenter IMAX theater to watch *Alamo: The Price of Freedom*. Head north to visit Pearl Brewery, a historic site that offers culinary classes and outdoor concerts.

One of the best ways to see the River Walk is by boat. Rio San Antonio Cruises runs affordable, narrated trips down the river on a daily basis.

3 THE ALAMO

300 Alamo Plaza, San Antonio, TX 78205. thealamo.org; alamoinfo@glo.texas.gov; 210-225-1391. 9 A.M. to 5:30 P.M. Check website for extended summer hours. Free admission.

Start your visit here at the Alamo Shrine, the iconic church where many of the defenders took their last stand against the Mexican troops. Every half hour, a ranger gives a brief historical talk. Volunteer docents located throughout the grounds are happy to answer any questions you have.

Other options for getting the most out of your visit include a 45-minute audio tour available for rent or a 1-hour guided battlefield tour costing $15 and available by advance reservation.

In the Long Barrack Museum, watch a short History Channel film for additional historical background, and visit the interpretative exhibit, *The Alamo: A Story Bigger than Texas*. End your trip with a quiet stroll through the shaded Alamo Gardens.

ITINERARIES

IF YOU HAVE 1 WEEK ...

Pick a base camp near either Austin or San Antonio, and take day trips to the other location. Visit the River Walk and the Alamo in San Antonio. Hang out in Austin's 6th Avenue District.

IF YOU HAVE 2 WEEKS ...

Spend a week at an Austin campground and a week at a San Antonio campground. In Austin, hike around Lady Bird Lake, visit the Lyndon Baines Johnson Presidential Library, and listen to live music. In San Antonio, tour Mission San José and the San Antonio Botanical Garden. Take a day trip to Fredericksburg.

IF YOU HAVE 3 WEEKS ...

Split your time evenly between a campground near Austin and a campground near San Antonio. In Austin, watch the races at Circuit of the Americas, and tour the Texas State Cemetery. In San Antonio, visit Mission Trail and the San Antonio Museum of Art. Day trip to the Enchanted Rock State Natural Area.

SOUTHWEST

SOUTHWEST

tucson,
arizona

With about 350 sunny days every year, it's no wonder Tucson is a hugely popular RV destination. This city has it all—phenomenal weather and beautiful views in a thriving urban environment. Food, art, shopping, and outdoor adventure await its visitors.

HIGHLIGHTS

★ Play a round of golf at the **Omni Tucson National Resort.**

★ Watch a Wild West gunfight at **Old Tucson Studios.**

★ Take a bus tour of retired Air Force planes at the **Pima Air and Space Museum.**

BEST TIME TO GO

April and October are the perfect times to visit, when you'll experience beautiful weather for outdoor activities without all the snowbirds.

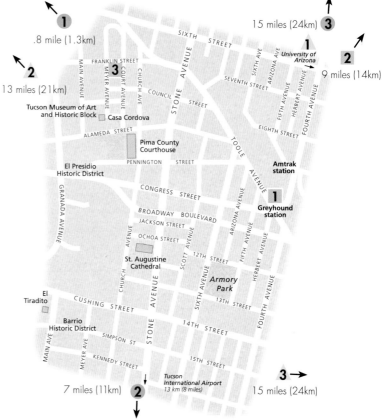

CAMPGROUNDS

① SENTINEL PEAK RV PARK

👨‍👩‍👧 👫 ♿ ⚰ 🚿 🔌 🚐 📶

450 N. Grande Avenue, Tucson, AZ 85745. sentinelpeakrv.com; info@sentinelpeakrv.com; 520-495-0175. $32 to $59. Pool, indoor playground, laundry, clubhouse, shuttle.

Located in the heart of Tucson, and at the foot of a Mountain, this urban campground is just steps away from the city's new light-rail system so you can park your RV and explore the city via streetcar.

The campground is small, but the sites are large and can accommodate big rigs. Cool off in the brand-new pool, or let the kids escape the summer heat at the indoor playground.

② TUCSON/LAZYDAYS KOA

👨‍👩‍👧 👫 ⚰ 🚿 🔌 🚐 📶

5151 S. Country Club Road, Tucson, AZ 85706. **koa.com/camp/tucson-lazydays**; tucson@koa.net; 520-799-3701. $25 to $50. Pool, hot tub, playground, snack bar.

The Tucson/Lazydays KOA is located right next door to a large RV dealership, so if you're looking to upgrade your rig (and who isn't?), this might be a fun place to set up base camp in Tucson.

The KOA does a nice job of combining kid-centered activities, such as arts and crafts time and movie nights, with adult-centered activities, such as beginner's yoga and Jazzercise. The on-site bar and grill is good for relaxing close to home after an exciting day in the city, and the fitness center and recreation room are classy and comfortable. The pool is nice but not amazing, and the covered playground is just good enough for smaller kids.

Lovely fruit trees add color and shade to the RV sites.

③ CATALINA STATE PARK CAMPGROUND

👨‍👩‍👧 👫 ♿ ⚰ 🚿 🔌

Catalina SP, 11570 N. Oracle Road, Tucson, AZ 85737. **azstateparks.com/parks/CATA**; 520-628-5798. $20 to $30. Gift shop, ranger station, exhibits, biking, equestrian area.

Visitors love the stunning natural setting of Catalina State Park at the base of the Santa Catalina Mountains. Some complain about the large shopping center across the street from the entrance, but others love the convenience. Either way, once you enter the park, the highway quickly disappears and the natural world takes over.

At the campground, most sites are large, level, and shaded, and you'll often spot wildlife right from your RV. The park contains more 170 species of birds, so keep your binoculars close. You also might see coyote, deer, and bobcat.

The park is packed with delightful multiuse hiking trails for biking and horseback riding. An equestrian staging area is also nearby for those who own horses.

THE FAMOUS SAGUARO CACTUS.

> The Tucson region has the world's largest concentration of the iconic saguaro cactus.

BIOSPHERE 2.

SOUTHWEST

> With the exception of the Amazon rainforest, Tucson is home to more bird species than any other place in the world.

RESTAURANTS

1 MAYNARD'S MARKET AND KITCHEN

400 N. Toole Avenue, Tucson, AZ 85701. maynardstucson.com; 520-545-0577. 7 A.M. to 9 P.M. $10 to $30. American.

Maynard's is a must-visit culinary destination in downtown Tucson, offering an upbeat atmosphere, comfortable seating, and delicious food. On the breakfast menu, you'll find biscuit sandwiches and burritos stuffed with applewood-smoked bacon and eggs. Lunch offers fresh café fare such as crudité platters, banh mi sandwiches, and classic BLTs.

The happy hour is a particularly popular among locals, who love the elevated bar menu featuring steak tartare, oysters, and mussels.

> Amateur spelunkers love to explore Peppersauce Cave and sign the guest book at the end of the path.

2 THE GRILL AT HACIENDA DEL SOL

5501 N. Hacienda Del Sol Road, Tucson, AZ 85718. haciendadelsol.com; fdesk@ haciendadelsol.com; 520-529-3500. Breakfast: Monday to Saturday 7 A.M. to 9 A.M.; lunch: Monday to Saturday 11 A.M. to 2 P.M.; dinner: Sunday to Thursday 5:30 P.M. to 9 P.M., Friday and Saturday 5:30 P.M. to 10 P.M.; Brunch: Sunday 9 A.M. to 2 P.M. $30 to $60. New American.

Regularly appearing on "best of" lists in local and national media, The Grill is the perfect place to celebrate a special occasion or splurge on a memorable vacation meal.

Wine is the real star here, with more than 900 labels and 6,000 bottles from which to choose. If you're not sure, the staff is happy to help you pick the perfect glass for your dinner. The menu features innovative dishes incorporating many ingredients from the resort's own gardens and citrus orchards. Sunday brunch offers a stunning assortment of delicacies ranging from prime rib to eggs Benedict and smoked salmon. Fill your plate with waffles, omelets, sushi, and blintzes, and sip a mimosa made with grapefruit picked and freshly squeezed that very morning.

3 EL CHARRO CAFÉ

311 N. Court Avenue, Tucson, AZ 85701. elcharrocafe.com; 520-622-1922. 10 A.M. to 9 P.M. $11 to $25. Mexican.

Eating amazing Mexican food while in Tucson is a must, and this iconic restaurant is the perfect place to do it. Said to be the oldest Mexican restaurant in continuous operation in America, many also claim it's where the chimichanga was invented.

History aside, the food is authentic and delicious. Try the carne seca followed by the churros.

SONORAN DESERT.

ATTRACTIONS

1 UNIVERSITY OF ARIZONA CAMPUS

UA Visitor Center, 811 N. Euclid Avenue, Tucson, AZ 85721. **universityrelations.arizona .edu;** visitor@email.arizona.edu; 520-621-5130. Monday to Friday 9 A.M. to 5 P.M.

The University of Arizona provides a number of attractions for visitors to experience, including a museum, arboretum, and planetarium. Choose a general interest tour, or explore the campus history and public art.

Head north of the city to take a tour of Biosphere 2, one of *TIME Magazine's* 50 must-see "wonders of the world."

2 ARIZONA-SONORA DESERT MUSEUM

2021 N. Kinney Road, Tucson, AZ 85743. **desertmuseum.org;** info@desertmuseum.org; 520-883-1380. Hours vary by season. Adults $19.50; seniors $17.50; youth $15.50; children $6; 3 and under free.

If possible, make this your first excursion when visiting Tucson. So much more than a museum, here you'll find 2 miles (3.2km) of walking paths that expose you to the region's native flora and fauna separated into various exhibit areas. Visit the Riparian Corridor, and see river otters, beavers, and bighorn sheep. Or head over to Cat Canyon, and try to spot the ocelots and bobcats. Interactive exhibits include a touch tank and walk-in aviary. Bring your camera to snap pictures of the hummingbirds feasting on the bountiful nectar around the grounds.

Plentiful dining options are available, including a food court, snack shop, coffee bar, and café.

3 SAGUARO NATIONAL PARK

3693 S. Old Spanish Trail, Tucson, AZ 85730. **nps.gov/sagu;** 520-733-5153. Visitor Center open 9 A.M. to 5 P.M. 7-day vehicle pass $10.

This national park is composed of two districts, the East and the West, separated in the middle by the city of Tucson. The scenic loop drives are a great introduction to both sides.

In the East section, start with the Cactus Forest Scenic Loop Drive, a one-way paved road that runs right through the heart of the saguaro forest and offers plenty of opportunities to take in the scenery and wildlife of the desert. The Bajada Loop Drive is a more rugged tour through the western section, but it's worth braving the dirt roads to spot the rock art and petroglyphs.

Tanque Verde Ridge Trail is a popular hike that leads you to the highest peak on the ridge and offers spectacular views of the Tucson basin.

ITINERARIES

IF YOU HAVE 1 WEEK ...

Start with a visit to the Arizona-Sonora Desert Museum. Drive the East and West districts of Saguaro National Park. Tour the University of Arizona campus, and play a round of golf. Shop the galleries in downtown Tucson.

IF YOU HAVE 2 WEEKS ...

All the above, plus visit the Pima Air and Space Museum. Watch a shootout at Old Tucson Studios. Take a tour of Biosphere 2. Hike Sentinel Peak (A Mountain), and take in the sweeping views of the city. Drive the Mt. Lemmon Scenic Byway.

IF YOU HAVE 3 WEEKS ...

All the above, plus visit the Mission San Xavier del Bac and hike in the Sabino Canyon. Take a sunset horseback riding tour at the Double R Ranch. Shop in the 4th Avenue District. Spend a day in wine country. Try your luck at the casinos.

grand canyon,
arizona

The Grand Canyon is what many people picture when imagining a trip "out west." The South Rim has the most popular destinations within the park, and the best RV campgrounds are nearby. The North Rim overall is more remote with fewer tourist spots.

HIGHLIGHTS

★ Travel the **Bright Angel Trail** by mule, making your way to **Plateau Point** for amazing river views.

★ View the ancient petroglyphs on a rafting tour down the **Colorado River.**

★ Ride the **Grand Canyon Railway** from Williams to Grand Canyon Village.

BEST TIME TO GO

The summer can be unbearably hot, and winter brings ice and snow. Stick with May and September if possible.

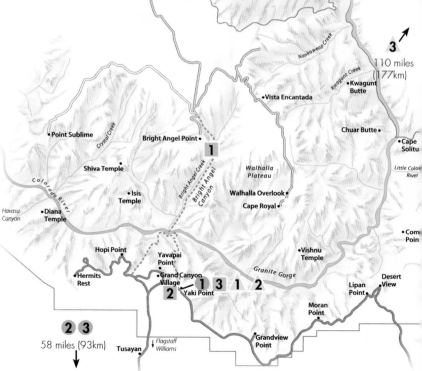

CAMPGROUNDS

① TRAILER VILLAGE RV PARK

🧍 🧍 ♿ 🐕 🛒 🔧 🚐

100 Market Plaza Road, Grand Canyon, AZ
86023. visitgrandcanyon.com/trailer-village-
rv-park; 928-638-1006. $36. Vending
machines, laundry, showers, ice.

The Trailer Village RV Park is short on
amenities but, considering that it has
full hookups, its location inside the
national park is unbeatable. Book
well in advance.

Sites are spacious and big-rig friendly.
Showers are only available at a
nearby campground, so plan on
using your RVs facilities.

The South Rim is only 1 mile (1.6km)
away and is accessible via the
Greenway Trail. Elk often like to walk
around the campground and say
hello.

GRAND CANYON VILLAGE.

COLORADO RIVER.

② GRAND CANYON RAILWAY RV PARK

🧍 🧍 ♿ 🐕 🛒 🔧 🚐

601 W. Franklin Avenue, Williams, AZ
86046. thetrain.com; info@thetrain.com;
800-843-8724. $40. Heated pool, spa,
horseshoes, playground, outdoor games.

The Grand Canyon RV Park is located
55 miles (88.5km) away from the
South Rim of the Grand Canyon, but
so are its competitors. This RV park
has an urban feel and is located only
2 blocks from Route 66 and
downtown Williams. It's a great
choice if you plan on taking the
historic train from Williams into the
Grand Canyon.

The paved roads are nice for riding
bikes, and kids will enjoy the indoor
pool, which is located a block away
at a hotel. The park also wins rave
reviews for the cleanliness of its
facilities. Buddy sites are available for
those who are traveling with family
and friends, and there's a community
fire pit for socializing with other
campers.

③ WILLIAMS/EXIT 167/CIRCLE PINES KOA

🧍 🧍 🧍 🐕 🚿 🔧 🚐 📶

1000 Circle Pines Road, Williams, AZ 86046.
koa.com/camp/Williams; circlepineskoa@
hotmail.com; 928-635-2626. April 1 to
October 31. $60 to $70. Pool, hot tub, mini-
golf.

If you're traveling with younger kids,
this might be your best bet for a base
camp near the Grand Canyon, which
is about 1 hour away. The kids will
love the indoor pool, large
playground, and bike rentals. Parents
will love the bike path right inside the
campground. Some sites are small,
and the highway is close by, so ask
for a quieter spot. Be sure to grab
breakfast at the Bear Trax Cafe.

The staff can help you plan your
excursions into the Grand Canyon by
train, helicopter, or airplane. If you
hike, you can take off right from the
campground for Dude Mountain. Or
you can ride your bicycles to historic
Route 66. Nearby stables also offer
horseback rides into a shaded forest.

Day trips to Sedona and Oak Creek
Canyon will make you fall in love
with northern Arizona.

> The Grand Canyon is
> 277 miles (445.8km) long
> with an average depth of
> 1 mile (1.6km).

The floor of the Grand Canyon contains the fossil footprints of more than 20 animal species, but no bones have ever been found.

RESTAURANTS

1 PHANTOM RANCH CANTEEN

N. Kaibab Trail, North Rim, AZ 86052. grandcanyonlodges.com/dining/phantom-ranch-canteen; 888-297-2757. Breakfast: 5 A.M. to 7 A.M.; dinner: 5 P.M. to 6:30 P.M. $20 to $45. American.

If you can manage to get to the Phantom Ranch Canteen at the bottom of the canyon, you'll have one of the more memorable dining experiences of your life. The Canteen is accessible only by foot, raft, or mule.

No lunch is served, and reservations for breakfast or dinner are required. Food is served family style, and the highlight for many guests is the stew, which has been served to hikers for more than 15 years.

MULE RIDE TO THE BOTTOM OF THE CANYON.

2 EL TOVAR DINING ROOM

Grand Canyon National Park, Village Loop Drive, Grand Canyon, AZ 86023. grandcanyonlodges.com; eltovar-dinner-res-gcsr@xanterra.com; 928-638-2631. 6:30 A.M. to 10 P.M. $11 to $30. American.

Located in the El Tovar Hotel, this restaurant offers the complete fine dining experience, with traditional décor and sophisticated menu options. Jackets aren't required, but shorts and flip-flops are discouraged.

The dining room and menu incorporate the history and culture of the area. Walls are painted with murals representing the customs of the four Native American tribes. Dishes include Southwestern influences in traditional American fare, such as the salmon tostada served with poblano black bean rice. The restaurant prides itself on its wine list, highlighting many local and regional wineries and winemakers that follow sustainable practices.

Not up for a fancy meal? Sit on the veranda outside and enjoy a drink and light fare while soaking in the view.

3 CANYON VILLAGE MARKETPLACE AND DELI

Market Plaza Road, Grand Canyon, AZ 86023. nps.gov/grca; 928-638-2262. May 21 to September 1. 6:30 A.M. to 9 P.M. $6 to $12. Deli.

This is the perfect place to stop before heading into the park for a day of exploration. Acting as a sort of general store for the nearby campground, it offers drinks, snacks, and deli sandwiches all in one place for very reasonable prices.

You might be tempted to pick up a souvenir as well.

Watch out for the Grand Canyon rattlesnake, whose pink hue blends in well with the color of the rocks.

ATTRACTIONS

1 CANYON VISTAS MULE RIDE

👨‍👩‍👧 👫

10 Albright Street, Grand Canyon, AZ 86023. grandcanyonlodges.com; 303-297-2757. 8 A.M. and 12 P.M. tours. $120.

Who doesn't want to see the Grand Canyon while riding a mule? This 4-mile (6.4km), 3-hour tour fills up more than a year in advance, so make your reservations early if this is on your to-do list.

The tour travels along the East Rim Trail and offers interpretative stops along the way. Full-day options are available as well.

2 GRAND CANYON VISITOR CENTER AND RIM TRAIL

👨‍👩‍👧 👫 ♿ 🐾

Grand Canyon National Park, AZ 86023. nps.gov/grca; 928-638-7888. 9 A.M. to 5 P.M. 7-day vehicle pass $30.

Starting your visit at the South Rim's Grand Canyon Visitor Center helps you plan your day and gives you a lot of information about the park. The center offers interactive trip planners, 3-D relief maps, and exhibits on the park's history.

From here, you can access the Rim Trail, one of the most popular ways to see views of the canyon. The trail is about 13 miles (21km) long, with many access points along the way, so it's an easy hike to customize.

Frequent shuttle stops mean visitors can walk for as long as comfortable, then hop off the trail and hitch a ride back to the visitor center.

3 COLORADO RIVER DISCOVERY

👨‍👩‍👧 👫

130 6th Avenue, Page, AZ 86040. raftthecanyon.com; info@coriverdiscovery.com; 928-645-9175. 7 A.M. to 1 P.M. $76 to $199.

Although many options for touring the Grand Canyon are available here, half-day rafting trips are the most popular ticket.

The rafting is an amazing experience, taking you through the Glen Canyon Dam access tunnel and providing stunning views of the cliffs soaring above the river. The guides give you more than just a pretty view, though. Along the way, they explain the geology and history of the region, the Native American heritage, and Southwestern water-supply issues. There's a stop on the tour to view ancient petroglyphs, and halfway through the journey, you'll dock at a beach for lunch and a swim in the river.

Full-day tour options are also available.

ITINERARIES

IF YOU HAVE 1 WEEK ...

Start your visit at Grand Canyon Village, exploring the exhibits, standing at Yavapai Point, and hiking the Rim Trail. Raft down the Colorado River. Ride the Grand Canyon Railway.

IF YOU HAVE 2 WEEKS ...

All the above, plus ride mules down the Bright Angel Trail and out to Plateau Point. Head up to the North Rim, and try the 4-mile (6.4km) round-trip hike to Supai Tunnel, starting at the North Kaibab Trailhead. Buy souvenirs at Kolb and Lookout studios, specializing in regional art.

IF YOU HAVE 3 WEEKS ...

All the above, plus take a day trip out to the Grand Canyon Skywalk, where you can look down through a glass floor at the canyon below. Climb to the top of the Desert View Watchtower. Try one of the many overnight backpacking trips offered, such as one out to Havasu Falls.

WEST

rocky mountain national park

This is one of the most visited national parks in the country, and with stunning drives, sweeping vistas, and diverse wildlife, it's easy to see why.

HIGHLIGHTS

★ Take a guided fly-fishing tour with the **Rocky Mountain Conservancy.**

★ Ride the **Estes Park Aerial Tramway** and then hike to the top of **Mount Prospect.**

★ Walk around **Bear Lake** at sunset and view the mountains reflected in the waters.

BEST TIME TO GO

Summer is the most popular time to visit, but plenty of people come in the winter for snowshoeing and cross-country skiing.

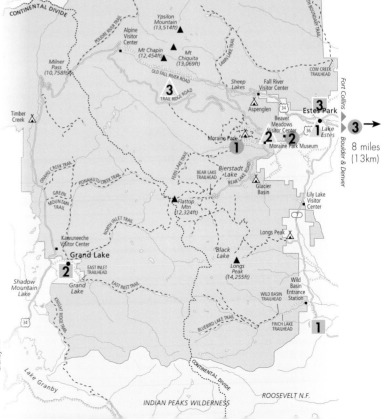

WEST

CAMPGROUNDS

① MORAINE PARK CAMPGROUND

Estes Park, CO 80517. nps.gov/romo/
planyourvisit/camping.htm; 970-586-1206.
$20. Shuttle buses, amphitheater, ranger-led
programs, hiking trails, food storage lockers.

If you're comfortable camping without
hookups and have an RV that's shorter
than 40 feet (12m), this is a great
option inside Rocky Mountain
National Park. The mountain views
from most sites are stunning, and you
can access terrific hiking right from
the campground.

Moraine Park Discovery Center and
Museum is within walking distance
and worth a visit. Shuttle service to
Estes Park and Bear Lake also is
available from the campground.

ELK IN THE PARK.

The Trail Ridge Road is the
highest continuously paved
road in America and
reaches over 12,000 feet
(3,600m).

② SPRUCE LAKE RV RESORT

1050 Mary's Lake Road, Estes Park, CO
80517. sprucelakerv.com; info@sprucelakerv
.com; 970-586-5342. April 15 to October 7.
$50 to $70. Heated pool, spa, playground.

This campground, located along the
banks of the Big Thompson River, has
an excellent location only 1 mile
(1.6km) from Rocky Mountain
National Park and 1½ miles (2.4km)
from Estes Park. You can walk to local
restaurants or take the shuttle into
town. There's also a well-stocked
pond with large trout, and good fly-
fishing is just steps away from your
campsite on the river.

Most sites are out in the open without
shade, but the views of the mountains
are fantastic. Elk are known to graze
both inside and outside of the park,
so have your camera ready. The pool
and hot tub are good enough for a
campground in the mountains, and
the playground is very nice.

PINE, SPRUCE, AND FIR ABOUND.

③ YOGI BEAR'S JELLYSTONE PARK CAMP-RESORT OF ESTES

5495 US 36, Estes Park, CO 80517.
jellystoneofestes.com; info@jellystoneofestes
.com; 970-658-2536. May 10 to September
30. $52 to $80. Heated pool, mini-golf.

If you're traveling with young children
and plan on spending downtime at
the campground, stay here. Your kids
will love the laser tag, mini-golf,
heated pool, and dances with the
characters. The owners and staff earn
high marks for excellent customer
service and seem heavily invested in
the guest experience.

The views of the mountains are
beautiful here, but the campground
has steep roads and some sites are
hard to access. Ask for one that's
easy to get to and away from the
highway noise.

Jellystone of Estes is a bit farther away
from the national park, but your kids
will be having so much fun, you won't
mind the extra drive.

WEST

About 30 miles (48km) of the Continental Divide runs through Rocky Mountain National Park, and the hike is a challenging one.

RESTAURANTS

1 MEADOW MOUNTAIN CAFE

441 CO Bus. 7, Allenspark, CO 80510. 303-747-2541. 7:30 A.M. to 2 P.M. $7 to $15. Bakery and deli fare.

This is the place to fill up with a hearty breakfast before hiking in the park, or to break for lunch if you're driving on the peak-to-peak road. Be prepared to enjoy the scenery while you wait for your food.

The coffee and pancakes are delicious. If you prefer savory morning dishes, the huevos rancheros is served with perfectly cooked eggs and a spicy green chile sauce. Try the burgers for lunch.

NUMEROUS HIKING TRAILS.

2 GRAND LAKE LODGE

15500 US Highway 34, Grand Lake, CO 80447. grandlakelodge.com; 970-627-3967. 8 A.M. to 9 P.M. $15 to $30. American.

Many national park visitors want to savor at least one meal at a restaurant with panoramic views. You might find better-reviewed cuisine in the Rocky Mountain region, but you certainly won't find better scenery.

Lunch might be your best bet, offering casual sandwiches, soups, and salads beside a beautiful lake framed by mountains. The Colorado lamb burger or the buffalo burger are great options if you want a twist on a standard menu offering. Or try a lunch portion of the buffalo meatloaf, a favorite for return visitors.

Dinner is a bit pricier, and the $14 burgers might alarm some guests. The steaks are very good though—well aged and properly prepared. A full cocktail menu also is available.

GORGEOUS, CLOUDY VIEWS.

3 NOTCHTOP BAKERY AND CAFÉ

459 E. Wonderview Avenue, Estes Park, CO 80517. thenotchtop.com; 970-586-0272. 7 A.M. to 3 P.M. $5 to $15. Baked goods, sandwiches.

Vegetarians and vegans, rejoice! You can find plenty of yummy options on the menu here. Gluten-free? That's no problem, either.

Dishes like fresh trout and eggs bring travelers in the door. Good, free Wi-Fi gets them to stay a while. The staff doesn't mind. The service is friendly, and they're happy to keep the coffee and pastries flowing.

The Beaver Meadows Visitor Center, a designated national landmark, was designed by Frank Lloyd Wright's architectural group in the 1960s.

ATTRACTIONS

1 COLORADO MOUNTAIN SCHOOL

341 Moraine Avenue, Estes Park, CO 80517. coloradomountainschool.com; info@ totalclimbing.com; 800-836-4008. 8 A.M. to 5 P.M. $90 to $195.

Colorado is popular with outfitters, but this one has an established track record for safety and professionalism.

Never climbed before? Take the beginner's half-day climbing tour. Want something more technical? Try the full-day rock-climbing course that covers the basics. Guided excursions are offered for every experience level.

2 ROCKY MOUNTAIN CONSERVANCY

48 Alpine Circle, Estes Park, CO 80517. rmconservancy.org; 970-586-0108. Check schedule of events for hours and pricing.

The Rocky Mountain Conservancy is a nonprofit organization operating within the park that offers tours and classes for visitors of all ages and interests.

If you prefer to enjoy the scenery while someone else drives, reserve a spot on the Grand Lake Safari or Trail Ridge Road Bus. You'll be taken to all the best sites on the tour and learn about the history, geology, and wildlife of the Rocky Mountains.

Or sign up for a daylong photography class that will allow you to expand your wildlife photography skills in the field with experts. For a truly unforgettable experience, schedule a private fly-fishing session in the subalpine meadows.

3 TRAIL RIDGE ROAD SCENIC DRIVE

Rocky Mountain National Park, Estes Park, CO 80517. nps.gov/romo; 970-586-1206. Late May to mid-October. 7-day vehicle pass $20.

The Trail Ridge Road runs 48 miles (77km) across the national park between Estes to the east and Grand Lake to the west, with 11 miles (17km) above the tree line for uninterrupted views of the magnificent mountains.

Like everything in this park, you'll enjoy the road more if you ride it early in the morning or later in the afternoon. In the middle of the day, parking lots for scenic lookouts get jammed with visitors. Don't miss the Alpine Visitor Center or Milner Pass.

You gain 4,000 feet (1,220m) of elevation in a matter of minutes on this road, so if you experience altitude sickness, you might want to wait a day or two into your visit before driving this highway.

ITINERARIES

IF YOU HAVE 1 WEEK ...

Drive the Trail Ridge Road from Estes to Grand Lake, making a stop at the Alpine Visitor Center. Visit Bear Lake at sunrise or sunset. Sign up for a class at the Rocky Mountain Conservancy. Take a rock climbing course.

IF YOU HAVE 2 WEEKS ...

All the above, plus hike the Emerald Lake Trail and Hallett Peak Trail. Drive the Old Fall River Road. Ride the Estes Park Aerial Tramway. Visit the Snowy Peaks Winery. Go whitewater rafting. See the Alluvial Fan. Take a dip in the chilly waters of Grand Lake.

IF YOU HAVE 3 WEEKS ...

All the above, plus hike the Lily Lake Trail and walk around Sprague Lake. Take a guided horseback riding tour with Moraine Park Stables or Sombrero Ranch. Learn about regional geology, and complete a junior ranger course at the Moraine Park Discovery Center. Visit the Holzwarth Historic Site.

arches
national park, utah

The national parks of Utah are a haven for lovers of outdoor recreation, and Arches is heaven for mountain bikers and off-roaders. Plan to spend plenty of time hiking, and dip into Canyonlands National Park to the south if time allows.

HIGHLIGHTS

★ See the petroglyphs above **Wolfe Ranch** at **Delicate Arch.**

★ Pack a picnic lunch, eat at **Devils Garden,** and hike to **Landscape Arch.**

★ Take a ranger-led tour through **Fiery Furnace** to scramble up rocks and walk along ledges.

BEST TIME TO GO

The wildflowers in late spring are beautiful, but rain brings mud and bugs. Late September offers relief from the heat and some brilliant foliage displays.

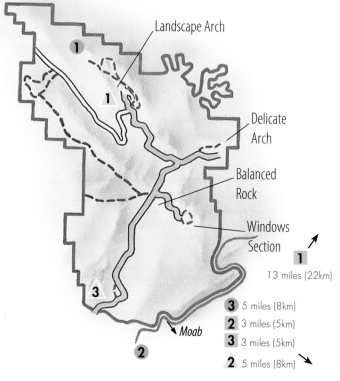

Landscape Arch

Delicate Arch

Balanced Rock

Windows Section

1 13 miles (22km)

3 5 miles (8km)
2 3 miles (5km)
3 3 miles (5km)
2 5 miles (8km)

↙ Moab

WEST

CAMPGROUNDS

① DEVILS GARDEN CAMPGROUND

Devils Garden Campground, Arches National Park. nps.gov/arch/planyourvisit/camping.htm; 435-719-2299. $20. Evening programs, picnic tables, grills.

This is spectacular, no-frills, national park service camping at its best. The campground is located deep in the heart of Arches National Park, where your rig is surrounded by otherworldly beauty. This is completely dry camping. There isn't even a dump station.

There are limitations on rig sizes and only 50 individual sites. Book early, and bring lots of water. Advanced planning and an adventurous spirit are required.

> Plenty of water, a hat, and lots of sunscreen are musts when hiking in this national park.

② MOAB VALLEY RV RESORT AND CAMPGROUND

1773 US 191, Moab, UT 84532; moabvalleyrv.com; moabvalley@highwaywestvacations.com; 435-259-4469. $31 to $60. Heated pool, hot tub, playground, dog park.

This is a solid choice for families who want to spend their mornings exploring Arches and Canyonlands and then spend the afternoons recharging at the campground. The pool and playground are nice for the kids, and Mom and Dad will enjoy the hot tub after hiking in the parks.

The sites are narrow, and if you have a larger rig, you might feel like you're on top of your neighbors. Road noise might also be an issue for light sleepers. The laundry and restroom areas are clean and modern, and customer service is solid and dependable. Cell service is good, and Wi-Fi is free.

Head into downtown Moab for dinner and then challenge the kids to a game of life-size checkers before bed.

BALANCED ROCK.

③ A.C.T. CAMPGROUND

1536 E. Mill Creek Drive, Moab, UT, 84532. actcampground.com; info@actcampground.com; 435-355-0355. $35 to $44. Adult education, community kitchens, writer's workshops.

This campground and environmental learning center is owned by a retired college professor and an environmental engineer whose passion for education and the natural world shows in every detail. The property has breathtaking 360-degree views of the La Sal Mountains and is less than 3 miles (4.8km) from downtown Moab. Arches and Canyonlands are both within striking distance.

The campground's location makes it an excellent pick for those who love outdoor adventures such as hiking, rock climbing, zip-lining, and mountain biking. RV sites are spacious, and communal areas abound. There's an active learning center, shared kitchen, and outdoor grill and patio area with fire pit.

LANDSCAPE ARCH.

WEST

The 71-foot-long (21.5m) Wall Arch came crashing down in 2008. Amazingly, no one was hurt.

RESTAURANTS

1 THE COWBOY GRILL

14 Highway 128, Moab, UT 84532. redcliffslodge.com; 435-259-2002. $25 to $50. Monday to Saturday 6:30 A.M. to 9:30 P.M.; Sunday 7 A.M. to 9:30 P.M. American.

A barbecue buffet lunch is on the deck from April through October, so make reservations for a table out there to enjoy amazing views of the Colorado River and red-rock cliffs while you eat. You also can order a picnic lunch to go if you're on your way into the park. Dinner is a more formal affair, and steak is the star of the show, so try the rib eye or T-bone.

Across the 76,000 acres (31,000ha) of the park are more than 2,000 arches, the most iconic of which is Delicate Arch.

2 QUESADILLA MOBILLA

89 N. Main Street, Moab, UT 84532. quesadillamobilla.com; 435-260-0289. Thursday to Monday 11 A.M. to 5 P.M. $5 to $10. Mexican.

Owners Carrie and Steven came up with the idea for their quesadilla food truck while camping, so this is the perfect place to nosh while on an RV trip near Moab. Beef, chicken, and veggies, served every which way, are sandwiched between tortillas. If you like heat, go with the fiery fungus.

3 SWEET CRAVINGS BAKERY AND BISTRO

397 N. Main Street, Moab, UT 84532. cravemoab.com; 435-259-8983. March to September 7 A.M. to 4 P.M.; October to February 8 A.M. to 3 P.M. $7 to $15. Bakery and deli.

Sweet Cravings might become a daily stop during your visit because of its delicious, convenient breakfast and lunch options.

For breakfast, pair a cup of organic coffee with a hearty breakfast burrito stuffed full of chorizo, sausage, potatoes, and eggs. Or try one of the many sweet options, including the homemade granola and yogurt, scones, and monkey bread.

The lunch menu offers sandwiches and panini served with homemade applesauce or coleslaw. If you're dining in, the strawberry chicken salad or daily quiche specials are healthy, satisfying choices.

This is the perfect spot to pick up lunch for one of the many picnic areas in Arches. No food vendors are located in the national park, so stock up before you head in for the day.

WINDOWS SECTION OF ARCHES.

ATTRACTIONS

1 FIERY FURNACE

Arches National Park, Moab, UT 84532. **recreation.gov**; 435-719-2299. 9 A.M. and 2 P.M. $8 to $16.

You have to make reservations in advance and pay an additional fee, but if you're up for a challenging ranger-led hike, this might end up being your favorite Arches experience.

Two hikes are offered a day, and the round-trip excursion takes about 3 hours. You'll appreciate the expertise of the ranger when navigating the canyons.

2 MOAB OUTDOOR RECREATION

Moab Information Center, 25 E. Center Street, Moab, UT 04532. **discovermoab.com**; 435-259-8825. Monday to Saturday 8 A.M. to 8 P.M.; Sunday 9 A.M. to 7 P.M. in summer; limited hours October to March.

The city of Moab has a thriving outdoor recreation culture and tons of outfitters, no matter what your sport of choice, and the Moab Information Center offers great suggestions for booking your adventure.

Mountain biking and four-wheeling are extremely popular, but if you're not experienced, be sure to join a guided tour, as the trail conditions can be challenging for novices.

Reserve far in advance if you want to raft, boat, or kayak the Colorado River.

Want a bigger adrenaline rush? Skydive over Canyonlands, or rock climb at Indian Creek. Set a slower pace by horseback riding in Castle Valley or playing a round of golf at the public Moab Golf Club.

3 SCENIC DRIVE AT ARCHES

Arches National Park Visitor Center, Arches National Park, UT 84532. **nps.gov/arch/index.htm**; 435-719-2299. Summer 7:30 A.M. to 6 P.M.; limited hours in fall, winter, and spring; closed December 25. 7-day vehicle pass $25.

Stop in at the visitor center and grab a road guide, which offers detailed information about all the stop-offs and hikes along the scenic drive. Many of the hikes in Arches are easily accessible and short, so it's worth it to plan plenty of time for the drive, stopping frequently to enjoy the view or take a quick walk.

Don't miss the Park Avenue overlook, displaying the great sandstone slabs that reach toward the sky. Then stop at Balanced Rock to witness the 55-foot-high (16.8m) rock perched on top of a 73-foot (22.3m) column, and take the short hike around the perimeter. In the Windows section, many short trails less than a mile long offer access to the arches. Delicate Arch is another must-see.

ITINERARIES

IF YOU HAVE 1 WEEK ...

Drive the entire scenic road, stopping and hiking at the Balanced Rock, the Windows section, and Delicate Arch. Take the ranger-led hike through Fiery Furnace. Shop downtown Moab, and take a rafting tour down the Colorado River.

IF YOU HAVE 2 WEEKS ...

All the above, plus hike at Landscape Arch and Devils Garden. Visit Wolfe Ranch, and see the ancient petroglyphs. Tour Park Avenue, and view the Tower of Babel. Mountain bike on the Salt Valley and Willow Springs roads. Take a guided horseback riding tour through Castle Valley.

IF YOU HAVE 3 WEEKS ...

All the above, plus explore Canyonlands National Park, starting your visit at the Island in the Sky Visitor Center. Take a four-wheel-drive backcountry tour through the Needles District. Hike the short trails to see Mesa Arch and Grand View Point overlook. Visit Dead Horse Point State Park.

zion and bryce canyon
national parks, utah

Zion and Bryce Canyon national parks offer very different visions of beauty. Zion is grand and sprawling, while Bryce is unusual and stunning.

HIGHLIGHTS

✱ Hike The **Narrows of Zion** by walking in the **Virgin River** at the bottom of a deep canyon.

✱ Take a guided Jeep tour at sunset into the heart of **Zion National Park.**

✱ Get up early, and head to **Sunrise Point** for a magical natural display in **Bryce National Park.**

BEST TIME TO GO

September is the ideal time to visit Zion and Bryce, when the temperatures are moderate during the day and cool at night.

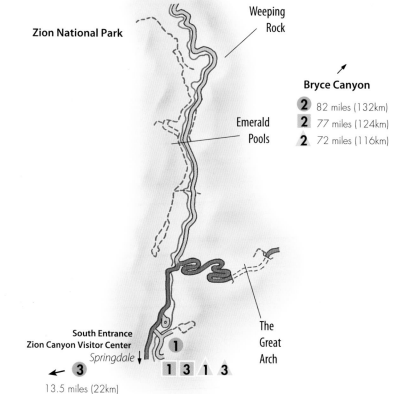

Zion National Park

Weeping Rock

Bryce Canyon

2 82 miles (132km)
2 77 miles (124km)
2 72 miles (116km)

Emerald Pools

The Great Arch

South Entrance
Zion Canyon Visitor Center
Springdale ↓

1

1 3 1 3

3

13.5 miles (22km)

WEST

CAMPGROUNDS

① WATCHMAN CAMPGROUND (ZION)

Watchmen Campground, Zion National Park, UT 84737. nps.gov/zion/planyourvisit/ watchman-campground.htm; *877-444-6777*. $18 to $20. Toilets, drinking water.

Travelers come from all over to camp at Watchman for its views of sandstone cliffs and its clear skies perfect for stargazing. Some sites are situated along the Virgin River, but any site here is good.

The campground has direct access to three hiking trails, and the main visitor center is nearby.

This is a rare national park campground with electric hookups, so you can run the AC on sweltering summer nights.

Traffic was such a problem in Zion National Park that the mandatory shuttle was introduced in 2000.

② CANNONVILLE/BRYCE VALLEY KOA

215 N. Red Rock Drive, Cannonville, UT 84718. **koa.com/camp/cannonville**; bvkoa@h-oh.com; 435-679-8988. $30 to $50. Pool, kamping kitchen, snack bar, pavilion, playground.

This KOA, located 12 miles (19km) from the entrance to Bryce Canyon National Park, serves as an excellent base camp for those seeking the comfort and convenience of a private campground. Situated in beautiful Bryce Valley, the views from most campsites are very good, especially at sunset.

The owners and staff are friendly and knowledgeable about the area, and the pancake breakfasts are great. A community kitchen is available for those traveling without one in their RV, and the camp store is stocked with all the basics. There's also a shared computer room for those needing a reliable connection. The pool is small but good enough for cooling off after a day of hiking in the park.

BRYCE CANYON ROCK FORMATIONS.

WALTER'S WIGGLES IN ZION.

③ ZION RIVER RESORT

551 E. Highway 9, Virgin, UT 84779. **zionriverresort.com**; zionrv@zrr.com; 888-466-8594. $50 to $65. Heated pool, spa, game room, playground, horseshoes, recreation hall.

There's nothing not to love about the Zion River Resort. This campground, located 15 minutes from Zion National Park, costs a little more than the local competition, but it's worth it. Beautiful mountains surround the property, and several sites are nestled along the Virgin River. The staff is friendly and well informed about the national park, and the hosts work hard to make everyone feel welcome.

The heated pool and spa are lovely, and the game room has a billiards table and comfortable seating for reading a book or playing board games. There's a community kitchen if you want to escape the RV and share a meal with other campers. Free coffee is served every morning.

WEST

One of the most endangered bird species, the California condor, is found in Zion National Park.

HOODOO IN BRYCE CANYON NATIONAL PARK.

RESTAURANTS

1 RED ROCK GRILL

Zion National Park Lodge, Springdale, UT 84767. zionlodge.com/dining; 435-772-7700. Breakfast 6:30 A.M. to 10:30 A.M.; lunch 11:30 A.M. to 3 P.M.; dinner 5 P.M. to 10 P.M. $10 to $35. American.

Zion Lodge's Red Rock Grill offers decent food in a convenient location in the park. If you're taking the shuttle and don't want to lug around a picnic lunch, this is a great place to stop. The atmosphere is on point, with stone walls and exposed wooden beams. A large outdoor dining terrace is also available.

Stick to the basics like hamburgers and bison meatloaf. Wraps, salads, and quesadillas are also great options for a light midday meal.

Early geologists named the columns and pinnacles of towering sandstone *hoodoos*, thinking the rock formations contained magical powers.

2 THE LODGE AT BRYCE CANYON RESTAURANT

UT 63, Bryce, UT 84764. brycecanyonforever .com; 435-834-8700. Breakfast 7 A.M. to 10 A.M.; lunch 11:30 A.M. to 3 P.M.; dinner 5:30 P.M. to 10 P.M. $10 to $35. New American.

The National Park Service's "Healthy Parks, Healthy People" initiative has inspired this establishment to provide as many healthy, sustainable, and organic food options as possible. That's definitely led to a more interesting and dynamic menu than is found in most national park dining restaurants.

Breakfast and lunch offer both buffet and à la carte options. Breakfast includes eggs, French toast, oatmeal, yogurt, and fresh fruit. During lunch, the buffet consists of soups, salads, and sandwiches. The elk chili is a house specialty and available daily.

More adventurous items appear at dinner, like the chile-lime baked game hen and the Utah trout topped with prickly pear cactus. Utah honey and local, seasonal vegetables are highlighted throughout the menu.

3 BIT AND SPUR RESTAURANT AND SALOON

1212 Zion Park Boulevard, Springdale, UT 84767. bitandspur.com; 435-772-3498. 5 P.M. to 12 A.M. $15 to $30. Mexican fusion.

A local favorite, this restaurant puts a spin on the standard Mexican fare found in most places. The quesadilla appetizer is stuffed with Brie, walnuts, apples, and jalapeños, and the coconut shrimp is served with tomato chutney. Entrées feature sweet potato tamales and chile-rubbed rib eye.

Be sure to take home a bottle of house-made fire lizard sauce or chile ketchup.

ATTRACTIONS

1 ZION OUTBACK SAFARIS

Springdale, UT 84767. **zionjeeptours.com;** info@zionjeeptours.com; 435-668-3756. 9 A.M. to 5 P.M. $45 to $65.

Get off the beaten path, and drive deep into the heart of Zion. Explore the west side of the park on a 2- or 3-hour tour, or book a private tour you can tailor to suit your fancy.

The guides are well versed on regional geography and history—and where to get the best pictures.

2 BRYCE CANYON SCENIC DRIVE

Bryce Canyon National Park, UT 84764. **nps.gov/brca;** 435-834-5322. Shuttle runs April to September 8 A.M. to 8 P.M. 7-day vehicle pass $30. Shuttle free with admission.

Bryce Canyon's scenic road is a round-trip journey of 38 miles (61km) with 13 viewpoints along the route. A quick trip takes at least 3 hours, so plan for longer if you're going to explore any of the stops more extensively.

The shuttle at Bryce Canyon isn't mandatory (unlike at Zion), but seriously consider taking it because the congestion in the park during the summer season can put a serious strain on the motorist.

Whether you take the shuttle or drive, go all the way to Rainbow Point and then stop at the viewpoints on your way back so you don't cross traffic to take in the scenery.

3 ZION CANYON SCENIC DRIVE

Zion National Park, Springdale, UT 84767. **nps.gov/zion;** 435-772-3256. Shuttle runs March to October 7 A.M. to 8 P.M. 7-day vehicle pass $30.

To travel the Zion Canyon Scenic Drive, you must use the park shuttle system. Shuttles run continuously during the day, and many visitors park in Springdale and avoid driving into the park at all.

Start your visit at the Zion Canyon Visitor Center, where you can map out a plan for the day. The next stop is Zion Human History Museum, which in addition to being educational, offers great views of the Bridge Mountain Arch and the Altar of Sacrifice.

If you're planning on hiking Emerald Pools Trail, you'll find the entrance at the Zion Lodge stop. If you want to hike Angels Landing or the West Rim Trail, get off at the Grotto. Weeping Rock offers a welcome water feature.

ITINERARIES

IF YOU HAVE 1 WEEK …

In Bryce Canyon, catch sunrise at Sunrise Point and then drive the entire scenic drive, stopping at all 13 viewpoints. In Zion, take a ranger-led hike on the Watchman Trail, and hike the West Rim Trail to Angels Landing. Go off-roading.

IF YOU HAVE 2 WEEKS …

All the above, plus hike the Rim Trail to Inspiration Point and the Silent City in Bryce Canyon. Also try the Peek-A-Boo Loop Trail full of twists and turns. In Zion, hike the Emerald Pools Trail from Zion Lodge. Take an ATV tour. Visit the St. George Dinosaur Discovery Site.

IF YOU HAVE 3 WEEKS …

All the above, plus hike the Bristlecone Loop Trail and Mossy Cave Trail in Bryce Canyon. In Zion, hike Weeping Rock Trail and Observation Point Trail. Take a 1-hour horseback riding tour from Zion Lodge. Visit Best Friends Animal Sanctuary. Shop in the galleries of Springdale.

las vegas

You might not consider traveling to Las Vegas in your RV, but you should. Dive into the glitz and glamor of the strip, try your hand with Lady Luck, and then retreat to the peace and quiet of your own abode on wheels.

HIGHLIGHTS

★ Enjoy the **fountain show** with choreographed music and lights at Bellagio.

★ Watch the **huge volcano** erupt every night to the sounds of the Grateful Dead at The Mirage.

★ Take a **gondola ride** and enjoy the singing of your gondolier at The Venetian.

BEST TIME TO GO

The spring and fall shoulder seasons are the best time for temperate weather and fewer crowds. Weekdays are also quieter than weekends.

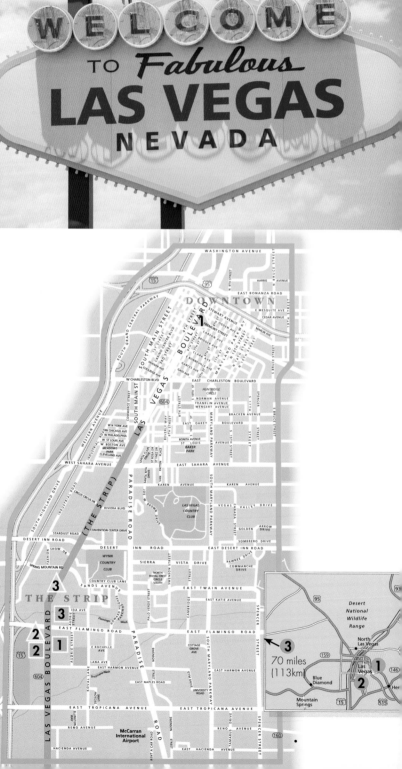

CAMPGROUNDS

1 LAS VEGAS RV RESORT

3890 S. Nellis Boulevard, Las Vegas, NV 89121. **lasvegasrvresort.com;** info@lasvegasrvresort.com; 702-451-8005. $30 to $50. Heated pool, spa, game room.

Don't forget to forget the kids. This RV resort does not allow whippersnappers under 18, which makes for a quiet and relaxing atmosphere minutes away from the madness of the strip.

A landscaped setting, a nice pool and spa, and 24-hour security make this a favorite among veteran RVers. Need to burn off some calories from too many buffets? Try the well-equipped fitness center. Roads are a little tight for the biggest of rigs, however.

FOUNTAINS AT BELLAGIO.

The Bellagio fountains get most of their water from the artisanal wells located under the city.

2 LVM RESORT

8175 Arville Street, Las Vegas, NV 89139. **lvmresort.com;** info@lvmresort.com; 866-897-9300. $60 to $100. Heated pool, spa, recreation hall, putting course, tennis courts.

The word *resort* isn't thrown about casually at this luxurious RV oasis in the desert. Everything about Las Vegas Motorcoach (LVM) is high end, including the price, which is well worth it.

Relax at the lovely pool or in one of the two whirlpools after a long day at the tables. If you're a fitness junkie, you can grab a game of tennis or try the fitness center. If you brought your clubs, try the 9-hole lighted putting course. Or just kick back and relax at your manicured site with a good book. The strip can be stressful, but nothing about LVM is, except for the occasional sound of planes overhead.

If you need a break from the casinos, head to the clubhouse for live entertainment or a shared meal with friends.

FAMOUS LAS VEGAS STRIP.

3 NEVADA TREASURE RV RESORT

301 W. Leslie Street, Pahrump, NV 89060. **nvtreasure.com;** frontdesk@nvtreasure.com; 800-429-6665. $40 to $65. Heated pool, spa, horseshoes, recreation hall, game room, activities.

This is a good option for families traveling with kids; just don't plan on swimming with them in the gorgeous two-level pool after 6 P.M. during adult-only hours.

The entire park is clean and comfortable, and the food at the on-site bar and grill is quite good. The sites are very attractive, and many have gazebos and grills. The sauna, steam room, and hot tub also are excellent. There's even a bowling alley. The staff is more than willing to help you select a restaurant or secure tickets for a show.

Be sure to grab complementary coffee and a newspaper each morning.

WEST

The famous cowboy of Fremont Street, Vegas Vic is the world's largest mechanical neon sign.

THE LUXOR.

RESTAURANTS

1 LE VILLAGE BUFFET

👪 👪 ♿

Paris Las Vegas, 3655 Las Vegas Boulevard South, Las Vegas, NV 89109. **caesars.com/paris-las-vegas**; 702-946-7000. 7 A.M. to 10 P.M. $25 to $35. New American.

Le Village offers high-end culinary items and ups the ante with a charming atmosphere. It's also the only buffet in town to take reservations.

The buffet resembles a French village, with cobblestone streets and Parisian architecture. Food is made to order at the individual stations. Create your own surf and turf with prime rib and snow crab legs, or if you have a sweet tooth, visit the crepe station or try the macaroons and crème brûlée.

2 LE CIRQUE

👪 ♿

3600 Las Vegas Boulevard South, Las Vegas, NV 89109. **bellagio.com/restaurants**; 877-234-6358. Tuesday to Sunday 5:30 P.M. to 10 P.M. $100 to $200. French American.

The food in Vegas is legendary, and many visitors want to experience at least one meal here they'll remember forever. Le Cirque is worth the splurge.

The atmosphere is elegant but comfortable and cozy, the service is attentive without being snotty, and the kitchen is happy to adjust for any food allergies.

The main Dégustation Menu changes with the season and often includes foie gras and caviar options, along with a fish and game course. The more affordable Pre-Theatre Menu offers optional sommelier wine pairing. Entire menus are developed for vegetarian and vegan diners. For a real treat, splurge on the Caviar and Truffle Menu.

Make reservations well in advance and then arrive early to enjoy a cocktail at the bar.

3 HASH HOUSE A GO GO

👪 👪 ♿

3535 Las Vegas Boulevard South, Las Vegas, NV 89109. **hashhouseagogo.com**; 702-254-4646. $10 to $30. American.

After a long night of clubbing your way down the strip, head to this 24-hour fun spot for heaping portions of any breakfast favorite you can name.

Those who love savory hashes will be in heaven with roast chicken, meatloaf, and pork tenderloin options, and grilled French toast satisfies the sweet tooth. Good luck picking one thing off the menu.

In the 1800s, Las Vegas was just a watering hole on the trail from Santa Fe to Los Angeles.

PARIS LAS VEGAS.

ATTRACTIONS

1 DEUCE DOUBLE-DECKER BUS

Las Vegas Strip, NV 89109. rtcsnv.com/transit; 800-228-3911. 2-hour pass $6; 24-hour pass $8.

If this is your first trip to Vegas, snag a seat on the top level of these city-operated double-decker buses to get a bird's-eye view of the world-famous strip.

The bus goes slowly as it crawls through the traffic, but that's okay because the people-watching and sightseeing are quite entertaining.

2 O BY CIRQUE DU SOLEIL

3600 Las Vegas Boulevard South, Las Vegas, NV 89109. cirquedusoleil.com; contact@ cirquedusoleil.com; 888-488-7111. Wednesday to Sunday 7 P.M. and 10 P.M. show times. $98 to $170.

With so many amazing shows in Vegas, it can be difficult to choose just one to see. Cirque du Soleil is a perennial favorite of Las Vegas visitors, and nothing else competes with the wow factor of any Cirque show. Its popularity also means it sells out every night, so book your tickets well in advance.

O defies explanation, introducing an aquatic element to the spectacle of music, lights, and nonstop jaw-dropping aerobatic feats.

Splurging on premium seats pays off, but if you want to stick with the base price, you won't be disappointed. The theater at the Bellagio is small, with no bad seats.

3 ATTRACTIONS ON THE STRIP

Las Vegas Information Center, 3150 Paradise Road, Las Vegas, NV 89109. lasvegas.com; 877-847-4858. Hours vary by attraction. Price varies by attraction.

Vegas has gone from being a gambler's mecca to a vacation destination for families, couples, and friends. Even if you have no interest in trying your luck at the slot machines or gaming tables, there's plenty to keep you busy in the casinos—many of which are designed like mini theme parks.

You can't miss the fountain show at the Bellagio, a free choreographed light, music, and water display. Visit Paris Las Vegas for an amusing spin on the City of Light, showcasing replicas of the Eiffel Tower and other famous Paris landmarks. Take a jaunt to Italy, and see the street performers at The Venetian—don't leave without taking a gondola ride in the canal. Finally, take time to smell the roses at the Wynn Conservatory.

ITINERARIES

IF YOU HAVE 1 WEEK …

Upon arrival, take the Deuce bus to see the whole Strip and venture to Fremont Street. Watch O by Cirque du Soleil. See the Bellagio fountain show and take a gondola tour at the Venetian. Let it ride at the Cosmopolitan Casino.

IF YOU HAVE 2 WEEKS …

All the above, plus visit the City of Light at Paris Las Vegas, watch the volcano erupt at The Mirage, and ride the Big Apple Rollercoaster at New York–New York. Venture off the strip, and play bingo at the Red Rock Casino. Tour the Mob Museum. Take a day trip to the Hoover Dam.

IF YOU HAVE 3 WEEKS …

All the above, plus wander through the Bellagio Conservatory and Botanical Gardens, and take a spin on the High Roller Ferris wheel. Tour the Neon Museum, and indulge your sweet tooth at M&M's World. Shop the Forum Shops at Caesars. Take a day trip to the Red Rock Canyon National Conservation Area.

WEST

san diego

With an average daily temperature of 70.5°F (21°C), San Diego offers delightful weather and beautiful views no matter when you visit. Plan on enjoying the city's pristine beaches, bays, parks, and shopping districts during your stay.

HIGHLIGHTS

★ Walk, bike, or skate the boardwalk from **Mission Beach** to **Pacific Beach.**

★ Get the lay of the land by taking an **Old Town Trolley Tour** around the city.

★ Watch a show at **The Old Globe** theater in **Balboa Park.**

BEST TIME TO GO

Southern California is beautiful year-round, but to enjoy warm weather and water without the crowds, visit in September or October.

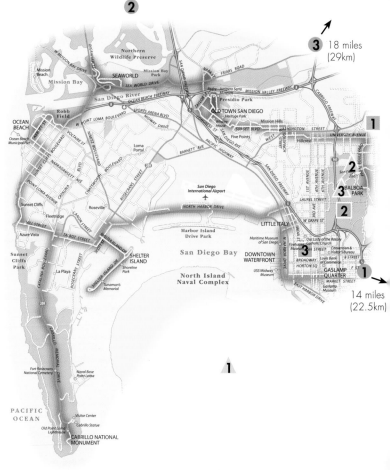

CAMPGROUNDS

1 SWEETWATER SUMMIT CAMPGROUND

👫 👫 🔨 🚿 🔌 🚐

3218 Summit Meadow Road, Bonita, CA. sandiegocounty.gov/parks/Camping/ sweetwater.html; 619-472-7572. $29 to $33. Showers, playground, amphitheater.

Located on a breezy hill with a view of Sweetwater Valley, this park wins rave reviews for its cleanliness, tranquility, and full-hookup sites at state park prices.

Kids love the tropical-themed aquatic playground, and active adults can enjoy a wide variety of attractive hiking trails.

Campsites are huge, and most are pull-thrus. The park can accommodate rigs of up to 45 feet (13m).

Downtown San Diego is about 20 minutes away, depending on traffic.

HIPPO AT THE SAN DIEGO ZOO.

> Marilyn Monroe's iconic beach resort scenes from *Some Like It Hot* were filmed at the Hotel del Coronado.

2 CAMPLAND ON THE BAY

👫 ♿ 🔨 🚿 🔌 🚐 📶

2211 Pacific Beach Drive, San Diego, CA 92109. campland.com; reservations@ campland.com; 800-422-9386. $40 to $400. Heated pool, marina, playground, game room, spa.

Campland on the Bay is big, bold, and boisterous. Don't come here for romantic walks on the beach; come here for nonstop family fun. Try the private beach overlooking Mission Bay, where kids can swim in an enclosed area, and families can relax around a bonfire at night. Watersports also reign supreme: ride personal watercraft, water bikes, stand-up paddleboards, and kayaks.

This is urban camping, and some sites are small, but that's the price you pay for a packed list of amenities and activities. Shoot some hoops, play table tennis, or skateboard in the campground's private park. Then catch a concert in their Central Park.

Want to make the campground splurge of a lifetime? Book the gated super site with private hot tub, patio, and grill.

HOTEL DEL CORONADO.

3 SANTEE LAKES RECREATION PRESERVE

👫 👫 ♿ 🔨 🚿 🔌 🚐 📶

9310 Fanita Parkway, Santee, CA 92071. santeelakes.com; santeelakes@padre.org; 619-596-3141. $40 to $50. Heated pool, lake, spa, playground, recreation hall, boat rentals.

Santee Lakes has 300+ full-hookup sites on seven different loops. But you'll still have to book this popular campground early because many locals like it for staycation spot. The park is set on seven manmade lakes, wildlife is abundant, and the bird-watching is excellent.

This isn't a quiet park. Most of the loops are packed with families who come to enjoy the large playgrounds and pools. Campers love the clubhouse, which sets a friendly tone by serving as a terrific gathering place for potluck dinners, family nights, live music, and morning coffee.

Depending on traffic, the campground is only 30 minutes from downtown San Diego and its beaches.

WEST

The world-famous San Diego Zoo, open since 1916, is one of only a few places in North America where you can see a giant panda.

BALBOA PARK.

RESTAURANTS

1 CARNITAS' SNACK SHACK

2632 University Avenue, San Diego, CA 92104. carnitassnackshack.com; 619-294-7675. 12 P.M. to 12 A.M. $10 to $25. New American.

The giant pig on the roof of this restaurant gives you a hint about its specialty. People line up down the block to order the triple threat pork sandwich and other smoked delicacies. The menu changes on a regular basis because local ranchers, farmers, and bakers supply the ingredients. Humane treatment of animals is a top priority for the owners, Sara and Hanis.

A wide assortment of local microbrews is offered, too.

2 THE PRADO AT BALBOA PARK

1549 El Prado, San Diego, CA. cohnrestaurants.com/theprado; 619-557-9441. Dinner Tuesday to Sunday 5 P.M. to close; lunch Monday to Friday 11:30 A.M. to 3 P.M.; Saturday and Sunday 11 A.M. to 3 P.M. $30 to $60. American fusion.

Indoor and outdoor dining areas, excellent service, and delicious food make this the perfect stop for lunch or dinner when visiting Balboa Park. If you have a dog, you'll love that you can dine on the patio with your pup after walking the grounds.

The bar serves reasonably priced specialty cocktails like the Irish mule and prickly pear margarita. The late-night happy hour features live music.

With the small and large portion options on the First Taste section of the menu, it's easy to create your entire meal out of small plates. Try the spicy calamari fries, whole-grain mustard steamed mussels, or the lobster and shrimp pot stickers. Or stick with one of the well-portioned entrées, like the chicken grits and gravy or the seasonal risotto.

3 KARL STRAUSS BREWING COMPANY

1157 Columbia Street, San Diego, CA 92101. karlstrauss.com; 619-234-2739. Monday to Thursday 11 A.M. to 10 P.M.; Friday 11 A.M. to 11 P.M.; Saturday 11:30 A.M. to 11 P.M.; Sunday 11:30 A.M. to 10 P.M. $15 to $35. Pub fare.

Located in the heart of downtown San Diego, this restaurant features solid pub fare, like ale-steamed mussels, that pairs nicely with the rotating craft brews on tap.

Beer pretzels, spicy hummus, and chile-lime fries are great happy hour options. Try a beer flight, take a tour, and fill up a growler to go.

Balboa Park is credited with popularizing many plant species, like the bird of paradise and the poinsettia.

ATTRACTIONS

1 CORONADO BEACH

919 Ocean Boulevard, Coronado, CA 92118. **coronadovisitorcenter.com**; 619-437-8788. Lifeguards on duty from 9 A.M. to dusk.

Many visitors stick to the white sands of Mission Beach, but if you want a quieter, more picturesque experience, drive over the bridge (or take the passenger ferry) to Coronado Beach.

Wander around the historic Hotel del Coronado, take a long walk along the beach, or rent bicycles to explore the 15 miles (24km) of dedicated bike trails.

2 SAN DIEGO ZOO

2920 Zoo Drive, San Diego, CA 92101. **sandiegozoo.org**; 619-231-1515. 9 A.M. to 9 P.M. $38 to $48.

One of the most famous in the world, the San Diego Zoo is home to almost 4,000 rare and endangered animals. Combine these creatures with more than 700,000 exotic plants, and you have a pretty awesome attraction.

Plan on arriving when it opens at 9 A.M. The crowds will be lighter, and the animals will be more active. Check the daily schedule to be sure you don't miss any interesting shows or feeding times.

The guided bus tour is a nice way to get acquainted with exhibits and overall layout of the park. The Skyfari Aerial Tram gives you another perspective of the beautiful zoo as it transports you through the air.

Don't miss the giant pandas, the polar bears, or the giraffe feeding.

3 BALBOA PARK

1549 El Prado, Balboa Park, San Diego, CA 92101. **balboapark.org**; bpoc@bpoc.org; 619-239-0512. Grounds open 24 hours a day; visitor center open daily 9:30 A.M. to 4:30 P.M.; museum hours vary by institution. Free park admission; some attractions charge entry fees.

A stunning array of activities and attractions are available at Balboa Park. In fact, you might end up spending a solid portion of your vacation on the grounds of this 1,200-acre (486ha) urban treasure.

The San Diego Air and Space Museum and Model Railroad Museum are big hits with the kids. Adults enjoy the Japanese Friendship Garden and the Museum of Art. Try to catch a performance at The Old Globe theater or the Marie Hitchcock Puppet Theater.

Take time to enjoy the miles of hiking and biking trails in the park. The playgrounds and dog parks are popular with the locals. You also can rent surreys.

ITINERARIES

IF YOU HAVE 1 WEEK ...

Visit the San Diego Zoo, and tour the San Diego Air and Space Museum and Japanese Friendship Garden in Balboa Park. Walk the boardwalk at Mission Beach, and visit Coronado Island.

IF YOU HAVE 2 WEEKS ...

All the above, plus visit the San Diego Museum of Art and the Inez Grant Parker Memorial Rose Garden in Balboa Park. Rent surreys, and ride the miles of bike paths. Experience the nightlife in the Gaslamp Quarter of the city. Visit the beaches of La Jolla Shores.

IF YOU HAVE 3 WEEKS ...

All the above, plus visit the Model Railroad Museum and Casa del Rey Moro Garden in Balboa Park. Watch a performance at The Old Globe. Visit Old Town, and eat at Cafe Coyote. Take a day trip to LEGOLAND California. Catch picture-perfect views of the city from the Cabrillo National Monument.

napa valley
and san francisco

San Francisco is one of the most diverse and eccentric cities in America, so relax and enjoy the vibe. Be sure to sample the abundance of food and wine in this culinary paradise.

HIGHLIGHTS

✷ Bundle up for a windy and often chilly walk across the **Golden Gate Bridge.**

✷ Buy a book at the legendary **City Lights Books,** founded by beat poet Lawrence Ferlinghetti.

✷ Tour the **Beaulieu Vineyard,** one of the oldest in Napa, and learn about the history of wine in the valley.

BEST TIME TO GO

You are never guaranteed perfect weather in San Francisco, but the best time to visit is between September and November, when you'll find warmer weather and fewer crowds.

WEST

CAMPGROUNDS

1 SAN FRANCISCO RV RESORT

👪 👫 ♿ 🧺 🚿 ⚡ 🚐 📶

700 Palmetto Avenue, Pacifica, CA 94044. sanfranciscorvresort.com; 877-570-2267. $53 to $86. Heated pool, spa, playground, clubhouse, laundry facilities.

The San Francisco RV Resort is not in San Francisco, and it is not a resort, but its oceanfront views and proximity to downtown are still unbeatable.

The sites are located in a parking lot–like setting atop a 60-foot (18m) bluff. Beyond amenities such as a pool, playground, and spa, there's not much else here. But who goes to San Francisco to hang out at a campground?

The staff knows the city well and is ready to help you explore.

SAN FRANCISCO CABLE CAR.

> The Golden Gate, a 1.7-mile (2.7km) suspension bridge, welcomes more than 10 million visitors each year.

2 NAPA VALLEY EXPO RV PARK

👫 ♿ 🧺 🚿 ⚡ 🚐 📶

601 Silverado Trail, Napa, CA 94559. napavalleyexpo.com/rv-park.php; rstockwell@ napavalleyexpo.com; 707-253-4900. $50. Laundry, recreation hall activities, outdoor games, bingo.

This RV park is within walking distance of downtown Napa, the Napa Valley Wine Train, and the Oxbow Public Market. Don't feel like walking? Hitch a ride on public transportation.

The park is part of the fairgrounds and next to a loud and busy highway, but the price is right, the location is good, and the facilities are clean. Individual sites are well sized and level, and the entire campground is big-rig friendly.

The popular Bingo Emporium is adjacent to the park, and the nearby Napa Valley Model Railroad Historical Society is open once a week. This is a great base camp for couples, but families with young kids should look elsewhere.

It can get very hot in Napa, and this campground has little shade. Plan accordingly.

NAPA VALLEY WINE COUNTRY.

3 SAN FRANCISCO NORTH/ PETALUMA KOA

👪 👫 ♿ 🧺 🚿 ⚡ 🚐 📶

20 Rainsville Road, Petaluma, CA 94952. koa.com/camp/san-francisco; koadesk@aol.com; 707-763-1492. $55 to $82. Pool, hot tub, tour shuttle, snack bar, bike rentals.

Situated between San Francisco and wine country, this campground is less than 40 miles (64km) from the Golden Gate Bridge. The May through October shuttle tours into the city are very popular among guests.

The pool, jumping pillow, and farm-themed playground keep little ones busy for hours, and teenagers will appreciate the wide variety of outdoor games, such as bocce ball, horseshoes, ring toss, and basketball. The whole family can enjoy karaoke nights and pancake breakfasts. The petting farm and hay-wagon rides give the campground a charming and rustic feel. With something fun for everyone, though, this campground might be too noisy for campers who are just looking for a good night's sleep.

A true foodie's paradise, San Francisco has more restaurants per capita than any other American city.

RESTAURANTS

1 FARMSTEAD AT LONG MEADOW RANCH

738 Main Street, Saint Helena, CA 94574. longmeadowranch.com; visit@ longmeadowranch.com; 707-963-4555. 11:30 A.M. to 9:30 P.M. $30 to $60. Farm to table.

You simply must have a farm-to-table dining experience while visiting Napa Valley, and this is a standout option in a region known for culinary excellence. Located in a restored barn on a cattle ranch and winery, the food celebrates the local agricultural harvest.

Enjoy the Weekly Traditions menu on Monday, Tuesday, and Wednesday, where family dishes like meatloaf and fried chicken are offered. Or enjoy the Growers Happy Hour during the week from 4 to 6 P.M.

2 BOULEVARD

1 Mission Street, San Francisco, CA 94105. boulevardrestaurant.com; info@ boulevardrestaurant.com; 415-543-6084. Monday to Friday 11 A.M. to 2:15 P.M.; Sunday to Thursday 5:30 P.M. to 10 P.M.; Friday and Saturday 5:30 P.M. to 10:30 P.M. $35 to $65. French American.

Considered one of the best restaurants in San Francisco, this is the perfect spot to celebrate a special occasion. The service is impeccable, but the food even more so. Watch the chefs prepare foie gras waffles and truffle-topped raviolis in the open kitchen.

The meat is often the star of the show here, and your quail, lamb, pork, and filet mignon will be cooked to perfection. Don't be afraid to order your favorite traditional mixed drink. The cocktails here are served strong and true.

Make reservations in advance, and specifically request to be seated by the windows that offer a stunning view of the Golden Gate Bridge. This might well be your most memorable experience in this unforgettable city.

INFAMOUS ALCATRAZ.

3 TARTINE BAKERY AND CAFE

600 Guerrero Street, San Francisco, CA 94110. tartinebakery.com; info@tartinebakery .com; 415-487-2600. Monday 8 A.M. to 7 P.M.; Tuesday and Wednesday 7:30 A.M. to 7 P.M.; Thursday to Saturday 7:30 A.M. to 8 P.M.; Sunday 9 A.M. to 8 P.M. $5 to $20. Bakery.

Brave the brusque service style and long lines to enjoy the best pastries in San Francisco. Baked goods are always emerging fresh from the oven, so don't be scared to ask what's warm and snap it up immediately.

Order a sandwich to enjoy on-site as well as plenty of goodies to take with you.

The wineries in Napa Valley pour more than $50 billion into the American economy every year.

ATTRACTIONS

1 NAPA VALLEY WINE TRAIN

1275 McKinstry Street, Napa, CA 94559. **winetrain.com**; 800-427-4124. Lunch 10:30 A.M. to 2:30 P.M.; dinner 5:30 P.M. to 9:30 P.M. $124 to $199.

With more than 400 winery tasting rooms in Napa Valley, it can be overwhelming to decide which ones to visit. Try this wine train tour as an alternative to driving from one winery to another.

The train offers gourmet lunch or dinner tours, but stick to the daytime train ride to see the best views.

2 GOLDEN GATE PARK

Golden Gate Park, San Francisco, CA 94121. **golden-gate-park.com**; 415-831-2700. Free park admission; certain attractions have entrance fees.

Steinhart Aquarium, de Young, Japanese Tea Garden, and California Academy of Sciences are some of the more popular attractions within this 1,000-acre (405ha) urban green space.

You also can climb to the top of Strawberry Hill and see views of Mount Tamalpais and the Golden Gate Bridge. Wander around the botanical garden, take a spin on the carousel, or enjoy the delightful fragrances of the rose gardens.

There's so much to do in Golden Gate Park, but many visitors simply choose a picnic lunch and people-watching. Hang out at the Music Concourse, and sample the goods from local food trucks that gather here.

3 ALCATRAZ

Alcatraz Island, San Francisco, CA 94133. **nps.gov/alca**; 415-561-4900. Tours offered every half hour beginning at 9 A.M.

There's no admission fee to tour Alcatraz, but you do have to take an Alcatraz Cruises ferry to get to the island. Be sure you buy your tickets in advance during the summer and holiday seasons.

Once at Alcatraz, check the daily exhibit schedule as soon as you arrive, as numerous programs are offered throughout the day. Rangers give talks on the natural history of the bay, infamous escapes, and the American Indian occupation.

The purchase of a ferry ticket includes an audio tour of the prison, and many exhibits and media presentations are offered. If you prefer a structured tour experience, consider taking the evening ferry ride, which offers a narrated history of Alcatraz and group tours from the dock to the cell house.

ITINERARIES

IF YOU HAVE 1 WEEK ...

Walk across the Golden Gate Bridge, and take a ride on the cable cars around San Francisco. Visit the Japanese Tea Garden, and tour Alcatraz. Ride the wine train in Napa Valley.

IF YOU HAVE 2 WEEKS ...

All the above, plus explore the touristy Fisherman's Wharf and the more gritty and authentic Mission District. Hike to the top of Twin Peaks. Eat your way through the Ferry Building Marketplace. Take a day trip to the Muir Woods National Monument, and marvel at the towering redwoods.

IF YOU HAVE 3 WEEKS ...

Consider splitting your time between the city and the valley, staying first at the San Francisco RV Resort and then moving to the Napa Valley Expo RV Park. Start in the city and get your fill of sightseeing and then escape to the valley for relaxing days filled with wine tours and farm-fresh food.

california gold rush tour

Gold was discovered in the western foothills of California's Sierra Nevada Range in 1848, attracting hundreds of thousands of pioneers to the area in an attempt to strike it rich. Today, the area is popular for historical sightseeing, plus hiking, biking, and rafting.

HIGHLIGHTS

★ Send a message over a working telegraph line at the **Capitol Mall** in Old Sacramento.

★ Take the Living History tour at **Empire Mine State Historic Park,** where guides in period dress re-create scenes from the past.

★ Pan for gold and gems at the **Hidden Treasure Gold Mine** in Columbia State Historical Park.

BEST TIME TO GO

Summer temperatures can soar above 100°F (38°C) degrees, and winter can bring lots of snow, so June or September are your best bets for warm, dry weather.

29 miles (47km)

CAMPGROUNDS

1 INN TOWN CAMPGROUND

9 Kidder Court, Nevada City, CA 95959. inntowncampground.com; dan@inntowncampground.com; 530-265-9900. $50 to $65. Pool, horseshoes, playground, walking trails, evening programs.

Inn Town Campground earns high marks for its unique location, which is deeply wooded but less than 2 miles (3.2km) from shopping, dining, and summer festivals in downtown Nevada City.

The Nevada County Narrow Gauge Railroad Museum is right next door, and train rides are available.

After hiking and exploring around the South Yuba River, head back to cook dinner at the community barbecue area, play a game of horseshoes, or take a dip in the pool.

GOLD BUG MINE IN PLACERVILLE.

James Wilson Marshall discovered the first flakes of gold in the America River in 1848, sparking the California gold rush.

2 49ER RV RANCH

23223 Italian Bar Road, Columbia, CA 95310. 49rv.com; stay@49rv.com; 209-532-4978. $40 to $55. Horseshoes, recreation hall, planned activities, hotdog roast, live music.

The facilities at this campground might not be world class, but the enthusiastic customer service is. The property has a unique rustic charm that will inspire your California gold rush road trip. Be sure to grab a free hotdog on Friday night, and catch some live music around the community campfire. Free gold panning lessons also are available.

The drive into the campground is hilly, and some sites are hard to back into, so call ahead for best directions. The expert staff will put you at ease.

The location is great with many nearby activities. Check out Columbia State Historic Park, Railtown 1897 State Historic Park, and Moaning Cavern. Bring comfortable shoes for the lovely Natural Bridges Hiking Trail. Black Oak Casino is also nearby.

SIERRA NEVADA RANGE FOOTHILLS.

3 PLACERVILLE KOA

4655 Rock Barn Road, Shingle Springs, CA 95682. koa.com/camp/Placerville; koa@koa-placerville.com; 530-676-2267. $50 to $70. Pool, bike rentals, snack bar.

This campground serves as a solid base camp for exploring California Gold Country and Old Town Sacramento. It's located near many wineries, Red Hawk Casino is right up the road (the buffet is very good), and the staff can arrange for a shuttle to pick you up and bring you home when you want. The property is located on a highway, but other than road noise, there's much to like.

The pool and hot tub are nice, and kids can enjoy mini-golf and bike rentals. They'll also love the miniature goats in the petting zoo.

On Sundays, breakfast is served right at the campground, and it makes for a good time to share your gold rush travel notes with other campers.

The owners are kind and helpful and like meeting their guests.

WEST

Many gold rush migrants, called 49ers, traveled historic Highway 49 to get to California.

RESTAURANTS

1 NEW MOON CAFE

203 York Street, Nevada City, CA 95959. thenewmooncafe.com; 530-265-6399. Lunch Tuesday to Friday 11:30 A.M. to 2 P.M.; dinner Tuesday to Sunday 5 P.M. to 8:30 P.M. $30 to $60. New American.

The menu at this upscale bistro in Nevada City changes seasonally to offer fresh and local ingredients. Organic salads feature roasted beets, grilled prawns, and candied walnuts. Small plates include the ravioli of the day, gnocchi, lamb, and pork belly. Full-size entrées highlight fresh, wild fish, duck, quail, and lamb.

2 OLD TOWN SMOKEHOUSE

1100 Front Street, Suite 140, Sacramento, CA 95814. oldtownsmokehouse.com; 916-492-9089. Monday 11 A.M. to 5 P.M.; Wednesday 11 A.M. to 3 P.M.; Thursday 11 A.M. to 5 P.M.; Friday to Sunday 11 A.M. to 8 P.M.; closed Tuesday. $10 to $20. Barbecue.

Don't miss this gem of a storefront that specializes in smoked meats and seafood. Track it down, enjoy a delicious lunch, and take some smoked salmon back to your RV.

The tri tip sandwich on a brioche bun is a favorite, as is the smoked shrimp po'boy. Outdoor seating is available.

3 COLUMBIA KATE'S TEAHOUSE, BAKERY AND BOUTIQUE

22727 Columbia Street, Columbia, CA 95310. columbiakates.com; manager@ columbiakates.com; 209-532-1885. Sunday to Thursday 11 A.M. to 4 P.M.; Friday and Saturday 10 A.M. to 4 P.M. $10 to $15. Sandwiches and pastries.

Stick with Columbia's gold rush theme at this teahouse, located in a charming refurbished 1880s barn. The tables are named after real mining claims, and the staff is happy to share local lore.

The restaurant offers a simple pastry or a hearty lunch. Choose from a variety of traditional tea combinations, including Kate's Tea, which comes with a pot of tea; a scone; a trio of cucumber, egg salad, and chicken salad sandwiches; a salad; and a macaroon. If you're famished from all your gold-panning, try the more filling chicken pot pie, meatloaf, or savory bread pudding. Save room for cake, pie, and lemon bars—all sweets are homemade on-site daily.

COLUMBIA STATE HISTORIC PARK.

The real economic beneficiaries of the gold rush were merchants, many of whom made fortunes outfitting the miners.

ATTRACTIONS

1 EMPIRE MINE STATE HISTORIC PARK

👪 👫 ♿ 🐕

10791 Empire Street, Grass Valley, CA 95945. **empiremine.org;** empiremine@parks .ca.gov; 530-273-8522. 10 A.M. to 5 P.M. Adults 17 and up $7; children 6 to 16 $3; 5 and under free; additional $2 fee for Cottage Living History tour.

Although you're free to explore the grounds yourself, the guided tours bring the past to life at this historic mine. Take 45- to 60-minute tours of the cottage grounds, mine yard, or gardens. Better yet, join one of the Living History tours, during which docents in period costume portray figures from the past.

The grounds are the perfect setting for a picnic lunch.

2 COLUMBIA STATE HISTORIC PARK

👪 👫 ♿

11255 Jackson Street, Columbia, CA 95310. **visitcolumbiacalifornia.com;** 209-588-9128. Town open 24 hours; most businesses operate 10 A.M. to 5 P.M. Free town tours; prices for attractions vary.

This is a state park and also a fully functioning town with restaurants, saloons, shops, and attractions all centered on the gold rush theme. Many visitors find the activities and souvenirs refreshingly affordable for a tourist stop.

Arrange your schedule to make the daily 11 A.M. town tour led by knowledgeable and enthusiastic volunteers. Shop for handmade leather goods at Ebler's Leather and Saddlery Emporium, and stock up on old-fashioned candies at Nelson's Columbia Candy Kitchen. Parrott's Blacksmith forges iron before your very eyes and will happily personalize a horseshoe with your name. Take a lesson and pan for gold at the Hidden Treasure Gold Mine.

3 OLD SACRAMENTO

👪 👫 ♿

Old Sacramento Visitor Center, 1002 2nd Street, Sacramento, CA 95814. **oldsacramento.com;** info@oldsacramento.com; 916-442-8575. Visitor center 10 A.M. to 5 P.M.

Old Sacramento is an eight-block section of the city located between Tower Bridge and I Street Bridge, home to clothing and jewelry boutiques, restaurants, and sweet shops. There's also an abundance of historically themed museums, walking tours, carriage rides, and living history theater programs. The folks at the visitor center can help you pick from the many available options.

The California State Railroad Museum entertains visitors of all ages, offering historical exhibits, train rides, and a train playroom for children. The Wells Fargo History Museum is small but worth visiting to see gold rush–era artifacts. Go under the city with Old Sacramento Underground Tours, or take a Classic Coach carriage ride to see the sites from street level.

ITINERARIES

IF YOU HAVE 1 WEEK …

Take the Cottage Living History tour at the Empire Mine State Historic Park and a guided tour of Columbia State Historic Park. Pan for gold at the Hidden Treasure Gold Mine. Visit the California State Railroad Museum, and take a ride on the train.

IF YOU HAVE 2 WEEKS …

All the above, plus hike the Hardrock Trails area and take the mine yard tour at Empire Mine State Historic Park. Shop in quaint downtown Nevada City. Visit the Wells Fargo History Museum. Whitewater raft on the American River, and bike along the American River Parkway. Take a day trip to South Lake Tahoe.

IF YOU HAVE 3 WEEKS …

All the above, plus fish for salmon and stripers in the Feather River outside Yuba City. Tour the Black Chasm Cavern outside Sacramento. Visit Marshall Gold Discovery State Historic Park, where the gold rush began. Rappel down into Moaning Cavern. Take a day trip to Indian Grinding Rock State Park.

yosemite national park

One of America's best loved national parks, Yosemite attracts millions of visitors from around the world each year. Granite peaks rise up thousands of feet from the valley floor, and waterfalls cascade over sheer cliffs. It's truly one of America's great wild places.

HIGHLIGHTS

★ Walk to the base of **Bridalveil Fall,** one of the first sights at the entrance to the valley.

★ Test your mettle on the 12-hour cable hike to the top of **Half Dome.**

★ Stand beneath the giant sequoia trees in the **Mariposa Grove.**

BEST TIME TO GO

May brings warm weather, blooming wildflowers, and waterfalls enhanced by melting snow. And of course, the summer crowds haven't yet arrived.

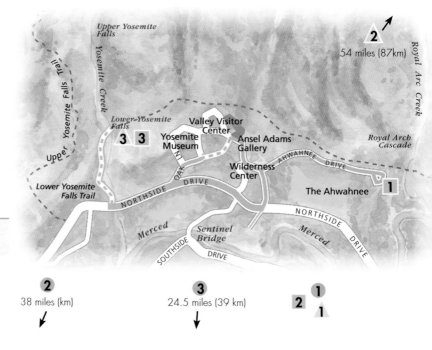

WEST

CAMPGROUNDS

1 UPPER PINES CAMPGROUND

Yosemite Valley, CA 95389. nps.gov/yose/
planyourvisit/upperpines.htm; 209-372-8502.
$26. Fire ring, picnic table, food locker, toilets.

At an elevation of 4,000 feet
(1,219m), Upper Pines is incredibly
beautiful, and incredibly hard to
book. Sites fill within minutes on the
first day they become available.

Bring your bike, and avoid the
headache of automobile travel in the
valley. Waterfalls, granite cliffs, and
ancient giant sequoias are all within
pedaling distance.

YOSEMITE VALLEY.

2 YOSEMITE RIDGE RESORT

7589 Highway 120, Groveland, CA 95321.
yosemiteridge.com; 800-706-3009. $25 to
$40. General store, restaurant, barbecue
pedestals, laundry, bathhouse, vintage cedar
showers.

Reserving a campsite inside Yosemite
can require luck, determination, or
divine intervention. Finding a good
campground outside the park also
can be challenging. Yosemite Ridge
scores points for being clean and well
run and offering roomy, full-hookup
sites. Shaded by a grove of trees, the
campground is quiet and peaceful.

Campers love the generous portions
at the nearby Buck Meadows
Restaurant and Bar, which is under the
same ownership. There's no pool on
the property, but the staff is happy to
direct you to Rainbow Pool, a lovely
swimming hole at the bottom of a
nearby waterfall.

In 1903, naturalist John
Muir led President
Theodore Roosevelt on a
3-day camping trip in
Yosemite, inspiring
Roosevelt to expand the
national parks.

EL CAPITAN.

3 YOSEMITE SOUTH/ COARSEGOLD KOA

34094 Highway 41, Coarsegold, CA 93614.
koa.com/camp/yosemite-south;
yosemitesouthkoa@gmail.com; 559-683-7855.
$50 to $65. Swimming pool, game room.

This KOA struggled to maintain its
facilities under the preceding owners,
but aggressive new ownership has
dramatic plans for improvement. It's a
fairly long drive from Yosemite
National Park, but if you aren't
camping at a national park
campground, that'll be the case just
about anywhere. Sites are spacious,
but there's road noise along the
highway, so ask for a quiet spot.

Kids enjoy swimming in the pool after
a long day of adventure in the
national park, and the game room
and outdoor theater also are good for
campground downtime.

The campground is set in the Sierra
Nevada foothills, and the charming
and rustic town of Coarsegold is
nearby.

WEST

Most of the 4 million annual visitors never leave Yosemite Valley, so take a hike—literally—if you want to escape the crowds.

SEQUOIA TREES AT YOSEMITE FALLS.

RESTAURANTS

1 AHWAHNEE DINING ROOM

ᵗᵗᵗ ᵗᵗ ♿

1 Ahwahnee Drive, Yosemite National Park, CA 95389. **yosemitepark.com**; 209-372-1489. Breakfast 7 A.M. to 10 A.M.; lunch 11:30 A.M. to 3 P.M.; dinner 5:30 P.M. to 9 P.M.; brunch Sunday 7 A.M. to 3 P.M. $30 to $50. American.

When presidents and dignitaries visit this iconic national park, Ahwahnee is where they eat.

The stately dining room harkens back to 1920s wilderness luxury, with exposed beams and floor-to-ceiling windows. Stone columns and etched wooden inlays complete the picture. Gaze out at the beautiful landscape while you enjoy the angus prime rib and an old-fashioned cocktail.

Day trippers and hikers should enjoy the casual lunch. A dress code is strictly enforced during dinner.

Hike a 2-mile (3.2km) round-trip trail to Yosemite Falls, the tallest waterfall in North America, with a 2,425-foot (739m) drop.

2 CURRY VILLAGE DINING

ᵗᵗᵗ ᵗᵗ ♿

Curry Village, Yosemite National Park, CA 95389. **yosemitepark.com**; 801-559-4884. Hours vary by restaurant. $5 to $20. American.

Curry Village is home to four dining establishments, so no matter when you're passing through, there's a suitable option.

Coffee Corner, open 6 A.M. to 10 P.M., brews Peet's Coffee, cappuccino, and espresso. For breakfast, try the oatmeal bar or grab a pastry to go. In the evening, indulge in a towering ice-cream sundae. Pizza Deck, open noon to 10 P.M., is a casual option for pizza, salads, and beers after a long day of hiking in the park. Meadow Grill serves more traditional pub fare like burgers and chicken sandwiches from 11 A.M. to 7 P.M. The menu at Curry Village Pavilion changes daily and features home-style cooking with comfort food sides and a salad bar. It's open 7 A.M. to 10 A.M. for breakfast, and dinner is served from 5:30 P.M. to 8 P.M.

3 DEGNAN'S DELI

ᵗᵗᵗ ᵗᵗ ♿

9006 Yosemite Lodge Drive, Yosemite National Park, CA 95389. **yosemite park.com**; 801-559-4884. 7 A.M. to 5 P.M. $7 to $9. Sandwiches.

Here you'll find both premade and made-to-order sandwiches, perfect to pack for your picnic lunch in the park. The sandwiches are reasonably priced and made with fresh ingredients.

Plenty of vegetarian options also are available, as is a wide variety of cold beverages, including local beers.

ATTRACTIONS

1 TIOGA ROAD

Tuolumne Meadows, Yosemite National
Park, CA 95389. nps.gov/yose; 209-372-4025.
Tuolumne Meadows Visitor Center 9 A.M. to
5 P.M. 7-day vehicle pass $30.

This scenic route bisects the park,
running east to west, north of Yosemite
Valley. Driving straight through takes
about 2 hours, but you should stop in
at the Tuolumne Meadows Visitor
Center and talk to a ranger about the
stunning hikes in the area. Options
are available for any ability level, and
the lack of crowds is refreshing.

2 RAFTING THE MERCED RIVER

Curry Village Recreation Center, Yosemite
National Park, CA 95389. yosemitepark.com;
209-372-4386. 10 A.M. to 3:30 P.M. $31.

Rafting the Merced River is another
way to escape the crowds and enjoy
some of the most iconic views in
Yosemite in a tranquil river setting. The
trip takes you through the heart of the
valley.

You can rent a four-person raft from
the Curry Village Recreation Center.
The price includes a return trip by
shuttle at the end of your float. Or use
your own raft, and pay a smaller fee
for the shuttle ride. Height and weight
guidelines are strictly enforced, so
carefully check them if you have small
children. No reservations are taken,
so arrive early.

3 VALLEY FLOOR TOUR

Yosemite Lodge at the Falls, Yosemite National
Park, CA 95389. yosemitepark.com;
209-372-4386. 10 A.M. to 3 P.M. Adults $25;
seniors $23; children $13.

Instead of fighting traffic congestion
and overly full parking lots, consider
seeing the Yosemite Valley by way of
a 2-hour ranger-led open-air tram tour.

You'll see all of Yosemite's most
famous attractions while also learning
about the history and geology of the
region. The tour includes discussion of
the park's flora and fauna, too. Stops
are made to view and photograph
Yosemite Falls, Half Dome, El
Capitan, Tunnel View, and Bridalveil
Fall.

Tours leave on the hour during the
summer from Yosemite Lodge at the
Falls, which is shuttle stop 8. During
the winter months the tours still run, but
in enclosed, heated buses.

Special evening tours are offered
periodically, so check the schedule or
call before your trip.

Reservations can be made online.

ITINERARIES

IF YOU HAVE 1 WEEK ...

Start at the Yosemite Valley Visitor
Center, and learn about the history
and geology of the park. Tour the
Yosemite Museum. Take a tram tour
of Yosemite Valley. Raft down the
Merced River. Hike to Yosemite Falls.
Have Sunday brunch at Ahwahnee.

IF YOU HAVE 2 WEEKS ...

All the above, plus visit the giant
sequoias in Mariposa Grove. Drive
the Tioga Road, take in the views
from Olmsted Point, and explore
Tuolumne Meadows. Take a sunrise
hike to Mirror Lake, walk Cook's
Meadow Loop, and swim in Tenaya
Lake. Eat dinner on the porch of the
Wawona Hotel.

IF YOU HAVE 3 WEEKS ...

All the above, plus visit the Ansel
Adams Gallery. Hike the Mist Trail to
Vernal Fall and the John Muir Trail.
Take the moderate walk to Sentinel
Dome. Take a personal fly-fishing
lesson with a Yosemite outfitter. Join
the lottery for a permit to hike up
Half Dome.

WEST

portland,
oregon

For such a casual city, Portland takes a lot of things very seriously, including its outdoor activities, artisanal food, fresh-roasted coffee, spirit distilleries, and microbrew beers. Arrive ready to put aside sightseeing and embrace sampling the local culture, preferably on foot or bicycle, like locals.

HIGHLIGHTS

★ Breathe in the heavenly floral aromas at the **International Rose Test Garden.**

★ Browse the stacks at **Powell's City of Books,** the largest new and used bookstore in the world.

★ Sip a cup of java at **Coava,** considered one of the best coffee roasters in the city.

BEST TIME TO GO

Although mild year round, summer is glorious in Portland, offering warm, dry weather and tons of outdoor festivals and celebrations.

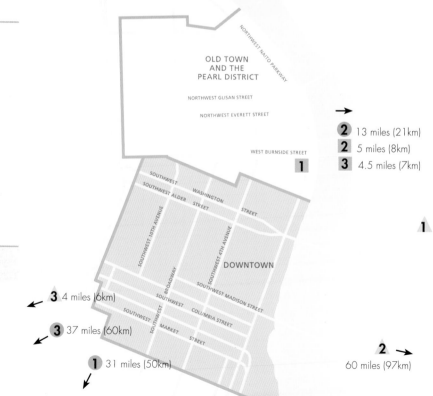

CAMPGROUNDS

1 PORTLAND–WOODBURN RV PARK

115 N. Arney Road, Woodburn, OR 97071. **woodburnrv.com;** info@woodburnrv.com; 888-988-0002. $42. Heated pool, playground, recreation hall, horseshoes, outdoor games.

This park is only 30 minutes from Portland and is big rig friendly. All sites and roads are paved, and the restrooms are clean. There's a nice heated pool for the kids to enjoy after exploring Portland. The campground is located next to Woodburn Premium Outlets, and a Starbucks is within walking distance.

This is a solid choice for exploring Portland.

PORTLAND JAPANESE GARDEN.

2 OLDE STONE VILLAGE RV PARK

4155 NE Three Mile Lane, McMinnville, OR 97128. **oldestonevillage.com;** oldestonevillage@comcast.net; 877-472-4315. $40. Heated pool, recreation hall, playground.

This park is universally loved and scores high marks in every area. It's clean, the staff is super-friendly and helpful, and the sites are large and level with concrete pads. Restrooms are also up to date and comfortable.

The pool, playground, tennis court, and clubhouse are excellent, so plan on spending time enjoying the campground. Dog owners will love all the large, grassy, walk areas. This also is a great spot for bike lovers, as a paved bike path takes off directly from the campground.

The location is excellent as well. Nearby McMinnville has a cute downtown and good restaurants, and you're within striking distance of Portland, wine country, Salem, and the coast. Don't miss a walk or bike ride to the Evergreen Aviation and Space Museum, where you can learn about general aviation, military aircraft, and space flight.

A color-coded map helps visitors navigate the 1.5 million new and used books at Powell's.

SEEMINGLY ENDLESS STACKS OF BOOKS AT POWELL'S.

3 PORTLAND FAIRVIEW RV PARK

21401 NE Sandy Boulevard, Fairview, OR 97024. **portlandfairviewrv.com;** customerservice@portlandfairviewrv.com; 877-777-1047. $45. Heated pool.

This park's proximity to Portland can't be beat. If you plan on spending most of your time in the city, and not in the campground, this makes a great base camp.

You'll see a good number of friendly seasonal campers at this clean park. You might hear some noise from airplanes and trains, but that's to be expected this close to the city.

You can catch a bus right outside the campground to take you to a metro train that brings you directly into Portland, so you won't necessarily need to tow your car to enjoy the city.

WEST

> The Japanese Garden, considered the most authentic outside of Japan, has stunning views of Mount Hood.

PORTLAND FARMERS MARKET.

RESTAURANTS

1 PORTLAND SATURDAY MARKET

👨‍👧 👨 ♿

2 SW Naito Parkway, Portland, Oregon 97204. **portlandsaturdaymarket.com;** info@ saturdaymarket.org; 503-222-6072. Saturday 10 A.M. to 5 P.M.; Sunday 11 A.M. to 4:30 P.M. Free admission; prices vary according to vendor. Food truck fare.

One of Portland's most famous attractions, this is also the country's largest continuously operating open-air market. Bring cash, and be prepared to sample the treats and take a bunch back to your RV. Check the events and music calendar before your visit.

Many types of cuisine are represented, including Hawaiian, Mexican, Guatemalan, Lebanese, and African fare. The gyros at Angelina's Greek Cuizina are almost perfect. For dessert try the PDX Original Elephant Ears.

2 COQUINE

👨 ♿

6839 SE Belmont Street, Portland, OR 97215. **coquinepdx.com;** 503-384-2483. Wednesday to Sunday 5 P.M. to 10 P.M. $35 to $75. New American.

Chef Katy Millard brings her global culinary experience to Portland and blends it perfectly with this city's local, earthy food sensibility. The restaurant is rather small, and they do accept reservations, so call ahead if possible.

The highlight of the experience here is the Chef's Choice Prix Fixe, a four-course tasting menu with a wine pairing option. A carnivore and vegetarian menu is available as well. In contrast to some upscale establishments, the portions here are ample and you won't have to eat a fast-food cheeseburger later to satisfy your appetite. An à la carte menu is available, and favorites include the crispy duck wings and the black cod. Celebrating a special occasion? Share the roasted organic whole chicken for two.

3 VOODOO DOUGHNUT

👨‍👧 👨 ♿

22 SW 3rd Avenue, Portland, OR 97221. **voodoodoughnut.com;** 503-241-4704. $1 to $5. Doughnuts.

You'll always find a line out the door of this cash-only 24-hour spot, but it's worth every minute of the wait.

You can order a plain glazed doughnut here (and you should!), but be sure to try one of the zany options on the menu, too, like the dirty snowballs or tangfastic.

Portland Farmers Market operates eight weekly markets throughout the city, including the famous Saturday flagship market.

ATTRACTIONS

1 PORTLAND'S DISTILLERY ROW

👫 ♿

SE Industrial District, Portland, OR 97221. **distilleryrowpdx.com**. Hours vary according to distillery. Distillery Row Passport $20.

The newest wave of craft production in Portland is in the world of spirits, and seven distilleries offer tours and tastings to show off their wares.

Buying a passport earns you entry into all the locations, or you can cherry-pick according to your favorite spirit. Tickets don't expire, so you can spread out your visits, but they do sell out, so buy in advance of your trip.

2 MOUNT HOOD

👪 👫 ♿ 🐕

27500 E Timberline Road, Timberline Lodge, OR 97028. **timberlinelodge.com**; 503-272-3311. Free admission; fee for some attractions.

Head east of the city about 60 miles (96km), and you'll find yourself at Mount Hood, the highest mountain in Oregon. The drive itself offers plenty of scenic overlooks, so pull over to soak in the view at Crown Point.

Stop in at Timberline Lodge, and ride the Magic Mile Sky Ride to an elevation of 7,000 feet (2,133m). There are easy hikes around the lodge, or you can venture a little farther and hike to Little Zigzag Falls. Up for a challenge? Complete the Paradise Park Loop hike, a mere 11.8 miles (19km) round-trip.

Skiing is available almost year round, even in summer, depending on snowfall.

3 WASHINGTON PARK

👪 👫 ♿ 🐕

1715 SW Skyline Boulevard, Portland, OR 97221. **washingtonparkpdx.org**; 503-823-2525. 5 A.M. to 10 P.M. Free admission; fee for some attractions.

Some of Portland's most popular attractions are located in this park, so you might find yourself returning again and again during your stay. A free shuttle loops around to all the sites, so you can leave a car or bike in one spot and get around quite easily.

Portland Japanese Garden is world famous and offers guided tours that help you appreciate the authentic elements on display. The Oregon Zoo is another highlight for visitors and emphasizes conservation and animal welfare in its education and exhibits. The International Rose Test Garden has more than 7,000 rose plants and 550 varieties on display. Free tours are given daily at 1 P.M.

Whatever attractions you decide to visit, bring a picnic lunch and enjoy sweeping views of the city.

ITINERARIES

IF YOU HAVE 1 WEEK ...

Shop the Portland Saturday Market, tour Portland Japanese Garden, and visit the International Rose Test Garden. Rent bikes and ride through Forest Park. Walk the grounds, and take a tour at the historic Pittock Mansion. Shop in Old Town.

IF YOU HAVE 2 WEEKS ...

All the above, plus take a day trip to Mount Hood, tour Timberline Lodge, and ride the Magic Mile Sky Ride. Visit the Oregon Zoo, and sample your way through Distillery Row. Shop Alberta Street's boutique shops and galleries. Take the Foodie Field Trip Tour by Cycle Portland Bike Tours.

IF YOU HAVE 3 WEEKS ...

All the above, plus take day trips to the Oregon Coast and the Columbia River Gorge. Tour the Lan Su Chinese Garden, the Oregon Museum of Science and Industry, and the Portland Children's Museum. Find locally crafted souvenirs at MadeHere PDX. Take a guided pub-crawl through the city.

WEST

coastal washington **lighthouse tour**

Dozens of lighthouses have been built to help guide seafarers along Washington's rugged, rocky coast, and many are still in use. Opportunities abound for educational tours and stunning photography.

HIGHLIGHTS

★ Climb to the top of **Grays Harbor Lighthouse,** the tallest in the state standing at 107 feet (32.6m).

★ Pack a picnic lunch and enjoy whale watching from dry land at **Lime Kiln Point State Park.**

★ Take the Keystone Ferry out to **Fort Casey State Park,** and tour the Admiralty Head Lighthouse.

BEST TIME TO GO

The Washington coast regularly experiences rainy, foggy, and windy conditions, so the best time to visit is in July or August, the warmest and driest months.

CAMPGROUNDS

① FORT CASEY HISTORICAL STATE PARK

1280 Engle Road, Coupeville, WA 98239. parks.state.wa.us/505/FortCasey; 888-226-7688. $25 to $40. Restroom, shower, ferry terminal, fishing, lighthouse, walking trails.

This campground is small (fewer than 40 sites) and somewhat run down, but it's beautiful, and some spots are directly on the beach. There's simply no better base camp for exploring the Admiralty Head Lighthouse.

Relax and watch the ferries roll in, and take in the expansive views of Admiralty Inlet and the Strait of Juan de Fuca. Pack your windbreaker; you'll be close enough to feel the salt spray off the water.

ADMIRALTY LIGHTHOUSE.

② CAPE DISAPPOINTMENT STATE PARK

224 Robert Gray Drive, Ilwaco, WA 98624. parks.state.wa.us/486/cape-dissapointment; 888-226-7688. $25 to $45. Bathrooms, showers, food delivery.

No one leaves disappointed from this coastal classic. The campground offers full hookups, and trails lead directly to the windswept beaches. The sites are large and level, and some even have ocean views. The entire campground is clean and well maintained.

You don't have to leave the park for great hiking, biking, lighthouse touring, and tide pool exploring—it's all right here.

Don't forget to take a day trip or two into Long Beach, a charming coastal town just 5 miles (8km) away. The Columbia River Maritime Museum in Astoria is also a short drive away and shouldn't be missed.

Many campers come for the first time to see the Lewis and Clark Interpretive Center, and return again and again for the beach and the ocean.

> The Point No Point Lighthouse is the oldest lighthouse in the Puget Sound and has been in continuous operation since its completion in 1879.

WEST POINT LIGHTHOUSE.

③ BAY CENTER/WILLAPA BAY KOA

457 Bay Center Road, Bay Center, WA 98527. koa.com/camp/bay-center; baycenterkoa@centurylink.net; 360-875-6344. April 3 to November 29. $40 to $55. Bike rentals, playground, geocaching, remote-control car track.

This KOA is a great location for exploring the lighthouses at Cape Disappointment and North Head at the mouth of the Columbia River.

The campground is very pretty with lots of trees and spacious sites, and the owners take a personal interest in ensuring their campers are happy. One of them grew up clam digging, and the campground has its own clam bed. A short nature trail leads down to the beach at Willapa Bay, where kids can play and dogs can run free. Sunsets are pretty.

After a day of exploring the scenic coastline, head back for volleyball, horseshoes, basketball, or badminton. Or just kick back and relax at an ice-cream social where you can meet other campers.

WEST

Cape Disappointment, at the entrance to the Columbia River, earned its name when explorer John Meares mistakenly sailed right past the river in 1788.

LIME KILN LIGHTHOUSE ON SAN JUAN ISLAND.

RESTAURANTS

1 OLEBOB'S SEAFOOD MARKET AND GALLEY RESTAURANT

👪 👫 ♿

151 Howerton Way, Ilwaco, WA 98624. olebobs.com; 360-642-4332. Sunday to Thursday 11 A.M. to 5:30 P.M.; Friday 11 A.M. to 7 P.M.; Saturday 10 A.M. to 7 P.M. $15 to $30. Seafood.

This seafood shack is just minutes away from both Cape Disappointment Lighthouse and North Head Lighthouse, making it the perfect place to break for lunch before heading north to the other three lighthouses along Highway 101, or for dinner if you're coming south.

Sit outside and marina views while you sample the baked oysters, a house specialty. Choose among the fresh catches of the day for your fish and chips platter. Beer and wine are available.

2 IVARS ACRE OF CLAMS

👪 👫 ♿

Pier 54 1001 Alaskan Way, Seattle, WA 98104. ivars.com/locations/acres-of-clams; 206-624-6852. Lunch Monday to Saturday 11 A.M. to 4 P.M. and Sunday 11 A.M. to 3 P.M.; dinner Monday to Thursday 4 P.M. to 10 P.M.; Friday and Saturday 4 P.M. to 11 P.M.; Sunday 3 P.M. to 10 P.M. $25 to $50. Seafood.

This waterfront seafood restaurant has been open on Seattle's Pier 54 for more than 70 years, and it recently got a facelift. It's the perfect place for lunch or dinner after exploring Discovery Park, home of the West Point Lighthouse.

Indoor and outdoor seating is available, and you can watch the ferries moving through Elliott Bay from many tables. Or order take-out and eat at picnic tables on-site. Be warned: diners feed french fries to the seagulls, making this an unappealing option for some patrons.

The basics are done well here. Try the chowder, prawns, or fish and chips. Or get fancy with bacon-wrapped halibut and wild sockeye salmon. Land lovers can find options as well.

3 DUCK SOUP INN

👫 ♿

50 Duck Soup Lane, Friday Harbor, WA 98250. ducksoupinn.com; hi@ducksoupinn.com; 360-378-4878. Wednesday to Sunday 5 P.M. to 10 P.M. $30 to $60. American.

Nestled in Friday Harbor, this romantic and quaint restaurant celebrates the landscape and bounty of San Juan Island, offering a seasonal menu that always features house-made sourdough bread and organic salads.

Roasted duck, pan-seared halibut, and farm-fresh pork are creatively prepared with fresh morels, nettles, or wild fennel. Reservations are highly recommended.

A hydrophone system is installed in the waters off San Juan Island, allowing scientists to listen to the sounds of orcas as they migrate through the area.

ATTRACTIONS

1 HIGHWAY 101 LIGHTHOUSES

👪 👫 ♿

Cape Disappointment State Park, 24 Robert Gray Drive, Ilwaco, WA 98624. **parks.state .wa.us/486/cape-dissapointment**; 360-642-3078. 6:30 A.M. to dusk. 1-day Washington State Park Discover Pass $10; annual pass $30.

Start your exploration at Cape Disappointment State Park, where you can visit the Lewis and Clark Interpretive Center perched above the Pacific Ocean on a 200-foot (61m) cliff. Also tour the Cape Disappointment Lighthouse and the North Head Lighthouse here.

Head north on 101 to climb Grays Harbor Lighthouse. Use the viewpoint 2 miles (3.2km) south of Ruby Beach to spot the Destruction Island Lighthouse 3 miles (4.8km) offshore.

2 SEATTLE LIGHTHOUSES

👪 👫 ♿

Fort Casey Historical State Park, 1280 Engle Road, Coupeville, WA 98239. **parks.state .wa.us/505/fort-casey**; 360-678-4519. 8 A.M. to dusk. 1-day Washington State Park Discover Pass $10; annual pass $30.

Start touring the lighthouses of the Seattle area by visiting Admiralty Lighthouse, located in Fort Casey Historical State Park. You can drive, but it's much more fun to take a ferry to the Keystone Ferry Landing. Call ahead to schedule a free educational tour, or tour the museum and fort on your own.

Mukilteo Lighthouse to the north of Seattle is charming and offers great views of the sound from the top. The light is still in operation and flashes every 5 seconds year round. West Point Lighthouse is in Discovery Park, a favorite destination for Seattle locals. In addition to the working lighthouse, you'll find trails, beaches, picnic areas, and bike paths.

3 SAN JUAN ARCHIPELAGO LIGHTHOUSES

👪 👫 ♿

Lime Kiln Point State Park, 1567 Westside Road, Friday Harbor, WA 98250. **parks.state .wa.us/540/lime-kiln-point**; 360-378-2044. 8 A.M. to dusk. 1-day Washington State Park Discover Pass $10; annual pass $30.

During peak whale-watching season (May to September) you can spot minke whales, orcas, seals, and sea lions daily from Lime Kiln Point State Park on San Juan Island, which is the home of the Lime Kiln Point Lighthouse. Drive south about 30 minutes from the state park to visit Cattle Point Lighthouse, where a short walk on an interpretative trail brings you to the tower.

Turn Point Lighthouse on Stuart Island is a bit trickier to visit. There's a public dock on the island for chartered vessels, and from there, it's a beautiful 2-mile (3.2km) hike to the lighthouse. Outer Island Excursions offers guided tours. It also offers tours to Patos Island Lighthouse, another destination that requires a boat ride and hike.

ITINERARIES

IF YOU HAVE 1 WEEK ...

Spend a full day driving Highway 101, stopping to see the lighthouses at Cape Disappointment, North Head, Grays Harbor, and Destruction Island. Head to Seattle to tour Admiralty Head, Mukilteo, and West Point. Visit San Juan Island, and see Lime Kiln Point and Cattle Point lighthouses.

IF YOU HAVE 2 WEEKS ...

All the above, plus head farther north on 101 and visit Cape Flattery and Slip Point lighthouses. In Seattle, add on visits to Point No Point and Point Robinson lighthouses. Hike at New Dungeness Lighthouse. Take a guided tour to Stuart Island and hike to Turn Point Lighthouse.

IF YOU HAVE 3 WEEKS ...

All the above, plus head a little farther off 101 to see the private residence that was once the Ediz Hook Lighthouse. While there, explore the coastal town of Port Angeles. In Seattle, add on visits to Browns Point and Alki Point lighthouses. Take a guided tour to Patos Island.

WEST

olympic national park,
washington

This diverse park is large and not easily traversed. Ninety-five percent is classified wilderness, and there's no through road. Extra planning ensures you see all the park's phenomenal beauty.

HIGHLIGHTS

★ Take the 1-hour ranger-led Meadow Walk at the **Hurricane Ridge Visitor Center.**

★ Explore the **Ruby Beach** tide pools in the coastal region of the park.

★ Earn a view of Mount Olympus by hiking the **Hoh River Trail.**

BEST TIME TO GO

June through September provide the warmest and driest weather. If you're wanting to spot wildlife, September is your best month.

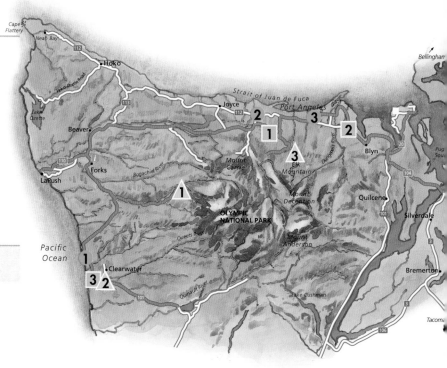

CAMPGROUNDS

1 KALALOCH CAMPGROUND

Highway 101, Mile Post Marker 157683, WA 98331. **nps.gov/olym/planyourvisit/camping .htm;** 360-565-3130. $14 to $36. Picnic tables, campfire rings, ranger programs.

If you have a smaller RV and love falling asleep to the sound of the ocean, Kalaloch is a magical place. Some sites even have water views, but beware of strong, cold winds coming off the ocean.

This campground isn't big rig–friendly. Only 9 sites can accommodate rigs longer than 40 feet (12m), and some sites can be uneven and challenging to access.

> Although Olympic is one of the most visited national parks, the fact that no road crosses through it keeps the crowds dispersed.

2 ELWHA DAM RV PARK

47 Lower Dam Road, Port Angeles, WA 98363. **elwhadamrvpark.com;** paradise@ elwhacreekrvpark.com; 360-452-7054. $40. Horseshoes, recreation hall, playground, outdoor games, pond.

The owners of this park are kind and energetic, and they take great care of their guests. The property is beautifully landscaped and filled with mature trees. Most sites are spacious and big rig–friendly, and the pull-thrus are extra long. Some sites are shaded, and some are in the open. Let them know your preference.

The campground has a rustic and family friendly feel, and the owner's children even run a dog-walking business so campers can spend their days exploring nearby Olympic National Park and Pacific beaches. Directly from the park, you can access hiking trails that lead to the Elwha River and the former dam site.

Campground Wi-Fi is very slow, but signals from major carriers are strong.

SOL DUC FALLS.

3 OLYMPIC PENINSULA/PORT ANGELES KOA

80 O'Brien Road, Port Angeles, WA 98362. **koa.com/camp/port-angeles;** portangeleskoa@ wavecable.com; 360-457-5916. March 1 to October 31. $40 to $80. Pool, hot tub, mini-golf, bike rentals.

This KOA is being refurbished by its new owners, who have added a new pavilion and deluxe patio sites. It's a good base for exploring nearby Olympic National Park and Vancouver Island in British Columbia. If you're traveling with kids, this is your best option. Ice-cream socials are held every Saturday night, and free hayrides around the park are given on a regularly scheduled basis. Look forward to the movie night and bingo night every weekend. And making tie-dye shirts is a blast. If you need a break from the kids, enjoy the mountain views from the adults-only hot tub.

A major highway borders one side of the campground, so if you're a light sleeper, ask for a site in a quieter section of the park.

VANCOUVER IS A FERRY RIDE AWAY AND WORTH A SIDE TRIP.

WEST

> The mountain goats in Olympic National Park can be aggressive. Rangers recommend staying at least 50 yards (46m) away from them.

RESTAURANTS

1 TOGA'S SOUP HOUSE

122 W. Lauridsen Boulevard, Port Angeles, WA 98362. **togassouphouse.com;** info@ togassouphouse.com; 360-452-1952. Monday to Friday 10 A.M. to 6 P.M. $8 to $15. Soups and sandwiches.

One of the best things you can do when visiting a national park is pick up a picnic lunch to eat while enjoying panoramic views at the end of a hike. Stop at Toga's Soup House and load up on delicious sandwiches, salads, and panini. The menu highlights seasonal and local fare and changes monthly.

Five homemade soups are available daily and include a variety of chilis, chowders, and vegetarian offerings. Ask to fill up your thermos.

> Olympic is home to the Northwest's largest unmanaged herd of Roosevelt elk, named to honor President Theodore Roosevelt and his efforts to conserve their habitat.

2 BLONDIE'S PLATE

134 S. 2nd Avenue, Sequim, WA 98382. **blondiesplate.com;** 360-683-2233. Sunday to Thursday 4 P.M. to 9 P.M.; Friday and Saturday 4 P.M. to 10 P.M. $15 to $35. Tapas.

Located in an old Episcopal church building, Blondie's serves small plate dishes with a Northwestern culinary point of view and offers a cozy and delightful place to dine after a day of hiking in the park.

Menu items range from light, vegetable-centered dishes to hearty, comfort food items. Starters like pan-fried oysters, sliders, and crostini topped with local mushrooms are sure to please. If you're in a coastal state of mind, enjoy the steamers or the crispy-skin salmon. Need a little comfort food to take off the chill? Try the roast chicken, macaroni and cheese, or risotto. The wine offerings are impressive for such a small restaurant, and gluten-free beers are available.

It's a small space that fills quickly, so make a reservation in advance.

ROOSEVELT ELK.

3 KALALOCH'S CREEKSIDE RESTAURANT

157151 US 101, Forks, WA 98331. **thekalalochlodge.com/Dine.aspx;** 360-962-2271. Breakfast 7 A.M. to 11 P.M.; lunch 11 A.M. to 5 P.M.; dinner 5 P.M. to 9 P.M. $15 to $50. American.

This is a park concession located in Lalaloch Lodge, with phenomenal scenery. Call ahead to ensure you get a table with a view of the ocean. Outdoor seating is available.

The seafood dishes on the dinner menu are favorites, so try the mussels, wild salmon, or halibut.

ATTRACTIONS

1 HOH RAIN FOREST

Upper Hoh Road, Forks, WA 98331. **nps.gov/olym**; 360-565-3130. Hours vary by season. Entrance included with park's $20 7-day vehicle pass.

On the west side of the park, this area receives up to 170 inches (432cm) of precipitation each year but is green, lush, and mostly dry during the summer months.

Start at the Hoh Rain Forest Visitor Center to map out your day and hike the two short nature trails. The 31-mile (50km) Hoh River Trail starts here as well.

2 WILDERNESS COAST

Kalaloch Ranger Station. **nps.gov/olym**. Open summer. Entrance included with park's $20 7-day vehicle pass.

Olympic National Park includes 73 miles (117.5km) of wilderness coastline, and Kalaloch, Ruby Beach, and Beach 4 on the southern end are the most popular. The Kalaloch Ranger Station, open through the summer, offers interpretative programs and access to an easy 1-mile (1.6km) loop trail. Be sure to check the tidal charts upon arrival to ensure you can enjoy the tide pools without getting trapped by incoming water.

You have to take a winding path to access Ruby Beach, but the effort is worth the views of driftwood, beach shrubs, and huge rocks rising out of the ocean. Keep your eyes peeled for sea otters, deer, and bald eagles.

3 HURRICANE RIDGE

Hurricane Ridge Road, Olympic National Park, WA 98362. **nps.gov/olym**; 360-565-3130. Hours vary by season. Entrance included with park's $20 7-day vehicle pass.

The Hurricane Ridge Visitor Center is located at the end of a 17-mile (27km) road that runs south of Port Angeles. Drive straight through, spend time at the visitor center, and then stop at chosen places along the drive back. An educational orientation movie and many ranger-led programs run frequently during the summer.

Many trails are accessible from the center, including the Cirque Rim, Big Meadow, and High Ridge, all under 1 mile (1.6km) round-trip. Hurricane Hill is a bit more challenging at 3 miles (4.8km) round-trip, leading to breathtaking views of the coast and mountains.

Visit early in the morning or late afternoon to see abundant wildlife. Olympic marmots are a favorite animal to spot, but also look for deer, bear, and mountain goats.

ITINERARIES

IF YOU HAVE 1 WEEK ...

Drive to Hurricane Ridge, and take a ranger-led walk. Hike Hurricane Hill and Klahhane Ridge. Visit Hoh Rain Forest, hiking the Hall of Mosses and the Spruce Nature Trail. Start your coastal explorations at the Kalaloch Ranger Station.

IF YOU HAVE 2 WEEKS ...

All the above, plus take the short hike to Sol Duc Falls. Go elk spotting on the Rain Forest Loop Drive, and see the 191-foot (58m) Sitka spruce in Quinault Rain Forest. Visit Lake Crescent, and hike to Marymere Falls. Splash around at Rialto Beach.

IF YOU HAVE 3 WEEKS ...

Consider driving the entire Olympic Peninsula Loop Drive, which is more than 300 miles (482km) and takes you through all four ecosystems in the park. Plan on spending at least 4 days in each area to fully explore the hiking and attractions. Explore the small towns of Sequim, Leavenworth, and Port Townsend.

glacier national park, montana

The stunning beauty of Glacier National Park outshines all competition. Despite its popularity, it's one of the few national parks that offers the feeling of solitude in nature, even at the busiest times.

HIGHLIGHTS

★ Ride in a historic wooden boat across **Swiftcurrent Lake** to see Grinnell Glacier.

★ Hike the 3-mile (5km) round-trip to **Hidden Lake Overlook** for the best chance to spot wildlife.

★ Picnic on the rocky beach of **Lake McDonald,** the largest lake in the park.

BEST TIME TO GO

For access to all the best drives and hikes in Glacier National Park, visit during July and August.

Kintla Lake

Goat Haunt

Bowman Lake

Quartz Lake

Polebridge

Logging Lake

Many Glacier

Lake Sherburne

Swiftcurrent Lake

1
1 St. Mary
3
← Going-To-The-Su Road

Logan Pass

Rising Sun
St. Mary Lake

Avalanche Creek

Lake McDonald
1

Jackson Glacier

Lake McDonald

2 Fish Creek

3 2

Harrison Lake

Two Medicine

Rocky Mountains

Apgar Visitor Center

2
22 miles (35km)

WEST

CAMGROUNDS

① ST. MARY CAMPGROUND

👪 👬 ♿ 🐕

St. Mary Campground, Glacier National Park, PO Box 123, West Glacier, MT 59936. **nps.gov/glac**; 406-732-7708. $20 to $23. Showers, toilets, amphitheater.

St. Mary is the largest campground on the east side of Glacier National Park, located near the visitor center and town of the same name. Along with Fish Creek, it's one of only two campgrounds in the park that accepts reservations. Shade is limited, but views of the mountains are stunning.

Only three sites accommodate RVs of up to 40 feet (12m). If you're traveling with a small RV, this place is ideal.

② FISH CREEK CAMPGROUND

👪 👬 ♿ 🐕

Fish Creek Campground, Glacier National Park, PO Box 128, West Glacier, MT 59936. **nps.gov/glac**; 406-888-7800. June 1 to September 6. $23. Toilets, showers, amphitheater, ranger programs.

This campground is on the western side of Glacier National Park and accepts reservations. The sites here are more shaded than those at St. Mary, and several have gorgeous views of Lake McDonald.

This is a large campground with more than 170 sites, but they're spacious and private. Amenities and activities are bare bones, but the campground's location in the park and its proximity to world-class day hikes such as Rocky Point Trail are unbeatable. Be sure to catch one of the nightly ranger-led programs at the amphitheater.

Although it's situated at an elevation of 3,500 feet (1,067m), summer temperatures can still be quite warm.

And this is bear country, so review safety precautions and food-storage regulations before you arrive.

> Glacier National Park had 150 glaciers in 1850. Now only 25 active glaciers remain.

GRINNELL GLACIER.

③ WEST GLACIER KOA

👪 👬 ♿ 🐕

355 Halfmoon Flats Road, PO Box 215, West Glacier, MT 59936. **koa.com/camp/west-glacier**; 406-387-5341. May 1 to September 30. $50 to $95. Pool, hot tub, snack bar, ice-cream shop.

Surrounded by stunning mountain views, this campground is so beautiful, KOA uses it for corporate photography shoots. If you want more amenities than what's available in the national park campgrounds, this is your place, and it's only 2.5 miles (4km) from Glacier.

After a long day of hiking in the park, take a dip in the pool or soak in the hot tub. Or enjoy the restaurant-quality "dinner with Gene" or ice cream at the on-site parlor. The twice-weekly wildlife slideshow presentations in the pavilion offer a unique window into the beauty of Glacier National Park.

Some of the sites are a little tight, but the deluxe patio sites are beautifully landscaped and private. Book early.

VIEWS FROM THE HIGHLINE TRAIL.

WEST

Water originating in Glacier National Park eventually ends up in the Hudson Bay, the Gulf of Mexico, and the Pacific Ocean.

RESTAURANTS

1 JOHNSON'S CAFE

21 Red Eagle Road, St Mary, MT 59417. johnsonsofstmary.com; info@johnsonsofstmary .com; 406-732-4207. Monday 7 A.M. to 9 P.M.; Tuesday to Sunday 7:30 A.M. to 9 P.M. $10 to $25. American.

This family owned café on the east side of the park has been a staple of St. Mary for more than six decades.

Meals can be served family style on big platters placed in the center of the table. Lunches and dinners come with homemade bread, soup, and salad. (Note that some diners complain pricing can be confusing for this option.) Fried chicken is a favorite for guests. You can also order à la carte burgers and sandwiches.

2 GLACIER HIGHLAND RESTAURANT

12555 Highway 2E, West Glacier, MT 59936. glacierhighland.com/restaurant; 406-888-5427. 7 A.M. to 9 P.M. $11 to $30. Diner.

This is a great diner option near the west entrance of the park. Want to load up on eggs, hash browns, and bacon before a day of hiking? Or maybe you need a hearty burger and fries after exploring the park all day. The service here is friendly and fast.

Be sure to save room for a piece of huckleberry pie.

3 BELTON GRILL DINING ROOM

12575 Highway 2E, West Glacier, MT 59936. beltonchalet.com; info@beltonchalet .com; 888-235-8665. 5 P.M. to 10 P.M.; tap room: 3 P.M. to 10 P.M. $30 to $50. New American.

Directly outside the west entrance to the park, this restaurant is situated in the Belton Chalet, a historic hotel built in 1910 and recently restored to celebrate its original grandeur.

The focus here is on giving guests a true Montana experience by using locally grown ingredients prepared by regional chefs. Summer menus and winter menus feature seasonally appropriate fare, and the wine list offers many organic selections. If you're a meat lover, don't miss the chance to taste grass-fed Montana beef prepared to perfection on the hotel's original boiler that's been converted into a barbecue grill.

Enjoy the views of the park while you eat on the large deck, or enjoy the more casual environment in the Tap Room.

PEACEFUL LAKE MCDONALD.

Glacier National Park is home to 13 campgrounds and more than 1,000 individual sites.

ATTRACTIONS

1 LAKE MCDONALD

👪 👫 ♿

288 Lake McDonald Lodge, Lake McDonald, MT 59921. **nps.gov/glac;** 406-888-7800. 7-day vehicle pass: summer $25, winter $15.

At 10 miles (16km) long and 500 feet (152m) deep, this glacier-carved lake is the largest in the park. It's also one of the loveliest places to spend a day. Relax on the shores soaking in the view, or rent a boat to enjoy the water.

Avalanche Lake and Trail of the Cedars are two popular hikes originating from this lovely spot.

2 GLACIER PARK BOAT COMPANY

👪 👫

Glacier National Park, MT 59903. **glacierparkboats.com;** info@glacierparkboats .com; 406-257-2426. May to September 9 A.M. to 8 P.M. Adults $16.75; children 4 to 12 $8.50.

Many glaciers in this national park can only be enjoyed by way of long and arduous hikes. If you want to see one of the park's bigger glaciers without that much effort, this company offers many different options.

Cross the Swiftcurrent Lake and Lake Josephine to awe at the breathtaking views in Many Glacier. Or take the boat cruise paired with a guided hike to Grinnell Glacier. The boat tour at St. Marys Lake gives you the chance

to see Sexton Glacier along with waterfalls and towering cliffs. Reservations are absolutely necessary to avoid being one of the many visitors left at the dock with each departing tour.

3 GOING-TO-THE-SUN ROAD

👪 👫 ♿

Glacier National Park, MT 59903. **nps.gov/ glac;** 406-888-7800. 7-day vehicle pass: summer $25, winter $15.

This 50-mile (80.5km) stretch of road, full of tight turns and precarious dropoffs, takes you to some of the most epic views in the park.

If you drive without stopping, the trip takes about 2 hours. But to fully experience why this is called the most beautiful road in America, plan for stops along the way. Don't miss the Weeping Wall, the Jackson Glacier Overlook, and Oberlin Bend.

You can take the national park shuttle instead of driving yourself. This allows you to enjoy the views instead of focusing on the white-knuckle driving. Many stops are along the way, and you can hop on and off at will. Other guided tours are available as well.

ITINERARIES

IF YOU HAVE 1 WEEK ...

First drive the Going-to-the-Sun Road, or take a guided tour to fully enjoy the views. Take a sunset boat tour on St. Marys Lake. Picnic at Lake McDonald. See Grinnell Glacier via guided boat and hiking tour.

IF YOU HAVE 2 WEEKS ...

All the above, plus hike the Iceberg Lake Trail and the Highline Trail. Rent a canoe, and paddle around Avalanche Lake. Visit Redrock Falls. Take a whitewater rafting tour on the Flathead River. Take a day trip to the Blackfeet Indian Reservation, or cross the border to Canada's Waterton Lakes National Park.

IF YOU HAVE 3 WEEKS ...

Consider splitting up your time by spending half your trip camping on the east side of the park near St. Mary and half your time on the west side near West Glacier. This keeps driving to a minimum so you can spend more time hiking, boating, fishing, and sightseeing.

yellowstone and grand teton
national parks

The proximity of these national parks offers a great opportunity to see two impressive parks in one trip. Although Yellowstone is more popular, many travelers swear the Grand Tetons is a more spectacular experience. Make time to visit both.

HIGHLIGHTS

★ Watch Old Faithful erupt 130 feet (40m) into the air from **Observation Point.**

★ Hike to **Artist Point** for a stunning view of the Grand Canyon of the Yellowstone.

★ Climb **Signal Mountain Summit Road,** and behold Teton Range and Jackson Hole Valley.

BEST TIME TO GO

June and September are ideal months for a visit due to the typically mild weather and light crowds, but weather is always a wild card so be prepared no matter when you visit.

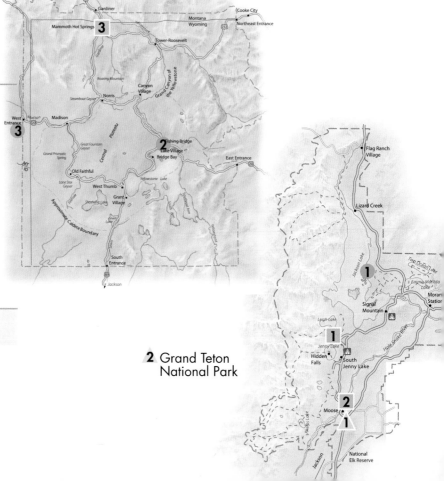

3 Yellowstone National Park

2 Grand Teton National Park

CAMPGROUNDS

① COLTER BAY VILLAGE RV PARK

100 Colter Bay Village Road, Moran, WY 83013. gtlc.com; reservations@gtlc.com; 307-543-2811. May 22 to September 20. $58 to $68. Showers, bathrooms, laundry.

Colter Bay is situated inside Grand Teton National Park, and its location can't be beat. This full-hookup campground is clean and entirely no frills, but who drives to Wyoming for pools and playgrounds? You'll wake up in the comfort of your own RV, surrounded by a magical landscape. For astonishing views of the mountains, take the 5-minute walk to Jackson Lake. Love kayaking? Many outfitters can get you set up.

Book early; sites fill up fast.

YELLOWSTONE'S MAMMOTH HOT SPRINGS.

② FISHING BRIDGE RV PARK

Fishing Bridge RV Park, Yellowstone National Park. nps.gov/yell/planyourvisit/fishingbridgecg.htm; 307-344-7311. May 8 to September 20. $46.75. General store, gas station.

This is the only campground located inside Yellowstone National Park that offers full hookups. Much like Colter Bay in Grand Teton, it's run by a concessionaire with spartan amenities and is all about the location. You'll be close to West Thumb, Hayden Valley, and the Grand Canyon of the Yellowstone.

RVs up to 40 feet (12m) long can be accommodated. Only hard-sided rigs are allowed—no tents and no pop-ups—because the park is located in bear country. Campfires aren't allowed for the same reason. Educate yourself about bear safety after booking your site—and plan on reserving well in advance.

A park ranger hosts evening programs at the amphitheater, and a general store and gas station are nearby.

> Yellowstone contains the largest concentration of free-roaming wildlife in the lower 48 states.

SNAKE RIVER IN THE TETONS.

③ YELLOWSTONE PARK/WEST ENTRANCE KOA

3305 Targhee Pass Highway, West Yellowstone, MT 59758. koa.com/camp/yellowstone-park; moreinfo@yellowstonekoa.com; 406-646-7606. May 22 to September 22. $55 to $80. Indoor pool, hot tub.

This KOA is only 5 minutes from Yellowstone's West Entrance and a short drive to Old Faithful and other park attractions. The campground is bustling and crowded in the summer, and sites near the highway are noisy. But the amenities are great, and the surroundings are beautiful.

Grab some pancakes and coffee from the Koffee Kabin before heading into the park. After a long day, relax in the indoor pool and hot tub. Mini-golf and bike rentals also are available. Barbecue is offered each evening if you don't feel like driving to dinner. Be sure to try the homemade fudge.

WEST

There are more than 300 geysers in Yellowstone, but the most popular is Old Faithful, which erupts approximately every 91 minutes.

GRAND PRISMATIC SPRING.

RESTAURANTS

1 JENNY LAKE LODGE DINING ROOM

North Jenny Lake Junction, Grand Teton National Park, WY 83013. **gtlc.com**; 307-733-4647. June 1 to October 1 6 A.M. to 9 P.M. $30 to $50. New American.

This restaurant in Grand Teton National Park offers everything from a casual breakfast and lunch to formal dinner requiring a jacket and reservations.

In all cases, the food is fresh and seasonal, and the menu options are perfectly paired with the wonderful views of Jenny Lake. The log cabin and large stone fireplace create a lovely ambiance for enjoying the huevos rancheros Benedict for breakfast or the grilled red trout for dinner.

2 DORNAN'S MOOSE CHUCKWAGON

10 Moose Street, Moose, WY 83012. **dornans.com**; 307-733-2415. Breakfast 7 A.M. to 11 A.M.; lunch 12 P.M. to 3 P.M.; dinner Sunday to Thursday 5 P.M. to 9 P.M. $11 to $30. American.

Open since 1948, Dornan's serves quirky cowboy cuisine in a casual setting with great views and outdoor seating. You'll know you've arrived when you spot the giant white teepee and smell the burning campfires.

For breakfast, enjoy all-you-can-eat sourdough pancakes or biscuits and sausage gravy. If you're visiting for lunch, you can't go wrong with the spur beef burger or the NY strip steak sandwich. The chuck wagon dinner is the real star of the show here, offering an all-you-can-eat spread of barbecue options. Pay a little extra for the ribs to go alongside your potatoes, beans, and salad, and enjoy cobbler for dessert.

On Monday nights, Dornan's hosts a free hootenanny, where local musicians perform.

3 MAMMOTH GENERAL STORE

1 Mammoth Upper Loop Road, Mammoth, Yellowstone National Park, WY 82190. **nps.gov/yell**; 406-586-7593. 8 A.M. to 5 P.M. $5 to $10. Deli.

Yellowstone is home to a surprising number of restaurants, but most serve average food accompanied by amazing scenery. You're better off picking up sandwiches here for a more affordable price and scouting out your own scenic dining location.

A great selection of beer and very yummy ice cream are also available.

Of all 50 states, Wyoming ranks fiftieth in population, with only 5 people per 1 square mile (1.5 square km).

JENNY LAKE IN THE GRAND TETONS.

ATTRACTIONS

1 BARKER-EWING SCENIC FLOAT TRIPS

Grand Teton National Park, WY 83012. **barkerewing.com;** floattrips@barkerewing.com; 800-365-1800. Call for schedule and reservations. $50 to $70.

Start your exploration at Cape Disappointment State Park, where you can visit the Lewis and Clark Interpretative Center perched above the Pacific Ocean on a 200-foot (61m) cliff. Also tour the Cape Disappointment Lighthouse and the North Head Lighthouse here. Then head north on 101 to climb Grays Harbor Lighthouse. Use the viewpoint 2 miles (3.2km) south of Ruby Beach to spot the Destruction Island lighthouse.

2 GRAND TETON NATIONAL PARK

Craig Thomas Discovery and Visitor Center. **nps.gov/grte/planyourvisit/ctdvc.htm;** 307-739-3399. Summer 8 A.M. to 7 P.M. 7-day vehicle pass $30.

The center has an educational introductory video and relief map of the park that helps you get situated and plan your explorations. Many visitors start with the scenic loop drive that hugs the base of the Tetons with plenty of pull-offs and wildlife viewing opportunities. Don't miss the Signal Mountain Summit Road that climbs an additional 800 feet (244m) to offer

sweeping views of Teton Range, Jackson Lake, and Jackson Hole Valley.

If you have time for one hike, take an early morning boat shuttle across Jenny Lake, and walk to Hidden Falls to see the 80-foot (24.5m) cascading waterfall. Or check out Inspiration Point for spectacular water views.

3 YELLOWSTONE NATIONAL PARK

Canyon Visitor Education Center. **nps.gov/yell/planyourvisit/canyonvc.htm;** 307-344-2550. Summer 8 A.M. to 8 P.M. 7-day vehicle pass $30.

Visitors should always begin trips to national parks by touring the interpretative exhibits at the visitor center and speaking with rangers about their itinerary. At the Canyon Visitor Education Center, you can watch videos and tour interactive exhibits that bring the geology of the park to life before you go out and explore the real deal.

Get to Old Faithful early in the morning to avoid the crush of tourists that will gather later in the day. Hike the South Rim Trail for the best lookout points to see the Grand Canyon of the Yellowstone. Walk the boardwalks at Mammoth Hot Springs, avoiding contact with the scalding waters. Stop at Hayden Valley for some of the best wildlife viewing in the park.

ITINERARIES

IF YOU HAVE 1 WEEK ...

In Yellowstone, pay a visit to Old Faithful, Mammoth Hot Springs, and the Grand Prismatic Spring. Hike the South Rim Trail for views of the Grand Canyon of the Yellowstone. In Grand Teton, raft the Snake River and drive the loop road.

IF YOU HAVE 2 WEEKS ...

Spend 1 week in Yellowstone doing all the above, plus have a picnic lunch and rent a boat at Yellowstone Lake. Drive the Grand Loop and stop at Hayden Valley. Then set up camp in the Tetons and take the Jenny Lake boat shuttle to Inspiration Point.

IF YOU HAVE 3 WEEKS ...

Split your time between both parks doing all the above, plus in Yellowstone, visit the Lower Geyser Basin and hike Uncle Tom's Trail. Take a guided horseback ride with Yellowstone Wilderness Outfitters. In Grand Teton, hike the Cascade Canyon Trail, and take a day trip into Jackson Hole for an aerial tram ride.

top photo spots in glacier, yellowstone, and grand teton

Capturing the beauty of America's stunning national parks is no easy task. A quality camera helps, but you also need to know where and when to take the best photographs. Here are some tips for snapping epic photos during your visits to Glacier, Yellowstone, and Grand Teton.

GLACIER NATIONAL PARK

Hidden Lake Overlook   Adventurous photographers will want to hike to Hidden Lake Overlook. You might spot a mountain goat on your way, so have your camera ready and keep a safe distance. At the overlook, the platform deck provides a stunning view of the lake and the surrounding mountains.

Wild Goose Island   This iconic view of a mysterious island on Saint Mary Lake, which is rimmed with glorious mountains, serves as a visual explanation for why Glacier is called the crown of the continent. It's easy to access from a turnoff at Saint Mary Lake.

Many Glacier Hotel   The environs of this hotel, built by the Great Northern Railway, offer many safe and easy opportunities for delightful photography. The mountains that surround Swiftcurrent Lake are imposing and make this sprawling hotel look miniscule. Take a boat across the lake if time allows.

YELLOWSTONE NATIONAL PARK

Upper and Lower Falls   The power of Lower Falls, almost twice the height of Niagara Falls, makes for an epic photography session. Frame your shots with the colorful rock of the Grand Canyon of the Yellowstone. Upper Falls is smaller but easily accessed. Make time for both.

Hayden Valley   Hayden Valley is the home of the largest rut of free-roaming bison in the world. The Yellowstone River and the mountains beyond form the perfect backdrop when photographing these majestic creatures. Use a telephoto lens, and stay at least 50 yards (46m) away. Bison might look docile, but they can be deadly.

Grand Prismatic Spring   The largest hot spring in Yellowstone is also its most beautiful. The center is a dark blue that lightens as the spring widens. It's often covered with steam, which can add an element of visual mystery to your pictures if the mist isn't too thick. For best photos, come at midday, when the sun is high.

GRAND TETON NATIONAL PARK

Jenny Lake   Named after a fur trapper's wife, this sparkling lake is easily accessed. The Tetons rise up dramatically in the background, and if the mountains are reflecting in the lake, your photos will be magical. Pick a morning with light winds so the reflections aren't blurry.

T. A. Moulton Barn   The Teton Range forms a majestic backdrop to the most photographed barn in the world. The mountains easily fill a close-up shot of this historic Mormon homestead. Drop farther back at sunrise and sunset, and let the clouds add spectacular color.

Snake River Overlook   Bring a wide-angle lens, and do your best Ansel Adams impersonation here. Arrive before sunrise to pick a spot with unobstructed views, and prepare to be amazed by an oxbow in the Snake River that seems to point upward toward the craggy Tetons.

Index